The ABCs of
Word 97

Second Edition

The ABCs of
Word 97
Second Edition

Guy Hart-Davis

SYBEX®

San Francisco • Paris • Düsseldorf • Soest

Associate Publisher: Amy Romanoff
Acquisitions Manager: Kristine Plachy
Acquisitions & Developmental Editor: Sherry Schmitt
Editor: Shelby Zimmerman
Technical Editor: Rob Sanfilippo
Book Designer: Design Site
Electronic Publishing Specialists: Stephanie Hollier, Kate Kaminski, Kris Warrenburg
Production Coordinator: Amy Eoff
Indexer: Lynnzee Elze Spence
Cover Designer: Design Site
Cover Photographer: Mark Johann

Screen reproductions produced with Collage Plus and Collage Complete. Collage Plus and Collage Complete are trademarks of Inner Media Inc.

SYBEX is a registered trademark of SYBEX Inc.

TRADEMARKS: SYBEX has attempted throughout this book to distinguish proprietary trademarks from descriptive terms by following the capitalization style used by the manufacturer.

Library of Congress Card Number: 96-70741
ISBN: 0-7821-1978-6

Manufactured in the United States of America

10 9 8 7 6 5 4 3 2 1

This book is dedicated to my parents.

Acknowledgments

I'd like to thank the following people for their help and support with this book: Amy Romanoff and Sherry Schmitt for getting the project going; Shelby Zimmerman for editing the manuscript skillfully and patiently; Rob Sanfilippo for reviewing the manuscript for technical accuracy; Stephanie Hollier, Kris Warrenburg, and Kate Kaminski for typesetting the book; Amy Eoff for coordinating the production of the book; and Lynnzee Elze Spence for creating the index.

Finally, thanks go to Died Pretty for *Free Dirt*.

Contents at a Glance

Table of Contents

Chapter 2: Formatting a Document 38

Introduction

Word 97 is the latest version of Microsoft's immensely popular word processing application. Word 97 builds on the success of previous versions of Word and adds a number of new features, such as on-the-fly grammar-checking, tighter integration with the other Office applications, and the ability not only to surf the World Wide Web but also to easily create Web pages.

What Will You Learn from This Book?

This book aims to teach you everything you need to know to use Word productively in your home or office.

Word has many features that you will not only never use but that you will also never even need to know about. This book discusses only the features that you're likely to use the most. If you need to learn to use an esoteric feature that Word offers, the knowledge you gain from this book will stand you in good stead for either puzzling out what each command and feature does or for determinedly ransacking the Help file.

How Much Do You Need to Know Already?

In order to be concise, this book assumes that you know the following about the Windows 95 and Windows NT 4 graphical user interface:

- How to use Windows and navigate its interface enough to start Word with either the keyboard or the mouse
- How to use Windows programs—how to start them and how to exit them; how to use the menus and dialog boxes to make choices; and how to get help whenever you need it by pressing the F1 key or clicking any convenient Help button

NOTE

In this book, *mouse* is a generic term that refers to any mouse, trackball, touchpad, pointing stick, joystick, finger-ring mouse, foot-pedal, 3-D motion sensor, infrared head-tracker, or other improbable pointing device you may be using. If you've got the Microsoft IntelliMouse, you'll be able to use some extra features as well.

- That you click toggle buttons (such as those for boldface and italic) to select them, and that they'll appear to be pushed in when they've been selected
- That you *select* a check box for an item by clicking in it to place a check mark there, and that you *clear* a check box by clicking in it to remove the check mark
- That you normally click the left (or primary) mouse button to choose an item or to perform an action, and that, in the Windows 95/NT 4 interface, you click the right (or secondary) mouse button to produce a *context* menu (sometimes called a *shortcut* menu) of commands suited to that item
- The basics of using the Windows Explorer for file management and how to manage files within Windows' common dialog boxes by using the commands on the context menu
- That Windows applications let you open multiple documents at the same time, and that you can switch among them by using the Window menu

How to Use This Book

This book is set up so that you can go straight to the topic you want and instantly learn what you need to know to get a specific task done. The chapters divide the material by topic; within each chapter, sections divide the material into easily manageable segments:

Chapter 1 shows you how to create and save documents, how to enter text and graphics, and how to exit Word.

Chapter 2 lays out how to format a document, from simple formatting to complex typesetting.

Chapter 3 talks about how to print different kinds of documents.

Chapter 4 demonstrates how to use Word's text-improvement features, such as spell-checking and grammar-checking.

Chapter 5 shows you how to work with headers and footers.

Chapter 6 illustrates how to use Find and Replace to change your documents.

Chapter 7 tackles multi-column text, in both columns and tables.

Chapter 8 tells you how to sort information in Word.

Chapter 9 delves into all sorts of mail-merge operations.

Chapter 10 examines Word's document-automation features, which can help you produce documents quickly and consistently.

Chapter 11 demonstrates Outline view, a great tool for putting together structured documents.

Chapter 12 shows you how to add tables of contents and indexes to your documents.

Chapter 13 discusses how to manage long publications with master documents and subdocuments.

Chapter 14 digs into the mysteries of fields.

Chapter 15 pries open the topic of macros and how you can use them to automate your documents.

Chapter 16 looks at how to create forms using Word.

Chapter 17 outlines how you can customize Word to suit your needs and your working habits.

Chapter 18 shares Word's workgroup features, from tracking changes through transmitting documents via e-mail.

Chapter 19 talks about Object Linking and Embedding (OLE) and Office Binders.

Chapter 20 shows you how to use Word to surf the Web or your company's intranet; how to create Web pages; and how to use WordMail as your e-mail editor in Outlook or Exchange.

The Appendix looks at installing Word on your computer.

The Glossary defines terms useful to understanding Word and what it does.

> **NOTE** Notes, Tips, and Warnings, each identified clearly with this shading and a key word, give you extra guidance on specific topics.

Conventions Used in This Book

This book uses a number of conventions to convey more information accurately in fewer pages:

- ➤ designates choosing a command from a menu. For example, *choose File ➤ Open* means that you should pull down the File menu and choose the Open command from it.
- + signs indicate key combinations. For example, *press Ctrl+Shift+F9* means that you hold down the Ctrl and Shift keys, then press the F9 key. Some of these key combinations are visually confusing, so you may need to read them carefully; for example, Ctrl++ means that you hold down Ctrl and press the + key (hold down the Ctrl and Shift together and press the = key).
- ↑, ↓, ←, and → represent the arrow keys that should appear in some form on your keyboard. The important thing to note is that ← is *not* the Backspace key (which on many keyboards bears a similar arrow). The Backspace key is represented by "Backspace" or "the Backspace key."
- **Boldface** indicates items that you may want to type in letter for letter.
- *Italics* indicate either new terms being introduced or variable information (such as a drive letter that will vary from computer to computer and that you'll need to establish on your own).

Chapter 1

GETTING STARTED WITH WORD

FEATURING

- **Setting up your screen**
- **Creating documents**
- **Entering and editing text**
- **Inserting and sizing graphics and frames**
- **Saving documents**
- **Opening documents**
- **Viewing documents**
- **Exiting Word**

In this chapter, we'll run through the basics of working with Word—creating, saving, and viewing documents, and finally, exiting Word. First, though, we'll set up your screen so that you're working comfortably.

This chapter assumes that Word is running. If it's not, start Word in the usual manner—click the Word button on the Programs Shortcut Bar; or click the Start button, choose Programs, and click Word; or use any shortcut or keyboard shortcut you've arranged in Windows 95 or Windows NT. If you haven't installed Word, turn to the Appendix for instructions on installing it smoothly and swiftly.

Setting Up Your Screen

Before we get into working with documents, let's quickly look at how Word appears on the screen (see Figure 1.1).

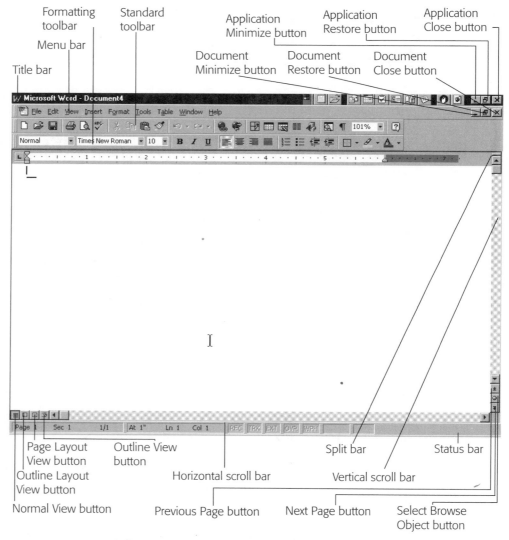

FIGURE 1.1: The elements of the Word window. The Office Shortcut Bar appears only if you have Microsoft Office installed and running on your computer.

Before you start work in Word, you may want to customize your screen. At a minimum, consider maximizing the Word window by clicking the Maximize button on the title bar, and then maximizing the document you're working on within the Word window by clicking the Document Maximize button. (Once you've maximized the Word window or the document window, Word will replace the Application Maximize button with an Application Restore button or the Document Maximize button with the Document Restore button; click a restore button to restore the window to its pre-maximized size.)

You may also want to use Zoom to enlarge or shrink the display. If so, skip ahead to the section titled *Viewing the Document* later in this chapter.

Displaying Toolbars

Word comes with a variety of toolbars containing buttons that give you quick access to actions—everything from italicizing your text to running a massive mail merge. By default, Word displays the Standard and Formatting toolbars, but you can easily choose to display other toolbars (such as the Tables and Borders toolbar or the Drawing toolbar) if you need them. Alternatively, you can hide the Standard and Formatting toolbars to give yourself more screen real estate.

To display and hide toolbars:

- With the mouse, right-click anywhere in the menu bar or in a displayed toolbar to display a list of toolbars. Check marks will appear next to the toolbars currently displayed. Click next to a displayed toolbar to hide it or next to a hidden toolbar to display it.

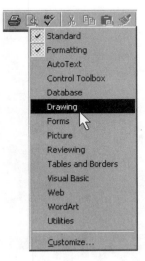

- With the keyboard, choose View ➤ Toolbars to display the list of toolbars. Again, check marks will appear next to those toolbars currently displayed. Use ↓ and ↑ to move the highlight to the displayed toolbar you want to hide or the hidden toolbar you want to display, then press ↵.

TIP

Don't display too many toolbars at once if you're using a low screen resolution, such as 640x480—you won't have much of the screen left for working in.

Moving and Reshaping Toolbars

Word can display its toolbars and the menu bar as either *docked* panels attached to one side of the screen or as free-floating panels that you can drag anywhere on your screen (see Figure 1.2).

To move a toolbar or the menu bar from its current position, click the move handle at its left end (or its top end, if it's positioned vertically) or click in any space in the toolbar or menu bar not occupied by a button or menu item and drag it to where you want it—either to one of the edges, in which case it will snap into position, or to the middle of the screen.

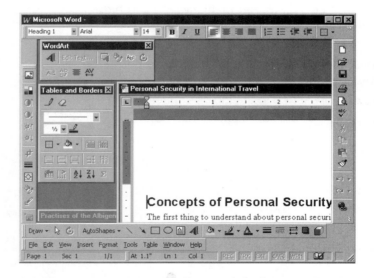

FIGURE 1.2:
You can display your toolbars at any extremity of the Word screen, or you can place them plumb in the middle.

TIP

You can also undock a docked toolbar (but not the menu bar) by double-clicking its move handle. To redock a floating toolbar (or the floating menu bar), double-click its title bar.

To reshape a floating toolbar or floating menu bar, move the mouse pointer over one of its borders until the pointer turns into a double-ended arrow, then click and drag to resize the toolbar. Because of the shape of their buttons or menu names, tool-bars and the menu bar resize in jumps rather than smoothly, like windows do.

Displaying and Hiding the Status Bar and Scroll Bars

The status bar at the bottom of the screen provides a host of information about the document you're working in—but it takes up space, so you may want to hide it from time to time. Word also has two scroll bars, one vertical and one horizontal, to help you negotiate the far reaches of your documents. While the vertical scroll bar is useful most of the time for moving through your documents—particularly if you don't get along with the roller on the IntelliMouse—you can often hide the horizontal scroll bar to free up a little room on the screen without sacrificing any functionality.

To display and hide the status bar and scroll bars:

1. Choose Tools ➤ Options to display the Options dialog box.
2. Click the View tab to bring it to the front of the dialog box if it's not already displayed.
3. In the Window group box, select the Status Bar, Horizontal Scroll Bar, and Vertical Scroll Bar check boxes to display the status bar and scroll bars, or clear the check boxes to hide the status bar and scroll bars.
4. Click the OK button to close the Options dialog box.

Displaying and Hiding the Rulers

To help you position your text optimally on the page, Word offers a horizontal ruler in Normal view and both horizontal and vertical rulers in Page Layout view and Print Preview.

You can either display the ruler onscreen all the time, or keep it hidden but available. To toggle the display of the ruler on and off, choose View ➤ Ruler. To pop up the horizontal ruler momentarily, move the mouse pointer to the thin light-gray bar at the top of the current document window.

The ruler will appear automatically so that you can view text positioning or work with tabs.

The ruler will disappear when you move the mouse pointer away from it.

To pop up the vertical ruler in Page Layout view or Print Preview, move the mouse pointer to the thin light-gray bar at the left edge of the current document window. The vertical ruler will appear automatically, and will disappear when you move the pointer away again.

NOTE You cannot display the ruler continuously in Online Layout view, but you can pop it up when you need it.

Creating a New Document

When you run Word, it opens a new document for you to work with based on the default template and names the document, *Document1*. To create a new document based on the default (Blank Document), click the New button on the Standard toolbar or press Ctrl+N. Word will open a new document named *Documentx—Document2*, *Document3*, and so on.

To create a new document based on a different template:

1. Choose File ➤ New. Word will display the New dialog box (see Figure 1.3).

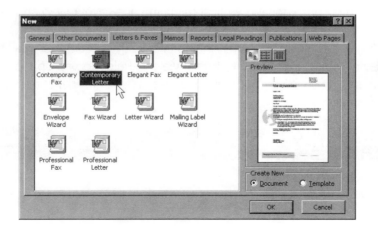

FIGURE 1.3:
To create a new document based on a template other than Blank Document, choose File ➤ New and select the template in the New dialog box.

2. In the New dialog box, choose the tab that contains the type of document you want to create: General, Legal Pleadings, Letters & Faxes, Memos, Other Documents, Reports, Publications, or Web Pages.

- If you didn't install all the templates that Word offers, you may not see all of these tabs in the New dialog box. Then again, if you or someone else has created more templates in another folder, you may see more tabs than those listed here.
- To see a preview of a template in the tab you chose, click a template. The preview will appear in the box on the right side of the New dialog box.

NOTE A *template* is a special type of document that you use to produce cookie-cutter documents. Templates can contain styles, AutoText entries, toolbars, and macros, all of which we'll get to in later chapters. By attaching a document to a different template, you can change its styles instantly, change its look completely, and virtually typeset it differently, in seconds. Take a look at the Preview box as you click some of the templates offered by word to get an idea of the different document designs available.

- You can choose between three views of the templates available by clicking any of the three buttons above the Preview box. The leftmost button gives the Large Icons view; the second gives the List view; the third gives the Details view.

TIP Details view offers the most information of the three views, and you can sort the templates by name, size, type, or date last modified by clicking the buttons at the top of the columns.

3. To start a document based on the template you've chosen, double-click the icon or listing for the template, or click it once and then click OK.

Working with Text, Graphics, and Text Boxes

Like most wordprocessing applications, Word's basic unit is the paragraph. These aren't paragraphs as people generally understand them: A paragraph in Word consists of a paragraph mark (made by pressing Enter) and any text (or graphic) between it and the previous paragraph mark (or the beginning of the document). In other words, a paragraph consists of anything (text, a graphic, space, or even nothing at all) that appears between two paragraph marks, up to and including the second paragraph mark. The previous sentence seems a strange way to describe it, but a paragraph mark with nothing between it and the previous paragraph mark is considered a full paragraph. You can treat each paragraph as a unit for formatting with styles (which we'll look at in Chapter 2) or for moving and copying.

> **TIP**
>
> If you're not seeing paragraph marks on your screen, click the ¶ button on the Standard toolbar. This is the Show/Hide ¶ button, and it toggles the display of spaces, tabs, paragraph marks, and the like. Some people find it easier to work with these marks displayed; others find them distracting. You can also display and hide these marks by pressing Ctrl+Shift+8.

Entering Text

To enter text into your document, simply position the insertion point where you want the text to appear and type it in. Word will automatically wrap text as it reaches the end of a line. Press the Enter key to start a new paragraph.

If you want to move to a new line without starting a new paragraph—for example, so there is no extra space between lines—press Shift+Enter to start a new line within the same paragraph.

As you reach the end of a page, Word will automatically break text onto the next page. If you want, you can start a new page at any point by inserting a page break. To do so, press Ctrl+Enter.

Insert and Overtype Modes

Word offers two modes for adding text to your documents: Insert mode and Overtype mode. In Insert mode (the default mode), characters you type are inserted into the text at the insertion point, pushing along any characters to the right of the insertion point. If you want to type over existing text in Insert mode, select the text using either the mouse or the keyboard (see the section *Selecting Text* in this chapter for instructions on selecting text) and type in the text you want to insert in its place. In Insert mode, the OVR indicator on the status bar is dimmed.

In Overtype mode, any character you type replaces the character (if any) to the immediate right of the insertion point. When Word is in Overtype mode, the OVR indicator on the status bar is active (darkened), as shown here.

To toggle between Insert mode and Overtype mode, double-click the OVR indicator on the status bar.

Inserting and Sizing Pictures

You can easily insert pictures of various types into Word documents. Once you've inserted them, you can resize them and crop them as necessary.

Inserting a Picture

To insert a picture at the insertion point:

1. Choose Insert ➤ Picture to display the Picture submenu.
2. Choose from the six options for inserting a picture: Clip Art, From File, AutoShapes, WordArt, From Scanner, or Chart. Here we'll choose From File and look at inserting a picture you have in a file. Word displays the Insert Picture dialog box (see Figure 1.4).

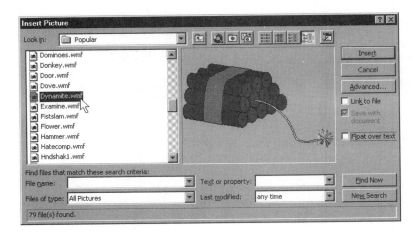

FIGURE 1.4:
In the Insert Picture dialog box, choose a picture to insert and click OK.

3. Navigate to the folder containing the picture you want using standard Windows techniques. Click the Up One Level button (or press the Backspace key with the focus in the folder list box) to move up one level of folders, or double-click the folders displayed in the main window to drill down through them to find the folder you want.
   - Word displays all the pictures that are in formats it recognizes, but you can restrict the display to certain types of graphics by choosing them from the Files of Type drop-down list.
4. Choose the picture file you want to insert from the main list box. If Word isn't displaying the Preview box, click the Preview button to display it and make sure you've got the right file.
5. If you want the picture to appear in text so that you can manipulate it as you would a character, clear the Float over Text check box. If the Float over Text check box is selected, Word will place the image on the drawing layer, where you can make it appear either in front of or behind text.
6. Click the Insert button to insert the picture into your document.

Resizing and Cropping Pictures

To resize a picture quickly, first click it to select it. Word will display the Picture toolbar (see Figure 1.5) and an outline around the picture with eight handles, one at each corner and one in the middle of each side. Drag a corner handle to resize the image proportionally; drag a side handle to resize the image only in that dimension (horizontally or vertically).

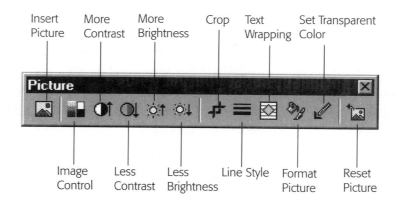

FIGURE 1.5: The Picture toolbar contains buttons for manipulating pictures quickly.

To crop a picture quickly (cut off part of it), click the picture to select it, then click the Crop button to select the cropping tool. The mouse pointer will change into cropping handles. Move the mouse pointer over one of the picture's handles, then drag inward or outward to crop the picture.

To resize or crop a picture more precisely:

1. Click the picture to display the outline and handles around it.
2. Click the Format Picture button or choose Format ➤ Picture to display the Format Picture dialog box (see Figure 1.6).

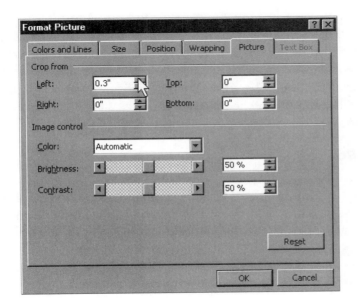

FIGURE 1.6:
The Format Picture dialog box lets you resize and crop pictures precisely.

3. To crop a picture, make sure the Picture tab is displayed (click on it if it isn't). Enter the amount you want to crop in the Left, Right, Top, and Bottom boxes in the Crop From area.
4. To resize the picture, click the Size tab to display it. Then either set Width and Height percentages in the Scale area, or enter the desired width and height, such as 1.46″ by 1.74″, in the Width and Height boxes in the Size and Rotate area.

> **TIP** The Lock Aspect Ratio check box in the Scale area of the Size tab controls whether the Height and Width boxes act in concert or independently.

5. Click the OK button to close the Picture dialog box and apply your changes.

Inserting, Positioning, and Formatting Text Boxes

To precisely position a picture in a document, use a text box. A *text box* is a container that Word uses to position items (pictures, text, and so forth.) in an exact place on the page. You can position a text box relative to a paragraph (so it moves with the text when the paragraph moves) or relative to the margin or page (so it remains in place even if the paragraph moves). The advantage of positioning a text box relative to the page rather than relative to one of the margins is that you can adjust the margins without the text box moving. Text boxes are held in place by *anchors*.

Inserting a Text Box

To insert a text box:

1. Choose Insert ➤ Text Box. Word will change the insertion point to a large + sign and, if you are in Normal view or Outline view, will switch to Page Layout view. (We'll look at the different views Word offers in *Viewing the Document* later in this chapter.)

2. Click and drag in the document to create a text box of the size you want, as shown here. The text box will appear with a thick shaded border, and Word will display the Text Box toolbar.

Now you can click inside the text box and insert a picture in it as described earlier in this chapter.

Sizing and Positioning a Text Box

To resize a text box quickly, click in it to display the text box border and then drag one of the sizing handles.

To position a text box quickly:

1. Click inside the text box to display the text box border and handles. Make sure that you've selected the text box rather than any picture inside it.

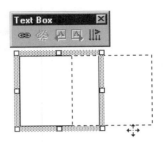

2. Move the mouse pointer onto the shaded border of the text box so that the pointer becomes a four-headed compass arrow attached to the normal mouse-pointer arrow.

3. Click and drag the text box to wherever you want to place it on the page. Here, I'm dragging a text box and its contents.

To resize and position a text box exactly:

1. Right-click the border of the text box and choose Format Text Box from the context menu to display the Format Text Box dialog box (see Figure 1.7).

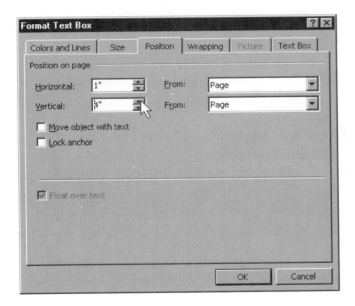

FIGURE 1.7:
Choose the text box's position on the page in the Format Text Box dialog box.

2. To resize the text box, click the Size tab to display it. You can then set the height and width either by entering measurements in the Height and Width boxes in the Size and Rotate area or by entering percentages in the Height and Width boxes in the Scale area. To resize the image proportionally, select the Lock Aspect Ratio check box; to resize the image differently in each dimension, clear the check box.

3. To reposition the text box, click the Position tab to display it. Specify a horizontal position by entering a measurement in the Horizontal box and specifying in the upper From drop-down list whether this is from the Margin, the Column, or the Page. Then specify a vertical position by setting a measurement in the Vertical box and specifying in the lower From drop-down list whether this is from the Margin, the Page, or the current Paragraph.

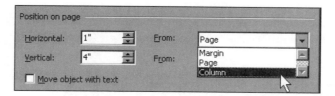

4. To allow a text box to move when the text it is attached to moves, select the Move Object with Text check box. For example, if you position a text box relative to a paragraph, select this check box; if you position a text box relative to the page, clear this check box. Toggling this check box changes the setting in the Vertical From drop-down list.

5. To lock the text box to the paragraph it belongs with (so you can't accidentally move it to another paragraph), select the Lock Anchor check box.

6. Click OK to close the Format Text Box dialog box and apply the settings to the text box.

Removing a Text Box

To delete a text box, select it by clicking on its border, then press the Delete button. This deletes both the text box and its contents. To preserve the contents of the text box, copy and paste them into the document before deleting the text box. (We'll look at copy and paste later in this chapter.)

Moving the Insertion Point

In Word, you can move the insertion point using either the mouse or the keyboard.

Using the Mouse

To position the insertion point using the mouse, simply move the insertion point to where you want it, and click to place the insertion point.

Use the roller on the IntelliMouse or the vertical scroll bar to move up and down through your document (as you drag the box in the scroll bar in a multipage document, Word will display a small box next to the scroll bar showing which page you're on). Use the horizontal scroll bar to move from side to side as necessary.

> **TIP**
>
> If you're continually scrolling horizontally in Normal view to see the full width of your documents, turn on Word's Wrap to Window option, which makes the text fit into the current window size, regardless of width. To turn on Wrap to Window, choose Tools ➤ Options, click the View tab, and select the Wrap to Window check box. Click OK to close the Options dialog box.

Click the Next Page and Previous Page buttons to move to the next page and previous page, respectively. Make sure that these buttons are black, which indicates that Word is browsing by pages. If they're blue, that means Word is browsing by a different item, such as sections or comments. To reset Word to browse by pages, click the Object Browser button between the Next and Previous buttons and choose the Browse by Page button in the Object Browser list, as shown here.

Using Keyboard Shortcuts

Word offers a number of key combinations which enable you to move the insertion point swiftly through the document without removing your hands from the keyboard. Besides ← to move left one character, → to move right one character, ↑ to move up one line, and ↓ to move down one line, you can use the following:

Keystroke	Movement
Ctrl+→	One word to the right
Ctrl+←	One word to the left
Ctrl+↑	To the beginning of the current paragraph or (if the insertion point is at the beginning of a paragraph) to the beginning of the previous paragraph
Ctrl+↓	To the beginning of the next paragraph
End	To the end of the current line
Ctrl+End	To the end of the document
Home	To the start of the current line

Ctrl+Home	To the start of the document
PageUp	Up one screen's worth of text
PageDown	Down one screen's worth of text
Ctrl+PageUp	To the first character on the current screen
Ctrl+PageDown	To the last character on the current screen

> **TIP** You can quickly move to the last three places you edited in a document by pressing Shift+F5 (Go Back).

Selecting Text

Word offers a number of different ways to select text: You can use the keyboard, the mouse, or the two in combination. You'll find that with certain equipment, some ways of selecting text work better than others; experiment to find which are the fastest and most comfortable methods for you.

Selecting Text with the Mouse

The simplest way to select text with the mouse is to position the insertion point at the beginning or end of the block you want to select, then click and drag to the end or beginning of the block.

> **TIP** Word offers an automatic word selection feature to help you select whole words more quickly with the mouse. When this feature is switched on, as soon as you drag from one word to the next, Word will select the whole of the first word and the whole of the second; when the mouse pointer reaches the third, it selects that too. To temporarily override automatic word selection, hold down the Alt key before you click and drag. To turn off automatic word selection, choose Tools ➤ Options to display the Options dialog box. Click the Edit tab to bring it to the front of the dialog box, and clear the When Selecting, Automatically Select Entire Word check box. Then click OK. To turn automatic word selection on, select the When Selecting, Automatically Select Entire Word check box.

You can also select text with multiple clicks:
- Double-click in a word to select it.
- Triple-click in a paragraph to select it.
- Ctrl-click in a sentence to select it.

In the selection bar on the left side of the screen (where the insertion point turns from an I-beam to an arrow pointing toward the right), you can click to select text as follows:
- Click once to select the line the arrow is pointing at.
- Double-click to select the paragraph the arrow is pointing at.
- Triple-click (or Ctrl-click once) to select the entire document.

Selecting Text with the Keyboard

To select text with the keyboard, hold down the Shift key and move the insertion point by using the keyboard shortcuts listed in the *Using Keyboard Shortcuts* section earlier in the chapter.

Selecting Text with the Extend Selection Feature

You can also select text by using Word's Extend Selection feature, though I can't recommend it—it takes longer and is clumsier than the other ways of selecting text. Press the F8 key once to enter Extend Selection mode; you'll see EXT appear undimmed on the status bar. Press F8 a second time to select the current word; a third time to select the current sentence; a fourth time to select the current paragraph; and a fifth time to select the whole document. Then press the Esc key to turn off Extend Selection mode. Alternatively, you can press F8 once to enter Extend Selection mode, and then extend the selection from the insertion point towards the end of the document by pressing the character to which you want to extend the selection: For example, each time you press **e**, Word extends the selection to the next letter "e." To extend to the next comma or period, press the comma or period key, respectively. To extend the selection to the end of the paragraph, press Enter.

Selecting Text with the Mouse and Keyboard

Word also offers ways to select text using the mouse and keyboard together. These techniques are well worth trying out, as you can quickly select awkward blocks of text—for example, if you want to select a few sentences from a paragraph or if you want to select columns of characters.

To select a block of text using the mouse and the keyboard, position the insertion point at the start (or end) of a block and click. Then move the insertion point to the end (or start) of the block—scroll if necessary with the IntelliMouse roller or the scroll bar, but don't use the keyboard—hold down the Shift key, and then click again.

To select columns of characters, hold down the Alt key and click and drag from one end of the block to the other (see Figure 1.8). This technique can be very useful for getting rid of extra spaces or tabs that your colleagues have used to align text.

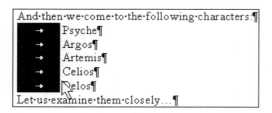

FIGURE 1.8:
To select columns of characters without selecting whole lines, hold down the Alt key and drag through the block.

NOTE Selecting text in a table works a little differently from selecting regular text, so we'll discuss that in Chapter 7.

Deleting Text

Word lets you delete text swiftly and easily:

- To delete a block of text, simply select it and press the Delete key.
- To delete the character to the left of the insertion point, press the Backspace key.
- To delete the character to the right of the insertion point, press the Delete key.
- To delete the word to the right of the insertion point, press Ctrl+Delete. This actually deletes from the insertion point to the beginning of the next word (or the end of the line, if the current word is the last one in the line), so if the insertion point is in a word when you press Ctrl+Delete, you won't delete the whole word.
- To delete the word to the left of the insertion point, press Ctrl+Backspace. Again, if the insertion point isn't at the end of the word, only the part of the word to the left of the insertion point will be deleted.

TIP

You can also delete selected text by choosing Edit ➤ Clear or by right-clicking in the selection and choosing Cut from the context menu that appears. (Some context menus—which are different for different elements of Word documents—don't have a Cut command.)

Cutting, Pasting, and Moving Text

You can easily copy and move text (and graphics) around your document either by using the Cut, Copy, and Paste commands or by using Word's drag-and-drop feature, which lets you copy or move text using your mouse.

Cut

The Cut command removes the selected text (or graphics) from the Word document and places it on the Windows Clipboard. From there, you can paste it into another part of the document. To cut the current selection, click the Cut button, right-click and choose Cut from the context menu, choose Edit ➤ Cut, or press Ctrl+X.

Copy

The Copy command copies the selected text (or graphics) to the Clipboard. From there, you can paste it into another part of the document. To copy the current selection, click the Copy button, right-click and choose Copy from the context menu, choose Edit ➤ Copy, or press Ctrl+C.

Paste

The Paste command pastes a copy of the Clipboard's contents into your Word document at the insertion point. To paste the contents of the Clipboard, right-click and choose Paste from the context menu, click the Paste button, choose Edit ➤ Paste, or press Ctrl+V.

Saving a Word Document

The first time you save a Word document, you assign it a name and choose the folder in which to save it. Thereafter, when you save the document, Word uses that name and folder and does not prompt you for changes to them—unless you decide to save the file under a different name, in which case you need to use the File ➤ Save As command rather than File ➤ Save. We'll get into this in a moment.

> **TIP** In Word 97, you can also save different versions of the same document in the same file. We'll look at this in detail in Chapter 18.

Saving a Document for the First Time

To save a Word document for the first time:

1. Click the Save button or choose File ➤ Save. Word will display the Save As dialog box (see Figure 1.9).

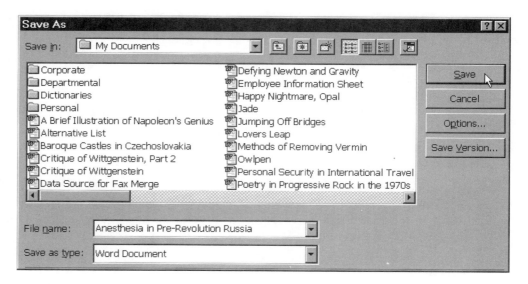

FIGURE 1.9: In the Save As dialog box, choose the folder in which to save your file, then enter a name for the file.

NOTE

In dialog boxes that show file names, you'll see file extensions (e.g., *.doc*) at the end of a Word file name only if you've chosen to see them in Windows Explorer. To display extensions in Explorer, choose View ➤ Options and clear the Hide MS-DOS File Extensions for File Types That Are Registered check box, then click the OK button.

2. In the Save In box at the top of the Save As dialog box, choose the folder in which to save the document.

- Navigate the Save As dialog box in the same way that you would any common Windows 95 dialog box—click the Up One Level button (or press the Backspace key with the focus on the folder list) to move up one level of folders, or double-click the folders displayed in the main window to drill down through them to the folder you want.
- Use the Look in Favorites button to quickly display the list of Favorite folders. (Click the Look in Favorites button again if you need to return to the folder you were viewing when you first clicked it.)

3. In the File Name text box, enter a name for your file.

- With Windows 95's and Windows NT's capacity for long filenames, you can enter a thorough and descriptive name—up to 255 characters, including the path to the file (i.e., the name of the folder or folders in which to save the file).
- You can't use the following characters in file names (if you do try to use one of these, Word will advise you of the problem):

Colon	:
Semicolon	;
Backslash	\
Forward slash	/
Greater-than sign	>
Less-than sign	<
Asterisk	*
Question mark	?
Double quotation mark	"
Pipe symbol	|

4. Click the Save button to save the file.

5. If Word displays a Properties dialog box for the document (see Figure 1.10), you can enter identifying information and any company name entered when Word was installed on the Summary tab. Change these as necessary.

- In the Title box, Word displays the first paragraph of the document (or a section of it, if it's long). You'll often want to change this.
- In the Author and Company boxes, Word displays the user name from the User Information tab of the Options dialog box.
- Use the Subject box to describe the subject of the document, and enter any key words that will help you remember the document in the Keywords box.
- Fill in other boxes as desired, then click OK to close the Properties dialog box and save the file.

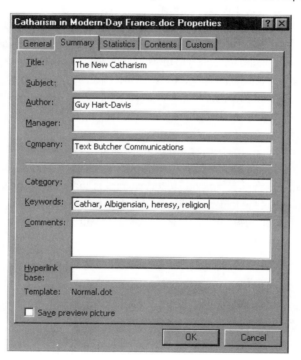

FIGURE 1.10:
Enter identifying information in the Properties dialog box if you want to.

TIP

Whether or not the Properties dialog box appears depends on the Prompt for Document Properties setting on the Save tab of the Options dialog box. To have Word automatically prompt you for summary information, choose Tools ➤ Options, click the Save tab, select the Prompt for Document Properties check box, and click OK.

Saving a Document Again

 To save a document that you've saved before, click the Save button, choose File ➤ Save, or press Ctrl+S (the shortcut for Save). Word will save the document without consulting you about the location or file name.

Saving a Document under Another Name

One of the easiest ways to make a copy of a Word document is to open it and save it under a different name. This technique can be particularly useful if you've made changes to the document but don't want to replace the original document—for example, if you think you might need to revert to the original document and you've forgotten to make a backup before making your changes. The Save As command can also be useful for copying a document to a different folder or drive—for example, if you want to copy a document to a floppy drive or to a network drive.

To save a document under a different name or to a different folder:

1. Choose File ➤ Save As to display the Save As dialog box.
2. Enter a different name for the document in the File name box, or choose a different folder in the Save In area.
3. Click the Save button to save the document.

If the folder you've chosen already contains a document of the same name, Word will ask whether you want to overwrite it. Choose Yes or No. If you choose No, Word will return you to the Save As dialog box so that you can choose a different name or different folder.

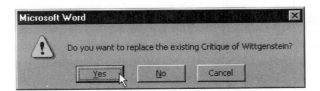

Opening a Word Document

To open a Word document:

1. Click the Open button on the Standard toolbar, choose File ➤ Open, or press Ctrl+O. Word will display the Open dialog box (see Figure 1.11).

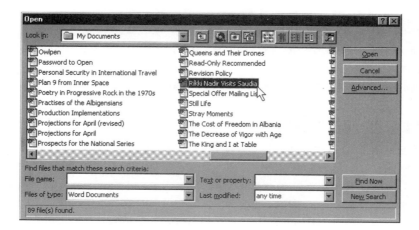

FIGURE 1.11:
In the Open dialog box, use the Look In box to navigate to the folder that contains the document you want to open, then highlight the document and click the Open button.

2. If you're already in the right folder, proceed to Step 3. If not, use the Look In box to navigate to the folder holding the document you want to open.
   - Move through the folders using standard Windows navigation: Click the Up One Level button (or press the Backspace key with the focus on the folder list) to move up one level of folders, or double-click a folder to drill down through it.
   - Click the Look in Favorites button (shown here on the left) to display your list of Favorite folders. Click it again to return to the folder you were in before you clicked it. Click the Add to Favorites button (shown here on the right) to add a folder or file to that list.

3. Choose the document to open, then click the Open button.

TIP

To open several documents at once, click the first one in the Open dialog box to select it. Then, to select contiguous documents, hold down Shift and click the last document in the sequence to select it and all the ones between it and the first document, and then click the Open button. To select noncontiguous documents, hold down Ctrl and click each document you want to open, and then click the Open button. (You can also combine the two methods of selection: First use Shift+click to select a sequence of documents, then use Ctrl+click to select others.)

Opening Word Documents Using Windows Techniques

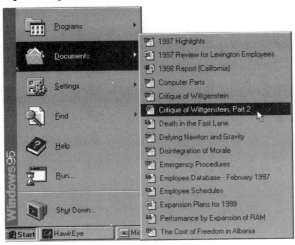

Windows 95 and Windows NT offer several ways to open a Word document quickly. If you've used the document recently, pop up the Start menu, choose Documents, and choose the document from the list of the fifteen most recently used files (as shown here). If Word is already open, Windows will just open the document for you; if Word isn't open, Windows will open Word and the document at the same time.

If you need to open a Word document frequently but can't be sure that it will always be among your fifteen-most-wanted files on the Start menu's Document menu, you can create an icon for it on the Desktop. To do so, either right-click the Desktop and choose New ➤ Shortcut and then Browse for the document in the Create Shortcut dialog box; or, more simply, open an Explorer window, find the Word document you want to keep handy, and right-drag it to the Desktop. Windows will invite you to create a shortcut to the document; go right ahead.

TIP

To quickly open one of the documents you worked on most recently from inside Word, pull down the File menu and choose one of the most recently used documents listed at the bottom of the menu. (By default, Word lists four files, but you can change this by using Tools ➤ Options, selecting the General tab, and changing the number in the Entries box for the Recently Used File List. Alternatively, you can turn off the display of recently used documents by clearing the Recently Used File List check box.

Finding Word Documents

The Open dialog box also lets you quickly search your computer for documents that match a certain description. This can be useful when you need to find a document whose name or location you've forgotten but whose contents you can remember.

Finding a Document from a Known Word

To find a Word document using a word you remember from the text of the document:

1. In the Open dialog box, navigate to the folder you think the document is in. (If you don't remember that, start with the drive you think the document is on.)

2. Make sure the File Name text box is blank. If it's not, click the New Search button to clear the details.

3. Make sure the Files of Type drop-down list shows the type of document you're looking for (e.g., *Word Documents*).

4. In the Text or Property drop-down list box, enter the text to search for (e.g., **surreal events**).

5. Click the Find Now button to start the search. If Word finds the document, it will highlight it in the dialog box. (If Word finds several files containing the text, you'll need to decide which one you want.) Click the Open button to open the file.

Finding a Document from Other Information

You can also search for a document using other known information, such as its contents, author, company, and so on. To do so:

1. Click the Advanced button to display the Advanced Find dialog box (see Figure 1.12).

2. In the Find Files that Match These Criteria box, check that Word is showing only appropriate criteria, such as Files of Type *is* Word Documents. To remove inappropriate criteria, highlight them and click the Delete button.

3. In the Define More Criteria group box, leave the And option button selected and choose the item to search for in the Property drop-down list: Application Name, Author, Category, Company, and so on. You'll recognize some of these as properties from the Properties dialog box.

4. In the Condition drop-down list, choose from the options available for the Property you chose. For example, if you chose Author in the Property drop-down list, you could choose Is (Exactly) from the Condition drop-down list to search by the whole author name or Includes Words to search by just part of the author name.

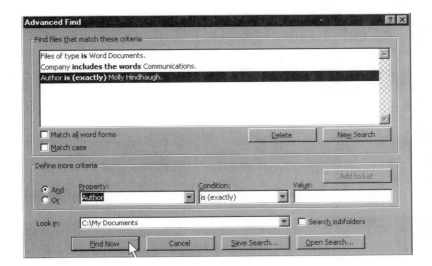

FIGURE 1.12:
The Advanced
Find dialog box
lets you find
lost files swiftly.

5. In the Value box, enter the value you're searching by. For example, when searching for a document by author, specify the author's name here.

6. Click the Add to List button to add this criterion to the list.

7. Add more criteria if necessary by repeating steps 3 through 6.

8. In the Look In drop-down list, specify the folder in which to start the search for the document. If the folder has subfolders, check the Search Subfolders box to the right of the Look In drop-down list if you want to search them as well.

9. Click the Find Now button to have Word search for the documents. If it finds any, it will display them in the Open dialog box, where you can open them as usual.

TIP

You can save search criteria by clicking the Save Search button in the Advanced Find dialog box, and you can open saved searches by clicking the Open Search button.

Viewing the Document

Word offers six main ways of viewing your documents, each of which has its strengths and its weaknesses:

- Normal view
- Online Layout view
- Page Layout view
- Print Preview
- Outline view
- Split-screen view

Normal View

Normal view provides the easiest view of the text and other elements onscreen and is probably the Word view you'll spend most of your time using. In Normal view, Word approximates the fonts and other formatting that you'll see when you print your document, but adapts the document so that you can see as much of it as possible on your screen. In Normal view, you don't see the margins of the paper, or the headers and footers, or the footnotes and annotations, and Word can wrap the text horizontally to the size of the window so that no text disappears off the side of the screen.

 To switch the document to Normal view, choose View ➤ Normal or click the Normal View button at the left end of the horizontal scroll bar.

> **NOTE** Another Word option some consider to be a separate view is Draft Font view, a relic of the Draft View of Word versions 2.*x* and earlier. Draft Font view, located in the Show area on the View tab in the Options dialog box, is now an option that you choose for Normal or Outline view. Draft font view uses standard fonts (with underline to indicate any form of emphasis, such as bold or italic) in order to speed up the display of text; for most purposes, it's hardly worth using in Word 97.

Online Layout View

Online Layout view, which is new in Word 97, is designed for creating and reading online documents. Online Layout view (see Figure 1.13) provides a left pane that displays the structure of the document (its headings) and a right pane that displays the text at an easily readable size, with features such as animated text and hyperlinks.

 To switch to Online Layout view, choose View ➤ Online Layout or click the Online Layout View button on the horizontal scroll bar.

NOTE **We'll look at Online Layout view in detail in Chapter 20.**

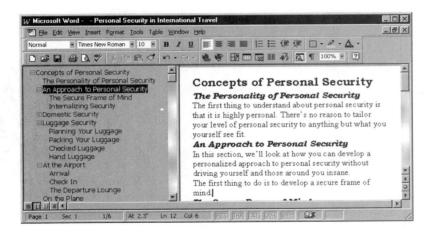

FIGURE 1.13:
Online Layout view provides special features for working with online documents.

Page Layout View

Page Layout view is useful for getting an idea of how your documents will look when you print them. In Page Layout view, Word shows you the margins of the sheet or sheets of paper you're working on, any headers or footers, and any footnotes or annotations. Word doesn't wrap text to the size of the window, as doing so would change the page from its print format.

To switch to Page Layout view, choose View ➤ Page Layout or click the Page Layout View button on the horizontal scroll bar. You'll see an approximation of the layout of your document, complete with margins (see Figure 1.14). If necessary, zoom to a more appropriate zoom percentage (see the section *Zooming the View* a couple of blocks south of here).

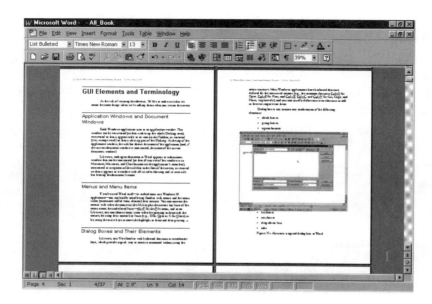

FIGURE 1.14:
Page Layout view shows you where each element in your document will really appear when printed.

Print Preview

Word's *Print Preview* provides a way for you to scan your documents on screen for formatting howlers before you immortalize them on dead trees. Print Preview shows you, as closely as Word can, the effect you'll get when you print your document on the currently selected printer. We'll look at Print Preview in detail in Chapter 3, *Printing a Document*.

Outline View

Word's *Outline view* lets you collapse your documents to a specified number of heading levels—for example, you could choose to view only the first-level heads in your documents or the first three levels of heads. Outline view is very useful for structuring long documents and is somewhat more complex than the other views. We'll examine it in detail in Chapter 11.

Split-Screen View

Word also offers Split-screen view, in which the screen is divided into two panes. You can use a different view in each pane (but not online layout view) and zoom each pane to a different zoom percentage.

To split the screen, choose Window ➤ Split. The mouse pointer will change to a double-headed arrow pointing up and down and dragging a thick gray line. Move the line up or down the screen to where you want to split it, and then click to place the line. Figure 1.15 shows a split window.

To remove the split screen, choose Window ➤ Remove Split.

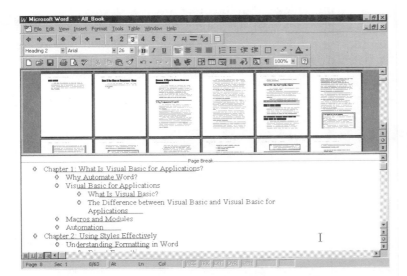

FIGURE 1.15:
Choose Window ➤ Split to split the screen into two panes. You can then work in a different view or at a different zoom percentage in each pane

> **TIP** To split the window in half quickly, double-click the split bar—the tiny horizontal bar at the top of the vertical scroll bar. Double-click the split bar that divides the screen to remove the split screen.

Zooming the View

In any of Word's views, you can use the Zoom feature to increase or decrease the size of the display to make it easily visible. Word lets you set any zoom percentage between 10% and 500% of full size.

You can use either the Zoom box on the Standard toolbar or the Zoom dialog box to set the zoom percentage.

Zooming with the Zoom Box on the Standard Toolbar

To zoom the view with the Zoom box on the Standard toolbar:

1. Display the Standard toolbar if it isn't visible.
2. Click the button to the right of the Zoom box to display a drop-down list of zoom percentages.
3. Choose a zoom percentage from the drop-down list or type in a different percentage (between 10% and 500%).

Zooming with the Zoom Dialog Box

To zoom the view with the Zoom dialog box:

1. Choose View ➤ Zoom to display the Zoom dialog box (see Figure 1.16).

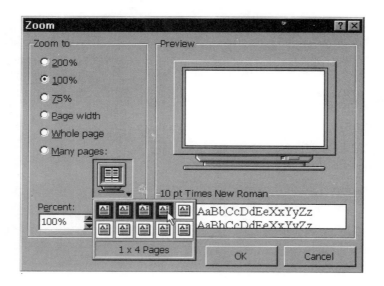

FIGURE 1.16:
In the Zoom dialog box, choose the zoom percentage you want in the Zoom To box.

2. In the Zoom To box, choose the zoom percentage you want:
   - To zoom to 200%, 100%, 75%, Page Width, or Whole Page (which is available only in Page Layout view and Print Preview), click the appropriate option button in the Zoom To box.
   - To display more than one page at a time (only in Page Layout view and Print Preview), click the monitor next to the Many Pages option button and drag through the grid it disgorges to indicate the configuration of pages you want to view: 2x2 pages, 2x3 pages, and so on.

- To display the page or pages at a precise zoom percentage of your choosing, adjust the setting in the Percent box at the bottom-left corner of the Zoom dialog box.

3. Click the OK button to apply the zoom percentage to the document.

Opening a Non-Word Document

Word can open files saved in a number of other formats, from plain-text ASCII files to spreadsheets (for example, Lotus 1-2-3) to calendar and address books.

> **NOTE**
>
> To open a file saved in a format other than Word, you need to have installed the appropriate converter so that Word can read the file. Generally speaking, the easiest way to tell if you have the right converter installed for a particular file format is to try to open the file; if Word cannot open it, you probably need to install another converter. Run the Word or Office Setup program again and choose to install the appropriate converter (see the Appendix for details on installation).

To open a document saved in a format other than Word:

1. Select File ➤ Open to display the Open dialog box.

2. Choose the folder containing the document you want to open.

3. Click the drop-down list button on the Files of Type list box at the bottom left-hand corner of the Open dialog box. From the list, select the type of file that you want to open. If Word doesn't list the file that you want to open, choose All Files (*.*) from the drop-down list to display all the files in the folder.

4. Choose the file in the main window of the Open dialog box, then click the Open button or press Enter to open the file.

Saving a Word Document in a Different Format

Not content with just letting you open a file saved in a different format, Word also lets you save files in formats other than Word.

> **NOTE** This procedure is dependent on your having the right converters installed. If you don't, you'll need to install them. To install another converter, run the Word or Office Setup program again and choose to install the appropriate converter.

To save an existing file in a different format:

1. Choose File ➤ Save As. Word will display the Save As dialog box.
2. Scroll down the Save as Type drop-down list and choose the file type you want to save the current document as.
3. If you want, enter a different file name for the file.
4. Click the Save button or press Enter.

> **NOTE** If you haven't saved the file before, you can choose File ➤ Save instead of File ➤ Save As to open the Save As dialog box. You'll also need to specify a name for the document (unless you want to accept Word's default name for it—Doc1.doc, Doc2.doc, and so on).

Now that you're up to speed on creating documents, entering text, and saving, it's time to get a little more fancy. In Chapter 2, we'll look at the different formatting options that you can use with Word to enhance your documents. But first, in case you've had enough for the day, let's quickly look at closing documents and exiting Word.

Closing Your Document

To close the current document, choose File ➤ Close, press Ctrl+F4, or click the Close button on the document window. If the document contains unsaved changes, Word will prompt you to save them and will close the document when you're finished.

If the document has been saved before and if there are no new changes, Word will simply close the document.

TIP   **To close all open documents at once, hold down one of the Shift keys on your keyboard, then, with your mouse, choose File ➤ Close All. (Interestingly enough, the Close All choice appears on the File menu even when you have only one file open in Word.)**

Exiting Word

When you've finished working in Word, exit it to get back to the Windows Desktop. Choose File ➤ Exit or click the Close button at the top-right corner of the Word window. If you have unsaved documents, Word will prompt you to save them; save them as described earlier in this chapter in the section *Saving a Word Document*. If you have open documents that you've saved but that you've subsequently changed without saving, Word will prompt you to save those changes.

Chapter 2

FORMATTING A DOCUMENT

- **Formatting characters and words**
- **Formatting paragraphs**
- **Creating and using styles**
- **Setting up the page**
- **Using Word's AutoFormat options**

Word supplies you with enough formatting options to sink a medium-sized battle cruiser—I mean, enough formatting options for you to typeset a long work of moderate complexity. The basic types of formatting options start with character formatting—how the individual letters look—and move through paragraph formatting—how paragraphs appear on the page—to style formatting—a combination of character and paragraph formatting, among other formatting—and finally, to page setup. In this chapter, we'll look at each of these types of formatting.

Character Formatting

Character formatting is formatting that you can apply to one or more characters. Character formatting consists of:

- character attributes, such as bold, italic, underline, and strikethrough (among others)
- fonts, such as Courier New, Times New Roman, and Arial
- point size—the size of the font
- character spacing, such as superscripts and subscripts (vertical spacing), and kerning (horizontal spacing)

You can apply character formatting in several ways—using the Font dialog box, using keyboard shortcuts, or using the Formatting toolbar. Each of these has advantages and disadvantages depending on what you're doing when you decide to start applying formatting and how much formatting you need to apply. Let's look at each of them in turn.

Character Formatting Using the Font Dialog Box

The Font dialog box offers you the most control over font formatting, providing all the character-formatting options together in one handy location.

To set character formatting using the Font dialog box:

1. Select the text whose formatting you want to change. If you want to change the formatting of just one word, place the insertion point inside it.
2. Right-click in the text and choose Font from the context menu, or choose Format ➤ Font, to display the Font dialog box (see Figure 2.1). If the Font tab isn't displayed, click it to bring it to the front of the dialog box.
3. Choose the formatting options you want from the Font tab.
   - In the Font list box, choose the font (or typeface) for the text.
   - In the Font Style list box, choose the font style: Regular, Italic, Bold, or Bold Italic.

> **NOTE** Watch the Preview box at the bottom of the dialog box to see approximately how your text will look.

   - In the Size box, choose the font size you want. To choose a font size that Word doesn't list, type it into the top Size box. For example, enter **13** to produce 13-point text. (Word offers 12-point and 14-point options in the list box.)

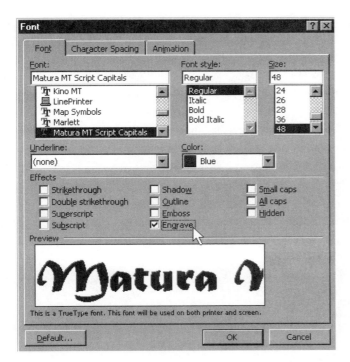

FIGURE 2.1:
The Font dialog box gives you quick access to all the character formatting options Word offers.

- In the Underline box, choose the underlining style you want. The styles are mostly self-explanatory, with the possible exception of these two: None removes any existing underline, while Words Only adds a single underline underneath words, with no underline underneath spaces.
- Select any special effects you want in the Effects area by clicking the check boxes for Strikethrough, Double Strikethrough, Superscript, Subscript, Shadow, Outline, Emboss, Engrave, Small Caps, All Caps, or Hidden. (Hidden text is invisible under normal viewing conditions and does not print unless you choose to include it.)
- Finally, choose a color for your text from the Color drop-down list. This will affect the text onscreen—and on printouts if you have a color printer.

4. For special effects, try adjusting the settings on the Character Spacing tab of the Font dialog box.

- The Spacing option controls the horizontal placement of letters relative to each other—closer to each other, or further apart. From the Spacing drop-down list, you can choose Expanded or Condensed, then use the up and down spinner arrows in the By box to adjust the degree of expansion or condensation. (Alternatively, simply click the spinner arrows and let Word worry about making the Spacing drop-list match your choice.) Again, watch the Preview box for a simulation of the effect your current choices will have.
- The Position option controls the vertical placement of letters relative to the baseline they're theoretically resting on. From the Position list, you can choose Normal, Raised, or Lowered, then use the spinner arrows in the By box to raise or lower the letters—or simply click the spinner arrows and let Word determine whether the text is Normal, Raised, or Lowered.
- To turn on automatic kerning for fonts above a certain size, select the Kerning for Fonts check box and adjust the point size in the Points and Above box if necessary.

> **NOTE**
>
> *Kerning* is the space between letters that prevents a letter from appearing too far from its neighbor. For example, if you type WAVE in a large font size without kerning, Word will leave enough space between the W and the A, and the A and the V, for you to slalom a small truck through. With proper kerning, you'll only be able to get a motorcycle through the gap.

5. To really enliven a document, try one of the six options on the Animation tab of the Font dialog box. Use these options in moderation for best effect.
6. When you've finished making your choices in the Font dialog box, click the OK button to close the dialog box and apply your changes to the selected text or current word.

Setting a New Default Font

To set a new default font for all documents that is based on the current template, make all your choices on the Font and Character Spacing tabs (and, in extreme cases, the Animation tab as well) of the Font dialog box, then click the Default button (on any tab). Word will display a message box to confirm that you want to change the default font. Click Yes to make the change.

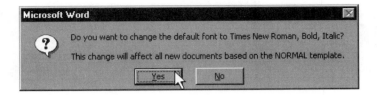

Character Formatting Using the Formatting Toolbar

The Formatting toolbar offers a quick way to apply some of the most used character formatting options: font, font size, bold, italic, underline, highlighting, and font color (see Figure 2.2).

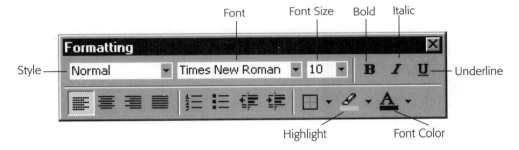

FIGURE 2.2: The Formatting toolbar provides a quick way to apply formatting to your documents.

To change fonts with the Formatting toolbar, select the text you want to affect, then click the drop-down list button on the Font box and select the new font from the list that appears.

- The fonts you've used most recently will be listed at the top of the list, with an alphabetical listing of all the fonts underneath that list.
- To move quickly down the list of fonts to the one you want, type the first letter of the font's name.

To change font size, select the text to change, then click the drop-down list button on the Font Size box and select the font size from the list that appears. To choose a font size that Word doesn't list, type it into the Font Size box and press Enter.

TIP To change the font or font size of just one word, you don't need to select it—just placing the insertion point within the word does the trick.

To apply bold, italic, or underline, select the text you want to emphasize, then click the Bold, Italic, or Underline button on the Formatting toolbar. When you've applied one of these attributes, the relevant button will appear to be pushed in.

NOTE To remove bold, italic, or underline, select the emphasized text, then click the Bold, Italic, or Underline button again to remove the formatting.

 To apply highlighting to one instance of text, select the text, then click the Highlight button.

To apply highlighting to several instances of text easily, click the Highlight button before selecting any text. Your mouse pointer will take on a little highlighter pen when moved into the document window. Drag this pen over text to highlight it.

To turn the highlighting off, click the Highlight button again or press the Esc key.

To change the color of the highlighting, click the drop-down list arrow next to the Highlight button and choose another color from the list. (The default color for highlighting is the classic fluorescent yellow—Enhanced French Headlamp, as it's known in the trade—beloved of anyone who's ever had a highlighter pen break in their shirt pocket.)

To remove highlighting, drag the highlighter pen over the highlighted text.

To change the font color of the current selection or current word, click the Font Color drop-down palette button and choose the color you want from the palette. You can then apply that color quickly to selected text by clicking the Font Color button.

Character Formatting Using Keyboard Shortcuts

Word offers the following keyboard shortcuts for formatting text with the keyboard. For all of them, select the text you want to affect first, unless you want to affect only the word in which the insertion point is currently resting.

Action	Keyboard Shortcut
Increase font size (in steps)	Ctrl+Shift+.
Decrease font size (in steps)	Ctrl+Shift+,
Increase font size by 1 point	Ctrl+]
Decrease font size by 1 point	Ctrl+[
Change case (cycle)	Shift+F3
All capitals	Ctrl+Shift+A
Small capitals	Ctrl+Shift+K
Bold	Ctrl+B
Underline	Ctrl+U
Underline (single words)	Ctrl+Shift+W
Double-underline	Ctrl+Shift+D
Hidden text	Ctrl+Shift+H
Italic	Ctrl+I
Subscript	Ctrl+=
Superscript	Ctrl+Shift+= (i.e., Ctrl++)
Remove formatting	Ctrl+Shift+Z
Change to Symbol font	Ctrl+Shift+Q

Paragraph Formatting

With paragraph formatting, you can set a number of parameters that influence how your paragraphs look:

- Alignment
- Indentation
- Line spacing
- Text flow
- Tabs

The sections of this chapter that follow discuss each of these paragraph formatting options in turn.

Setting Alignment

Word offers you several ways to set paragraph alignment: You can use the alignment buttons on the Formatting toolbar, or the keyboard shortcuts, or the options in the Paragraph dialog box. Using the buttons on the Formatting toolbar is the easiest way, and the one you'll probably find yourself using most often, so we'll look at that first.

Setting Alignment Using the Formatting Toolbar

To set alignment using the Formatting toolbar:

1. Place the insertion point in the paragraph that you want to align. To align more than one paragraph, select all the paragraphs you want to align.
2. Click the Align Left, Center, Align Right, or Justify button on the Formatting toolbar (see Figure 2.3).

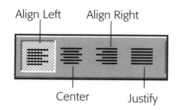

Align Left   Align Right

Center   Justify

FIGURE 2.3:
Use the alignment buttons to align text quickly.

Setting Alignment Using Keyboard Shortcuts

When you're typing, the quickest way to set the alignment of paragraphs is by using these keyboard shortcuts:

Shortcut	Effect
Ctrl+L	Align left
Ctrl+E	Center
Ctrl+R	Align right
Ctrl+J	Justify

Setting Alignment Using the Paragraph Dialog Box

The third way to set alignment—and usually the slowest—is to use the Paragraph dialog box. Why discuss this? Because you're very likely to be making other formatting changes in the Paragraph dialog box, so sometimes you may find it useful to set alignment there too.

To set alignment using the Paragraph dialog box:

1. Place the insertion point in the paragraph you want to align. To align several paragraphs, select all the paragraphs that you want to align.
2. Right-click and choose Paragraph from the context menu, or choose Format ➤ Paragraph to display the Paragraph dialog box (see Figure 2.4).
3. Choose the alignment you want from the Alignment drop-down list.
4. Click the OK button to close the Paragraph dialog box.

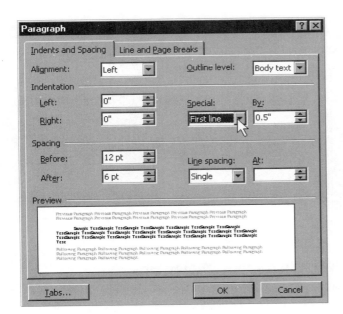

FIGURE 2.4:
In the Paragraph dialog box, you can set many paragraph-formatting options, including alignment.

Setting Indents

As with setting alignment, you can set indents in more than one way. Again, the quickest way is with the ruler, but you can also use the Paragraph dialog box and some obscure keyboard shortcuts.

Setting Indents with the Ruler

To set indents using the ruler, click and drag the indent markers on the ruler (see Figure 2.5).

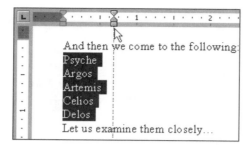

FIGURE 2.5:
Click and drag the indent markers on the ruler to change the indentation of the current paragraph or selected paragraphs.

- The first-line indent marker specifies the indentation of the first line of the paragraph (this could be a hanging indent).
- The left indent marker specifies the position of the left indent.

NOTE To move the left indent marker and first-line indent marker together, drag the left indent marker by the square box at its base rather than by the upward-pointing mark. Dragging by the upward-pointing mark will move the left indent marker without moving the first-line indent marker.

- The right indent marker specifies the position of the right indent.

Setting Indents with the Paragraph Dialog Box

Depending on whether you have a graphical or literal mindset, you may find setting indents in the Paragraph dialog box easier than setting them with the ruler.

To set paragraph indents with the Paragraph dialog box:

1. Place the insertion point in the paragraph for which you want to set indents. To set indents for several paragraphs, select all the paragraphs you want to set indents for.
2. Right-click and choose Paragraph from the context menu, or choose Format ➤ Paragraph to display the Paragraph dialog box.
3. Make sure the Indents and Spacing tab is selected (if it's not visible, click it to bring it in front of the Line and Page Breaks tab).
4. In the Left box, enter the distance to indent the paragraph from the left margin.
5. In the Right box, enter the distance to indent the paragraph from the right margin.

6. In the Special box, choose from (none), First Line, and Hanging:
   - (none) formats the paragraph as a regular paragraph, with indents controlled solely by the Left and Right settings.
   - First Line adds an indent to the first line of the paragraph. This indent is in addition to the Left setting. For example, if you choose a Left setting of 0.5" and a First Line setting of 0.5", the first line of the paragraph will be indented one inch. By using a first-line indent, you can avoid having to type a tab at the beginning of a paragraph.
   - Hanging makes the first line of the paragraph hang out to the left of the rest of the paragraph. (Excessively logical people call this an *outdent*.) Hanging indents are great for bulleted or numbered paragraphs—the bullet or number hangs way out to the left of the paragraph, and the wrapped lines of the paragraph align neatly with the first line.
   - Figure 2.6 illustrates the different types of indentation Word provides for paragraphs.

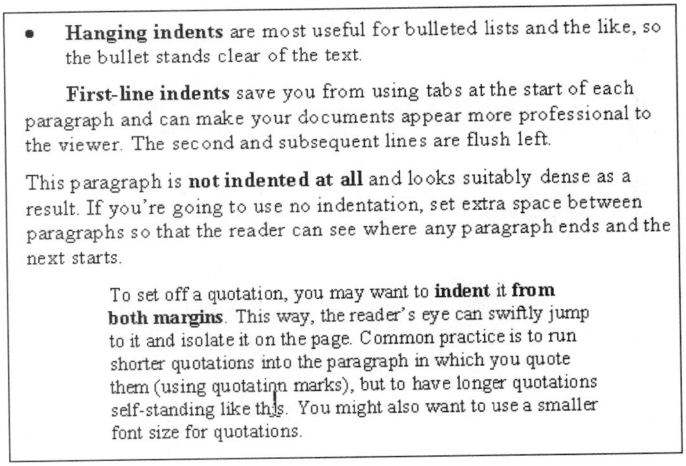

- **Hanging indents** are most useful for bulleted lists and the like, so the bullet stands clear of the text.

  First-line indents save you from using tabs at the start of each paragraph and can make your documents appear more professional to the viewer. The second and subsequent lines are flush left.

  This paragraph is **not indented at all** and looks suitably dense as a result. If you're going to use no indentation, set extra space between paragraphs so that the reader can see where any paragraph ends and the next starts.

  > To set off a quotation, you may want to **indent it from both margins**. This way, the reader's eye can swiftly jump to it and isolate it on the page. Common practice is to run shorter quotations into the paragraph in which you quote them (using quotation marks), but to have longer quotations self-standing like this. You might also want to use a smaller font size for quotations.

FIGURE 2.6:
Word provides these different types of indentation for formatting paragraphs.

7. If you chose a Special setting of First Line or Hanging, enter a measurement in the By box.
8. Click the OK button to close the Paragraph dialog box.

> **TIP**
>
> When setting indents, you can use negative values for Left and Right indents to make the text protrude beyond the margin. Negative indents can be useful for special effects, but if you find yourself using them all the time, you probably need to adjust your margins. One other thing—for obvious reasons, you can't set a negative hanging indent, no matter how hard you try.

Setting Indents by Using Keyboard Shortcuts

Here are the keyboard shortcuts for setting indents:

Indent from the left	Ctrl+M
Remove indent from the left	Ctrl+Shift+M
Create (or increase) a hanging indent	Ctrl+T
Reduce (or remove) a hanging indent	Ctrl+Shift+T
Remove paragraph formatting	Ctrl+Q

Choosing Measurement Units

You may have noticed that the measurement units (inches, centimeters, and so on) in the Paragraph dialog box on your computer are different from those in the screens shown here—for example, you might be seeing measurements in centimeters or picas rather than in inches.

If so, don't worry. Word lets you work in any of four measurements: inches, centimeters, points, and picas. Points and picas—$\frac{1}{72}$ of an inch and $\frac{1}{6}$ of an inch, respectively—are most useful for page layout and typesetting, but if you're not doing those, you might want to switch between inches and centimeters. (Sooner or later, we'll all be using centimeters, I'm told.)

To change your measurement units:

1. Choose Tools ➤ Options to display the Options dialog box.
2. Click the General tab to bring it to the front.
3. Choose Inches, Centimeters, Points, or Picas as your measurement unit from the Measurement Units drop-down list.
4. Click the OK button to close the Options dialog box.

Setting Line Spacing

You can change the line spacing of your documents by using either the Paragraph dialog box or keyboard shortcuts:

1. Place the insertion point in the paragraph you want to adjust or select several paragraphs whose line spacing you want to change.

    *   To select the whole document quickly, choose Edit ➤ Select All, or hold down the Ctrl key and click once in the selection bar at the left edge of the Word window. Alternatively, press Ctrl+5 (that's the 5 on the numeric keypad, not the 5 above the letters R and T).

2. Right-click in the selection and choose Paragraph from the context menu, or choose Format ➤ Paragraph, to display the Paragraph dialog box (shown in Figure 2.4).

3. If the Indents and Spacing tab isn't at the front of the Paragraph dialog box, click it to bring it to the front.

4. Use the Line Spacing drop-down list to choose the line spacing you want.

Line Spacing	Effect
Single	Single spacing, based on the point size of the font
1.5 lines	Line-and-a-half spacing, based on the point size of the font
Double	Double spacing based on the point size of the font
At least	Sets a minimum spacing for the lines, measured in points. This can be useful for including fonts of different sizes in a paragraph, or for including in-line graphics
Exactly	Sets the exact spacing for the lines, measured in points
Multiple	Multiple line spacing, set by the number in the At box to the right of the Line Spacing drop-down list. For example, to use triple line spacing, enter **3** in the At box; to use quadruple line spacing, enter **4**

5. If you chose At Least, Exactly, or Multiple in the Line Spacing drop-down list, adjust the setting in the At box if necessary.

6. Click the OK button to apply the line spacing setting to the chosen text.

> **TIP**
>
> To set line spacing with the keyboard, press **Ctrl+1** to single-space the selected paragraphs, **Ctrl+5** to set 1.5-line spacing, and **Ctrl+2** to double-space paragraphs.

Setting Spacing Before and After Paragraphs

As well as setting the line spacing within any paragraph, you can adjust the amount of space before and after any paragraph to position it more effectively on the page. So instead of using two blank lines (i.e., two extra paragraphs with no text) before a heading and one blank line afterwards, you can adjust the paragraph spacing to give the heading plenty of space without using any blank lines at all.

TIP The easiest way to set consistent spacing before and after paragraphs of a particular type is to use Word's *styles*, which we'll discuss later in this chapter.

To set the spacing before and after a paragraph:

1. Place the insertion point in the paragraph whose spacing you want to adjust, or select several paragraphs to adjust their spacing all at once.
2. Right-click and choose Paragraph from the context menu, or choose Format ➤ Paragraph to display the Paragraph dialog box (shown in Figure 2.4).
3. Make sure the Indents and Spacing tab is foremost. If it isn't, click it to bring it to the front.
4. In the Spacing box, choose a Before setting to specify the number of points of space before the selected paragraph. Watch the Preview box for the approximate effect this change will have.
5. Choose an After setting to specify the number of points of space after the current paragraph. Again, watch the Preview box.

NOTE The Before setting for a paragraph adds to the After setting for the paragraph before it; does not change the After setting. For example, if the previous paragraph has an After setting of 12 points, and you specify a Before setting of 12 points for the current paragraph, you'll end up with 24 points of space between the two paragraphs (in addition to the line spacing you've set).

6. Click the OK button to close the Paragraph dialog box and apply the changes.

TIP

To quickly add or remove one line's worth of space before a paragraph, press Ctrl+0 (Ctrl+zero).

Using the Text Flow Options

Word offers six options for controlling how your text flows from page to page in the document. To select these options, click in the paragraph you want to apply them to, or select a number of paragraphs. Then choose Format ➤ Paragraph to display the Paragraph dialog box, click the Line and Page Breaks tab to bring it to the front of the dialog box (unless it's already at the front), and select the options you want to use:

Widow/Orphan Control	A *widow* (in typesetting parlance) is when the last line of a paragraph appears on its own at the top of a page; an *orphan* is when the first line of a paragraph appears by itself at the foot of a page. Leave the Widow/Orphan Control box checked to have Word rearrange your documents to avoid widows and orphans.
Keep Lines Together	Tells Word to prevent the paragraph from breaking over a page. If the whole paragraph will not fit on the current page, Word moves it to the next page.

WARNING

If you write long paragraphs, choosing the Keep Lines Together option can produce painfully short pages.

Keep with Next	Tells Word to prevent a page break from occurring between the selected paragraph and the next paragraph. This options can be useful for making sure that a heading appears on the same page as the paragraph of text following it, or that an illustration appears together with its caption, but be careful not to set Keep with Next for body text paragraphs.
Page Break Before	Tells Word to force a page break before the current paragraph. This is useful for making sure that, for example, each section of a report starts on a new page.

Suppress Line Numbers	Tells Word to turn off line numbers for the current paragraph. This applies only if you are using line numbering in your document.
Don't Hyphenate	Tells Word to skip the current paragraph when applying automatic hyphenation.

When you've chosen the options you want, click the OK button to apply them to the paragraph or paragraphs.

Setting Tabs

To align the text in your documents, Word offers five kinds of tabs:

- Left-aligned
- Centered
- Right-aligned
- Decimal-aligned
- Bar

Setting Tabs Using the Ruler

The quickest way to set tabs for the current paragraph, or for a few paragraphs, is to use the ruler (choose View ➤ Ruler to display the ruler if it isn't visible, or simply pop it up by sliding the mouse pointer onto the gray bar at the top of the screen once you've selected the paragraphs you want to work on).

Adding a Tab

To add a tab:

1. Display the ruler if necessary.
2. Place the insertion point in a single paragraph or select the paragraphs to which you want to add the tab.
3. Choose the type of tab you want by clicking the tab selector button at the left end of the ruler to cycle through left tab, center tab, right tab, and decimal tab.
4. Click on the ruler in the location where you want to add the tab. The tab mark will appear in the ruler.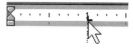

TIP   When adding a tab, you can click with either the left or the right mouse button. For moving or removing a tab, only the left button works. Don't ask.

Moving a Tab

To move a tab, display the ruler if necessary, then click the tab marker and drag it to where you want it.

Removing a Tab

To remove a tab, display the ruler if it's not visible, then click the marker for the tab you want to remove and drag it into the document. The tab marker will disappear from the ruler.

Setting Tabs Using the Tabs Dialog Box

When you need to check exactly where the tabs are in a paragraph, or if you set too many tabs in the ruler and get confused, turn to the Tabs dialog box to clear everything up.

First, place the insertion point in a single paragraph or select the paragraphs whose tabs you want to change, then choose Format ➤ Tabs to display the Tabs dialog box (see Figure 2.7) and follow the procedures described in the next sections.

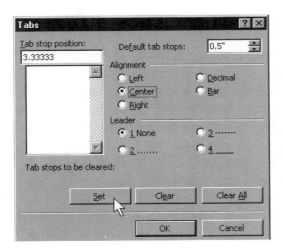

FIGURE 2.7:
The Tabs dialog box gives you fine control over the placement and types of tabs in your document.

Setting Default Tabs

To set a different spacing for default tabs, adjust the setting in the Default Tab Stops box at the top of the Tabs dialog box. For example, a setting of 1" will produce tabs at 1", 2", 3", and so on.

TIP

To quickly display the Tabs dialog box, double-click on an existing tab in the bottom half of the ruler. (If you double-click in open space in the bottom half of the ruler, the first click will place a new tab for you; if you double-click in the top half of the ruler, Word will display the Page Setup dialog box.) You can also get to the Tabs dialog box quickly by clicking the Tabs button on either panel of the Paragraph dialog box.

Setting Tabs

To set tabs:

1. Enter a position in the Tab Stop Position box.
   - If you're using the default unit of measurement set in the copy of Word you're using, you don't need to specify the units.
   - If you want to use another unit of measurement, specify it: 2.3"(or 2.3 in), 11 cm, 22 pi, 128 pt.
2. Specify the tab alignment in the Alignment box: Left, Center, Right, Decimal, or Bar. (Bar inserts a vertical bar—|—at the tab stop.)
3. In the Leader box, specify a tab leader if you want one: periods, hyphens, or underlines leading up to the tabbed text. (Periods are often used as tab leaders for tables of contents, between the heading and the page number.)
4. Click the Set button.
5. Repeat steps 1 through 4 to specify more tabs if necessary.
6. Click the OK button to close the Tabs dialog box and apply the tabs you set.

Clearing Tabs

To clear a tab, select it in the Tab Stop Position list and click the Clear button. Word will list the tab you chose in the Tab Stops to Be Cleared area of the Tabs dialog box. Choose other tabs to clear if necessary, then click the OK button.

To clear all tabs, simply click the Clear All button, then click the OK button.

Moving Tabs

To move tabs using the Tabs dialog box, you need to clear them from their current position and then set them elsewhere—you can't move them as such. (To move tabs easily, use the ruler method described earlier in this chapter.)

Language Formatting

You can format text as if it were written in a language other than English. Not only can you spell-check the text written in other languages, but you can also use the Find feature to search for text formatted in those languages for quick reference. (Chapter 4 discusses spell checking, while Chapter 6 discusses the Find feature.)

To format selected text as if it were another language:

1. Choose Tools ➤ Language ➤ Set Language to display the Language dialog box (see Figure 2.8).

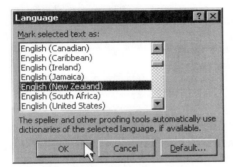

FIGURE 2.8:
In the Language dialog box, choose the language in which to format the selected text, and then click OK.

2. In the Mark Selected Text As list box, choose the language in which to format the text.

3. Click OK to apply the language formatting to the selected text.

> **NOTE**
>
> The (no proofing) language choice tells Word not to spell-check the text. This can be very useful for one-off technical terms that you don't want to add to your custom dictionaries (which we'll look at in Chapter 4). But if you find the spelling checker suddenly failing to catch blatant spelling errors, check the language formatting of the text in question.

Borders and Shading

If a part of your text, or a picture, or indeed the whole page, needs a little more emphasis, you can select it and add borders and shading:

1. Choose Format ➤ Borders and Shading to display the Borders and Shading dialog box (see Figure 2.9).

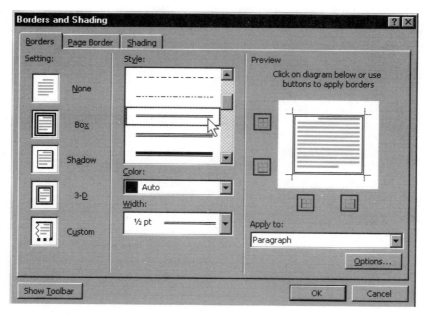

FIGURE 2.9: Apply borders and shading to items from the Borders and Shading dialog box.

2. On the Borders tab, choose the type of border you want to add from the options displayed:
   - In the Setting area, choose one of the settings, such as None, Box, Shadow, Grid (for tables and cells), 3-D (not available for tables and cells), or Custom. Watch the effect in the Preview demonstration box.
   - Next, choose the type of line you want from the Style list, choose a color from the Color drop-down list, and choose a weight from the Width drop-down list if you want. To change one of the lines, click the appropriate icon in the Preview area to apply it or remove it.

- For text, you can choose Text or Paragraph in the Apply To drop-down list below the Preview area. If you apply the border to a paragraph, you can specify the distance of the border from the text by clicking the Options button and specifying Top, Bottom, Left, and Right settings in the Border and Shading Options dialog box, then clicking OK.

3. On the Page Border tab, choose the type of border you want to add to the page. The controls on this tab work in the same way as those described in step 2. The important difference is that the Apply To drop-down list allows you to choose between Whole Document, This Section, This Section—First Page Only, and This Section—All Except First Page. Again, clicking the Options button displays the Border and Shading Options dialog box, which allows you to place the border precisely on the page.

4. On the Shading tab, choose the type of shading to add:
   - Choose the color for the shading from the Fill palette.
   - Choose a style and color for the pattern in the Style and Color drop-down list boxes in the Patterns area.
   - Finally, use the Apply To list to specify whether to apply the shading to the paragraph or just to selected text.

WARNING Any shading over 20% will completely mask text on most black-and-white printouts (even if it looks wonderfully artistic onscreen).

5. Click OK to close the Borders and Shading dialog box and apply your changes to the selection.

TIP To remove borders and shading, select the item, then choose Format ➤ Borders and Shading to display the Borders and Shading dialog box. To remove a border, choose None in the Setting area on the Borders tab; to remove a page border, choose None in the Setting area on the Page Border tab; and to remove shading, choose None in the Fill palette and Clear in the Style drop-down list on the Shading tab. Click OK to close the Borders and Shading dialog box.

Style Formatting

Word's *paragraph styles* bring together all the formatting elements discussed so far in this chapter—character formatting, paragraph formatting (including alignment), tabs, language formatting, and even borders and shading. Each style contains complete formatting information that you can apply with one click of the mouse or one keystroke.

> **NOTE** Word also offers *character styles*, which are similar to paragraph styles but contain only character formatting. Character styles are suitable for picking out elements in a paragraph formatted with paragraph styles.

Using styles not only gives your documents a consistent look—every Heading 1 paragraph will appear in the same font and font size, with the same amount of space before and after it, and so on—but also saves you a great deal of time in formatting your documents.

You can either use Word's built-in styles—which are different in Word's various predefined templates—or create your own styles. Every paragraph in Word uses a style; Word starts you off in the Normal style unless the template you're using dictates otherwise.

Applying Styles

To apply a style, place the insertion point in the paragraph or choose a number of paragraphs, then click the Style drop-down list button on the Formatting toolbar and choose the style you want from the list.

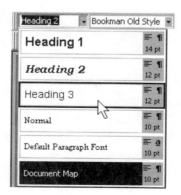

TIP **Some of the most popular styles have keyboard shortcuts: Ctrl+Shift+N for Normal style; Ctrl+Alt+1 for Heading 1, Ctrl+Alt+2 for Heading 2, Ctrl+Alt+3 for Heading 3; and Ctrl+Shift+L for List Bullet.**

You can also apply a style by choosing Format ➤ Style to display the Style dialog box (see Figure 2.10), choosing the style in the Styles list box, and clicking the Apply button.

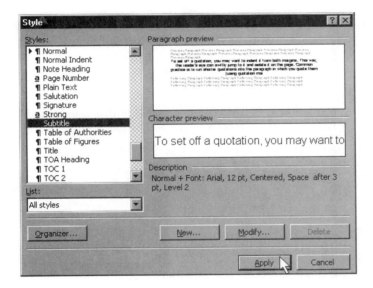

FIGURE 2.10:
To apply a style, choose it in the Styles list box and click the Apply button.

To tell which style paragraphs are in, you can display the *style area*, a vertical bar at the left side of the Word window that displays the style name for each paragraph.

Heading 1	Concepts of Personal Security
Heading 2	*The Personality of Personal Security*
Main Text	The first thing to understand about personal security is that it is your level of personal security to anything but what you yourse

To display the style area, choose Tools ➤ Options to display the Options dialog box and click the View tab to bring it to the front. Enter a measurement in the Style Area Width box in the Window area, and then click OK.

To alter the width of the style area once you've displayed it, click and drag the dividing line. To remove it, drag the dividing line all the way to the left of the Word window.

> **NOTE** **You cannot display the style area in Page Layout view or Print Preview.**

Creating a New Style

As you can see in the Styles list box shown in Figure 2.10, Word's templates come with a number of built-in styles. If they're not enough for you, you can create your own styles in three ways: by example, by definition, and by having Word do all the work for you.

Creating a New Style by Example

The easiest way to create a style is to set up a paragraph of text with the exact formatting you want for the style—character formatting, paragraph formatting, borders and shading, bullets or numbers, and so on. Then click the Style drop-down list, type the name for the new style into the box, and press Enter. Word will create the style, which you can immediately select from the Style drop-down list and apply to other paragraphs as necessary.

Creating a New Style by Definition

The more complex way of creating a style is by definition:

1. Choose Format ➤ Style to display the Style dialog box.
2. Click the New button. Word will display the New Style dialog box (see Figure 2.11).
3. Set the information for your new style:
   - In the Name box, enter a name for the style. Style names can be a decent length—Word will accept over 100 characters—but you'll do better to keep them short enough to fit in the Style box on the Formatting toolbar. If your style name is over 20 characters long, you should probably rethink your naming conventions.
   - In the Based On drop-down list box, choose the style on which you want to base the new style. Bear in mind that if you change the other style later, the new style will change too. The Preview box will show what the Based On style looks like.
   - In the Style Type box, choose whether you want a paragraph style or a character style.

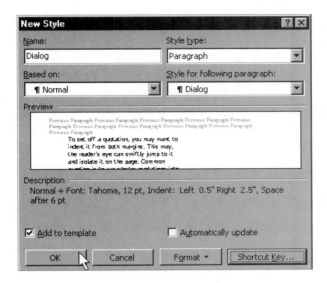

FIGURE 2.11:
Creating a new style
in the New Style
dialog box

- In the Style for Following Paragraph box (which is not available for character styles), choose the style that you want Word to apply to the paragraph immediately after this style. For example, after the Heading 1 style, you might want Body Text, or after Figure, you might want Caption. But for many styles you'll want to continue with the style itself.

4. To adjust the formatting of the style, click the Format button and choose Font, Paragraph, Tabs, Border, Language, Frame, or Numbering from the drop-down list. This will display the dialog box for that type of formatting. When you've finished, click the OK button to return to the New Style dialog box.

NOTE Some of these dialog boxes, such as Character, Paragraph, and Tabs, we've already looked at in this chapter; others we'll examine in subsequent chapters.

5. Repeat step 4 as necessary, selecting other formatting characteristics for the style.
6. Select the Add to Template check box to add the new style to the template.
7. Select the Automatically Update check box if you want Word to automatically update the style when you change it. (We'll look at this option more in a minute.)

8. To set up a shortcut key for the style, click the Shortcut Key button. Word will display the Customize Keyboard dialog box. With the insertion point in the Press New Shortcut Key box, press the shortcut key combination you'd like to set, click the Assign button, then click the Close button.

WARNING Watch the Currently Assigned To area of the Customize Keyboard dialog box when selecting your shortcut key combination. If Word has already assigned that key combination to a command, macro, or style, it will display its name there. If you choose to assign the key combination to the new style, the old assignment for that combination will be deactivated.

9. In the New Style dialog box, click the OK button to return to the Style dialog box.
10. To create another new style, repeat steps 2 through 9.
11. To close the Style dialog box, click the Apply button to apply the new style to the current paragraph or current selection, or click the Close button to save the new style without applying it.

Having Word Create Styles Automatically

Creating styles yourself can get tedious—why not have Word create them for you? And when you change the formatting of a paragraph that has a certain style, you can have Word update the style for you, so that every other paragraph that has the same style takes on that formatting too.

To have Word automatically create styles for you:

1. Choose Tools ➤ AutoCorrect to display the AutoCorrect dialog box.
2. Click the AutoFormat as You Type tab to display it.
3. In the Automatically as You Type area at the bottom of the tab, select the Define Styles Based on Your Formatting check box. (This is selected by default.)
4. Click the OK button to close the AutoCorrect dialog box.

Once you've set this option (or if it was set already), Word will attempt to identify styles you're creating and will supply names for them. For example, if you start a new document (with paragraphs in the Normal style, as usual) and bold and center the first paragraph, Word may define that bolding and centering as a Title style. If you simply increase the font size, Word may call that paragraph Heading 1 instead. This sounds creepy, but it works surprisingly well; and if it doesn't suit you, you can easily turn it off by clearing the Define Styles Based on Your Formatting check box.

Modifying a Style

You can modify a style by example and by definition. You can also choose to have Word automatically identify and apply changes you make to the style.

Modifying a Style by Example

To modify a style by example, change the formatting of a paragraph that currently has the style assigned to it, then choose the same style again from the Style drop-down list. Word will display the Modify Style dialog box (see Figure 2.12). Make sure the Update the Style to Reflect Recent Changes option button is selected, then click the OK button to update the style to include the changes you just made to it. If you want Word to automatically update the style without displaying this dialog box when you make changes in the future, select the Automatically Update the Style from Now On check box first.

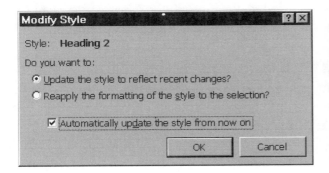

FIGURE 2.12:
In the Modify Style dialog box, choose OK to update the style to reflect changes you just made to it. If you want Word to automatically update the style in the future, select the Automatically Update the Style from Now On check box first.

Modifying a Style by Definition

Modifying a Word style by definition is similar to creating a new style, except that you work in the Modify Style dialog box, which offers one option less than the New Style dialog box offers—you don't get to choose whether the style is a paragraph style or a character style because Word already knows which it is.

Open the Style dialog box by choosing Format ➤ Style, then choose the style you want to work on from the Styles list. (If you can't see the style you're looking for, make sure the List box at the bottom-left corner of the Style dialog box is showing All Styles rather than Styles in Use or User-Defined Styles.)

Click the Modify button. Word will display the Modify Style dialog box. From there, follow steps 3 through 9 in the Creating a New Style by Definition section (except for selecting the style type) to modify the style, and step 11 to exit the Style dialog box.

Removing a Style

Removing a style is much faster than creating one. Simply open the Style dialog box by choosing Format ➤ Style, select the style to delete in the Styles list, and click the Delete button. Word will display a message box confirming that you want to delete the style; click the Yes button.

You can then delete another style the same way, or click the Close button to leave the Style dialog box.

> **TIP**
>
> **Two things to keep in mind here: You can't delete a Heading style once you've started using it. Second, when you delete a style that's in use (other than a Heading style), Word applies the Normal style to those paragraphs.**

Using the Style Gallery

Word provides the Style Gallery to give you a quick overview of its many templates and the myriad styles they contain. To open the Style Gallery, choose Format ➤ Style Gallery. Word will display the Style Gallery dialog box (see Figure 2.13).

To preview a template in the Preview Of box, select it in the Template list box. Then choose the preview you want in the Preview box:

- Document shows you how your current document looks with the template's styles applied.
- Example shows you a sample document that uses the template's styles.
- Style Samples shows each of the styles in the document.

To apply the template you've chosen to your document, click the OK button. Alternatively, click the Cancel button to close the Style Gallery.

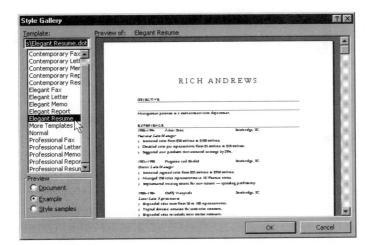

FIGURE 2.13:
The Style Gallery dialog box gives you a quick view of the styles in Word's templates.

Page Setup

If you're ever going to print a document, you need to tell Word how it should appear on the page. You can change the margins, the paper size, the layout of the paper, and even which printer tray it comes from (which we'll look at in Chapter 3, Printing a Document).

> **NOTE** The best time to set paper size is at the beginning of a project. While you can change it at any time during a project without trouble, having the right size (and orientation) of paper from the start will help you lay out your material.

To alter the page setup, double-click in the top half of the horizontal ruler (or anywhere in the vertical ruler) or choose File ➤ Page Setup to display the Page Setup dialog box, then follow the instructions for setting margins, paper size, and paper orientation in the next sections. (If you want to change the page setup for only one section of a document, place the insertion point in the section you want to change before displaying the Page Setup dialog box.) Alternatively, you can choose This Point Forward from the Apply To drop-down list on any tab of the Page Setup dialog box to change the page setup for the rest of the document.

Setting Margins

To set the margins for your document, click the Margins tab in the Page Setup dialog box (see Figure 2.14). In the boxes for Top, Bottom, Left, and Right margins, use the spinner arrows to enter the measurement you want for each margin; alternatively, type in a measurement.

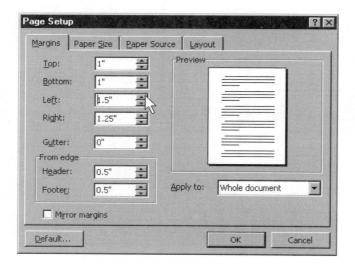

FIGURE 2.14:
The Margins tab of the Page Setup dialog box

If you're typesetting documents (rather than simply using the word processor to put them together), you may want to select the Mirror Margins check box. This makes the two inner-margin measurements the same as each other, and the two outer-margin measurements the same as each other, and changes the Left and Right settings in the column under Margins in the Page Setup dialog box to Inside and Outside, respectively.

The Gutter measurement is the space that your document will have on the inside of each facing page. For example, if you're working with mirror-margin facing pages, you could choose to have a Gutter measurement of 1″ and Inside and Outside margins of

1.25 inches. That way, your documents would appear with a 1.25" left margin on left-hand pages, a 1.25" inch right margin on right-hand pages, and a 2.25" margin on the inside of each page (the gutter plus the margin setting).

Use the Preview in the Page Setup dialog box to give you an idea of how your document will look when you print it.

Setting Paper Size

Word lets you print on paper of various sizes, offering a Custom option to allow you to set a paper size of your own, in addition to various standard paper and envelope sizes.

To change the size of the paper you're printing on, click the Paper Size tab of the Page Setup dialog box (see Figure 2.15).

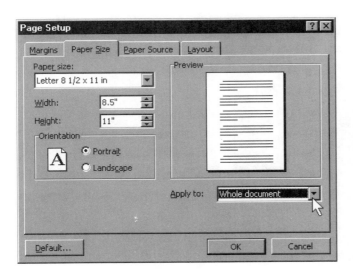

FIGURE 2.15:
The Paper Size tab of the Page Setup dialog box

In the Paper Size drop-down list box, choose the size of paper you'll be working with (for example, Letter 8½ x 11). If you can't find the width and height of paper you want, use the Width and Height boxes to set the width and height of the paper you're using; Word will automatically set the Paper Size box to Custom Size.

Setting Paper Orientation

To change the orientation of the page you're working on, click the Paper Size tab of the Page Setup dialog box (shown in Figure 2.15) and choose Portrait or Landscape in the Orientation group box. (Portrait is taller than it is wide; Landscape is wider than it is tall.)

Section Formatting

Often you'll want to create documents that use different page layouts, or even different sizes of paper, for different pages. Word handles this by letting you divide documents into *sections*, each of which can have different formatting characteristics. For example, you could use sections to set up a document to contain both a letter and an envelope, or to have one-column text and then multi-column text, and so on.

Creating a Section

To create a section:

1. Place the insertion point where you want the new section to start.
2. Choose Insert ➤ Break. Word will display the Break dialog box (see Figure 2.16).

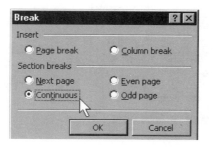

FIGURE 2.16:
In the Break dialog box, choose the type of section break to insert, and then click the OK button.

3. Choose the type of section break to insert by clicking an option button in the Section Breaks area:
   - **Next Page** starts the section on a new page. Use this when you have a drastic change in formatting between sections—for example, an envelope on one page and a letter on the next.

- **Continuous** starts the section on the same page as the preceding paragraph. This is useful for creating layouts with differing numbers of columns on the same page.
- **Even Page** starts the section on a new even page.
- **Odd Page** starts the section on a new odd page. This is useful for chapters or sections that should start on a right-hand page for consistency.

4. Click the OK button to insert the section break. It will appear in Normal view and Outline view as a double dotted line across the page containing the words *Section Break* and the type of section break:

··Section Break (Continuous)··

The Sec indicator on the status bar will indicate which section you're in:

| Page 12   Sec 7   12/16 |

> **TIP**
> You can change the type of section break on the Layout tab of the Page Setup dialog box: Place the insertion point in the relevant section, then choose File ➤ Page Setup, select the type of section you want from the Section Start drop-down list on the Layout tab, and click the OK button.

Deleting a Section

To delete a section break, place the insertion point at its beginning (or select it) and press the Delete key.

> **WARNING**
> When you delete a section break, the section before the break will take on the formatting characteristics of the section after the break.

Using AutoFormat

To automate the creation of documents, Word offers automatic formatting with its AutoFormat features: AutoFormat regular, which applies styles when you choose the Format ➤ AutoFormat command, and AutoFormat As You Type, which applies automatic formatting to paragraphs as you finish them.

To set AutoFormat options:

1. Choose Tools ➤ AutoCorrect to display the AutoCorrect dialog box.

2. Click the AutoFormat tab or AutoFormat As You Type tab of the AutoCorrect dialog box. Figure 2.17 shows the AutoFormat As You Type tab.

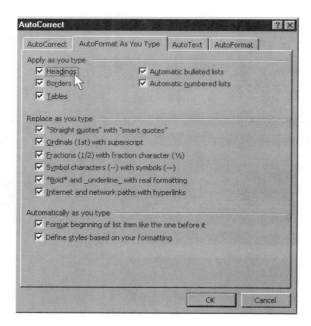

FIGURE 2.17:
On the AutoFormat As You Type tab (and the AutoFormat tab, which is not shown here) set the autoformatting options you want.

3. In the Apply or Apply As You Type box, select the check boxes next to the autoformatting options you want to use. For AutoFormat the options are: Headings, Lists, Automatic Bulleted Lists, and Other Paragraphs; and for AutoFormat As You Type the options are: Headings, Borders, Tables, Automatic Bulleted Lists, and Automatic Numbered Lists.

Headings	Word applies Heading 1 style when you press Enter, type a short paragraph starting with a capital letter and not ending with a period, and press Enter twice; and Heading 2 when that paragraph starts with a tab.
Automatic Numbered Lists	Word creates a numbered list when you type a number followed by a punctuation mark (such as a period, hyphen, or closing parenthesis), and then a space or tab and some text.
Automatic Bulleted Lists	Word creates a bulleted list when you type a bullet-type character (e.g., a bullet, an asterisk, a hyphen) and then a space or tab followed by text.
Borders	Word adds a border to a paragraph that follows a paragraph containing three or more dashes, underscores, or equal signs: Dashes produce a thin line for dashes, underscores produce a thick line, and equal signs produce a double line.
Tables	Word creates a table when you type an arrangement of hyphens and plus signs (e.g., + -- + -- + -- +). This is one of the more bizarre and inconvenient ways of creating a table; we'll look at better ways in Chapter 8.
Other Paragraph	Word applies styles based on what it judges your text to be.

> **NOTE** You can stop the automatic numbered or bulleted list by pressing Enter twice.

4. Choose Replace or Replace As You Type options as necessary.

5. In the Automatically As You Type area of the AutoFormat As You Type tab, select the Format Beginning of List Item Like the One Before It check box if you want Word to try to mimic your formatting of lists automatically. Select the Define Styles Based on Your Formatting check box if you want Word to automatically create styles whenever it feels that it's appropriate.

6. In the Always AutoFormat area of the AutoFormat tab, select the Plain Text WordMail documents check box if you want Word to automatically format plain-text e-mail in WordMail. (We'll look at WordMail in Chapter 20.)

7. Click the OK button to close the AutoCorrect dialog box.

AutoFormat As You Type options will now spring into effect as you create your documents.

If you decide to use the regular AutoFormat feature instead of AutoFormat As You Type, create your document and then choose Format ➤ AutoFormat. Word will display an AutoFormat dialog box (see Figure 2.18), which lets you access the AutoFormat dialog box to refine your predefined AutoFormat settings if necessary. Choose a type of document from the drop-down list, then click the OK button to start the autoformatting.

FIGURE 2.18:
In the AutoFormat dialog box, choose a type of document and whether you want to review the changes Word proposes, then click the OK button.

Like I said at the beginning of the chapter, Word offers enough formatting options to sink a medium-sized battle cruiser. If you've just read through this chapter in sequence, congratulations and take a rest. Then turn the page for Chapter 3, which deals with printing Word documents and is (mercifully) much shorter.

Chapter 3

PRINTING A DOCUMENT

- **Using Print Preview**
- **Printing documents**
- **Printing envelopes**
- **Printing labels**

Once you've written, set up, and formatted your documents, you'll probably want to print them. As it does with its other features, Word offers a wealth of printing options. Printing can be as simple as clicking one button to print a whole document, or as complicated as choosing which parts of your document to print, what to print them on, how many copies to print, and even what order to print them in.

In this chapter, we'll look first at how to use Word's Print Preview mode and how to nail down any glaring deficiencies in your text before you print it. Second, we'll tackle straightforward printing. And finally, we'll move on to the tricky stuff—envelopes and labels.

Using Print Preview

Before you print any document, you'll do well to use Word's Print Preview mode to establish that the document looks right before you print it.

To use Print Preview, click the Print Preview button or choose File ➤ Print Preview. Word will display the document in Print Preview mode (see Figure 3.1).

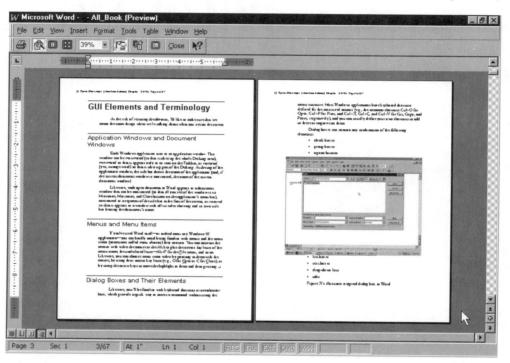

FIGURE 3.1: In Print Preview mode, Word displays your document as it will appear when you print it.

In Print Preview mode, Word displays the Print Preview toolbar (see Figure 3.2) which has the following buttons:

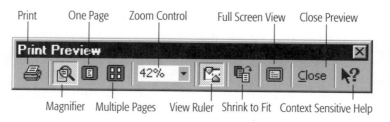

FIGURE 3.2: The Print Preview toolbar offers quick access to the Print Preview features.

Print	Prints the current document using the default print settings.
Magnifier	Switches between Magnifier mode and Editing mode. In Magnifier mode, the pointer appears as a magnifying glass containing a plus sign (when the view is zoomed out) or a minus sign (when the view is zoomed in). In Editing mode, the pointer appears as the insertion point, and you can use it to edit as usual.
One Page	Zooms the view to one full page.
Multiple Pages	Zooms the view to multiple pages. When you click the Multiple Pages button, Word displays a small grid showing the display combinations possible—one full page; two pages side by side; three pages side by side; two pages, one on top of the other; four pages, two on top, two below, and so on. Click the arrangement of pages you want. Click and drag to the right or bottom to extend out to more columns or rows of pages.
Zoom Control	Determines the size at which you view the document. Use the drop-down list to choose the zoom percentage that suits you.
View Ruler	Toggles the display of the horizontal and vertical rulers on and off.
Shrink to Fit	Attempts to make your document fit on one fewer page (by changing the font size, line spacing, and margins). This is useful when your crucial fax strays a line or two onto an additional page and you'd like to shrink it down.
Full Screen Views	Maximizes Word and removes the menus, status bar, scroll bars, and so on, from the display. This is useful for clearing more screen real estate to see exactly how your document looks before you print it.
Close Preview	Closes Print Preview, returning you to whichever view you were in before.
Help	Adds a question mark to the pointer so that you can click any screen element and receive pop-up help.

I'll let you explore Print Preview on your own, but here's one thing to try: Click and drag the gray margin borders in the rulers to quickly adjust the page setup of the document.

To exit Print Preview, click the Close button on the Print Preview toolbar to return to the view you were in before you entered Print Preview, or choose File ➤ Print Preview.

Printing a Document

Once you've checked a document in Print Preview and fixed any aberrations, you're ready to print it. Next, you need to choose whether to print the whole document at once or only part of it.

Printing All of a Document

The easiest way to print a document in Word is simply to click the Print button on the Standard toolbar. This prints the current document without offering you any options—to be more precise, it prints one copy of the entire document in page-number order (1, 2, 3, and so forth) to the currently selected printer.

You can also print the whole of a document by using the procedure described in the next section and choosing All in step 2.

Printing Part of a Document

If you want to print only part of a document, don't click the Print button. Instead, choose File ➤ Print to display the Print dialog box (see Figure 3.3).

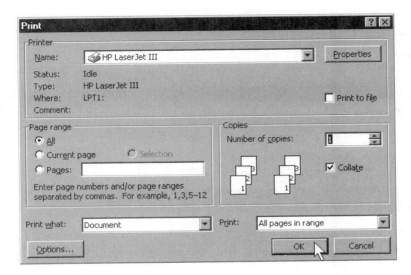

FIGURE 3.3:
In the Print dialog box, choose the printer you want to use, which pages you want to print, and the number of copies you want. Then click the OK button to print.

1. First, make sure the printer named in the Name drop-down list of the Printer group box is the one you want to use. If it's not, use the drop-down list to select the right printer.

2. Next, choose which pages to print in the Page Range group box by clicking one of the option buttons:
    - **All** prints the whole document.
    - **Current Page** prints the page on which the insertion point is currently located.
    - **Selection** prints only the selected text in your document. If you haven't selected any text, this option button will be dimmed.
    - **Pages** lets you print individual pages by number or a range (or ranges) of pages. Use commas to separate the page numbers (e.g., **1, 11, 21**) and a hyphen to separate page ranges (e.g., **31-41**). You can also combine the two: **1, 11, 21-31, 41-51, 61**.

> **TIP**   To print from a particular page to the end of the document, you don't need to know the number for the last page of the document—simply enter the page number followed by a hyphen (e.g., 11-).

3. If you want to print only odd pages or even pages, use the Print drop-down list at the bottom-right corner of the Print dialog box to specify Odd Pages or Even Pages. This can be useful for printing two-sided documents.

4. Choose how many copies of the document you want to print by using the Number of Copies box in the Copies area.

   • You can also choose whether to collate the pages or not–if you collate them, Word prints the first set of pages in order (1, 2, 3, 4, 5) and then prints the next set and subsequent sets; if you don't collate them, Word prints all the copies of page 1, then all the copies of page 2, and so on.

5. When you've made your choices in the Print dialog box, click the OK button to send the document to the printer.

Printing on Different Paper

So far we've looked only at printing on your default-sized paper (for example, 8½ x 11" paper). Sooner or later you're going to need to print on a different size of paper, be it to produce a manual, an application to some bureaucracy, or a tri-fold birthday card. Not only can you use various sizes of paper with Word, but you can use different sizes of paper for different sections of the same document, as discussed in Chapter 2.

When you want to print on paper of a different size, you will need to set up your document suitably–paper size, margins, and orientation. (Look back to the *Page Setup* section of Chapter 2 for more details on this if you need to.)

Next, choose the paper source for each section of your document.

Choosing a Paper Source

If you're writing a letter or a report, you may want to put the first page on special paper. For example, the first page of a letter might be on company paper that contains the company's logo, name, address, and URL, while subsequent pages might be on paper that contains everything but the URL.

To choose the paper source for printing the current section of the current document:

1. Choose File ➤ Page Setup, or double-click either in the top half of the horizontal ruler or anywhere in the vertical ruler to display the Page Setup dialog box, then click the Paper Source tab (see Figure 3.4).

2. In the First Page list box, choose the printer tray that contains the paper for the first page. (If your printer has only one tray, choose Manual Feed so that you can feed the page of different paper separately from the main tray.)

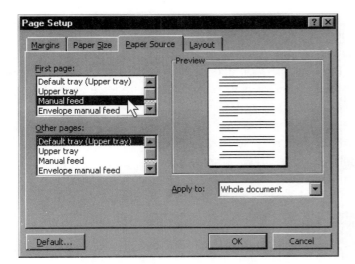

FIGURE 3.4:
Choose the printer trays for the various sections of a document on the Paper Source tab of the Page Setup dialog box.

3. In the Other Pages list box, choose the printer tray that contains the paper you want to use for the remaining pages of the document. Usually, you'll want to choose Default Tray here, but on occasion you may want to use either another tray or Manual Feed for special effects.

4. In the Apply To drop-down list box, choose the section of the document that you want to print on the paper you're choosing. (The default is Whole Document unless the document contains sections, in which case the default is This Section. You can also choose This Point Forward to print from the selection point through the rest of the document on the paper you're choosing—the page containing the selection point being the "first page" and the rest of the document being the "other pages.")

5. Click the OK button to close the Page Setup dialog box and save your changes.

NOTE   To set the paper source for another section of the document, click in that section and repeat the above steps.

Setting a Default Paper Source

If you always print from a different paper tray than your copy of Word is set up to use, you'd do well to change it. This might happen if you always needed to use letterhead on a networked printer that had a number of paper trays, and your colleagues kept filling the default paper tray with unflavored white bond.

To set your default paper source:

1. Choose File ➤ Page Setup, or double-click in the top half of the horizontal ruler (or anywhere in the vertical ruler), to display the Page Setup dialog box.
2. Click the Paper Source tab to display it.
3. Make your selections in the First Page list box and Other Pages list box.
4. Choose an option from the Apply To drop-down list if necessary.
5. Click the Default button. Word will display a message box asking for confirmation of your choice.

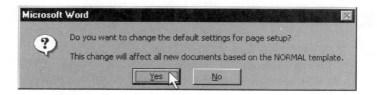

6. Click Yes. Word will close the Page Setup dialog box and make the change.

Printing Envelopes

Printing envelopes has long been the bane of the computerized office. Envelopes have been confusing to set up in word processing applications and—worse—they tend to jam in laser printers and inkjet printers (and that's not even mentioning what dot-matrix printers think of envelopes). There have been four traditional ways of avoiding these problems: hand-write the labels, use a typewriter, use window envelopes, or use sheets of labels. If none of these methods appeals to you, read on.

To print an envelope:

1. Choose Tools ➤ Envelopes and Labels. Word will display the Envelopes and Labels dialog box (see Figure 3.5).
   - If Word finds what it identifies as an address in the current document, it will display it in the Delivery Address box. If you don't think Word will find the address hidden in the document—for example, if the document contains more than one address, or the address is not broken over several lines into a typical address format—highlight the address before choosing Tools ➤ Envelopes and Labels.

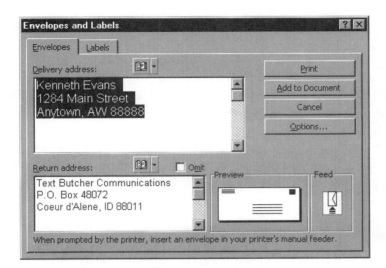

FIGURE 3.5:
Word displays any address it finds in the document—or the address you selected—in the Delivery Address box on the Envelopes tab of the Envelopes and Labels dialog box.

2. If Word hasn't found an address in the document, you'll need to choose it yourself.

    • To include a recently used address, click the Insert Address drop-down list button in the Envelopes and Labels dialog box and choose the name from the drop-down list.

    • To include an address from an address book, click the Insert Address button and choose the address book from the *Show Names* From The drop-down list in the Select Name dialog box. If you aren't logged on to e-mail, you will be prompted to choose a messaging profile before the Select Name dialog box is displayed. Then choose the name, either by typing the first characters of the name into the Type Name or Select from List text box or by selecting it from the list box. Click the OK button to insert the name in the Delivery Address box of the Envelopes and Labels dialog box.

    • Alternatively, type the name and address into the Address box.

3. Check the return address that Word has inserted in the Return Address box. Word automatically picks this information out of the User Information tab of the Options dialog box. If the information is incorrect, you can correct it in the Return Address box, but you'd do better to correct it in the Options dialog box if you regularly work with the computer you're now using. (Choose Tools ➤ Options, then click the User Information tab.) If no address is entered on the User Information tab of the Options dialog box, Word will leave the Return Address box blank.

- You can also use the Insert Address button's drop-down list to insert a recently used address or click the Insert Address button and choose a name in the Select Name dialog box.

- Alternatively, you can omit a return address by checking the Omit check box.

4. Next, check the Preview box to see how the envelope will look and the Feed box to see how Word expects you to feed it into the printer. If either of these is not to your liking, click the Options button (or click the Preview icon or the Feed icon) to display the Envelope Options dialog box (see Figure 3.6).

5. On the Envelope Options tab of the Envelope Options dialog box (yes, this gets weird), use the Envelope Size drop-down list to choose the size of envelope you're using. (Check the envelope's packaging for the size before you get out your ruler to measure an envelope.)

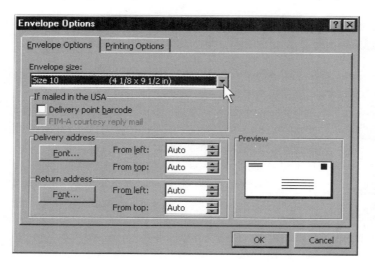

FIGURE 3.6:
In the Envelope Options dialog box, use the Envelope Options tab to set the size of the envelope and the fonts for the delivery address and return address. Use the Printing Options tab to set the feed method you want to use with your printer.

6. If you want to customize the look of the addresses, use the options in the Delivery Address group box and Return Address group box. The Font button in these boxes opens the Envelope Address dialog box (which you'll recognize as a version of the Font dialog box we looked at in Chapter 2). Choose the font and effects you want, then click the OK button to close the dialog box. Use the From Left and From Top boxes in the Delivery Address box and Return Address box to set the placement of the address on the envelope. Watch the Preview box to see how you're doing.

7. On the Printing Options tab of the Envelope Options dialog box, Word offers options for changing the feed method for the envelope—you have the choice of six different envelope orientations; the choice of placing the

envelope Face Up or Face Down in the printer; and the choice of Clockwise Rotation. Again, choose the options you want. Click the OK button when you're satisfied.

WARNING If your printer is set up correctly, Word should be able to make a fair guess at how you'll need to feed the envelope for the printer to print it correctly. You probably won't need to change the settings on the Printing Options tab of the Envelope Options dialog box unless you find that Word won't print your envelopes correctly.

8. You can now print the envelope you've set up by clicking the Print button in the Envelopes and Labels dialog box, or by adding it to the current document by clicking the Add to Document button.

- If you choose the Add to Document button, Word places the envelope on a new page at the start of the document and formats the page to require a manual envelope feed. When you print the document, you'll need to start the printer off with a manually fed envelope; once the envelope has printed, Word will resume its normal feeding pattern for the rest of the document (unless that too has abnormal paper requirements).

Printing Labels

If you don't want to mess with feeding envelopes into your printer and betting that it won't chew them up, sheets of labels provide a good alternative. What's more, Word makes it easy to set up labels.

NOTE In this section, we'll look at how to set up labels for one addressee—either a single label, or a whole sheet of labels with the same address on each. For sheets of labels with a different address on each label, see Chapter 9, *Mail Merge*.

1. If the current document contains the address you want to use on the label, select the address.

2. Choose Tools ➤ Envelopes and Labels to display the Envelopes and Labels dialog box (see Figure 3.7) and select the Labels tab if it isn't currently displayed.
- If you selected an address in step 1, or if Word found an address on its own, Word will display it in the Address box.

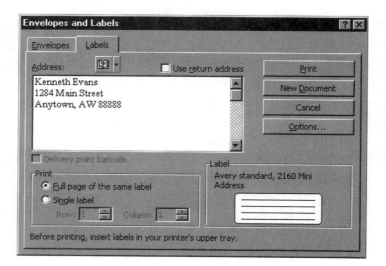

FIGURE 3.7:
In the Envelopes and Labels dialog box, click the Labels tab if it isn't displayed.

3. First, choose the type of labels you want. The current type of label is displayed in the Label box in the bottom-right corner of the Envelopes and Labels dialog box. To choose another type of label, click the Options button (or click anywhere in the Label group box). You'll see the Label Options dialog box (see Figure 3.8).
- Choose the type of printer you'll be using: Dot Matrix, or Laser and Ink Jet.
- Choose the printer tray that you'll put the label sheets in by using the Tray drop-down list.
- Choose the category of label by using the Label Products drop-down list: Avery Standard, Avery A4 and A5 Sizes, MACO Standard, or Other. (Other includes labels by manufacturers other than Avery and MACO.)
- In the Product Number list box, choose the type of labels you're using—it should be on the box of labels. The Label Information group box will show the details for the type of labels you've selected in the Product Number list box.
- For more details on the labels you've chosen, or to customize them, click the Details button to display the Information dialog box. Click OK when you're done.

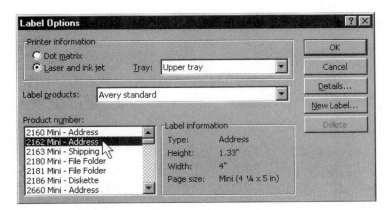

FIGURE 3.8:
In the Label Options dialog box, pick the type of label you want to use.

- Click the OK button in the Label Options dialog box to return to the Envelopes and Labels dialog box. It will now display the labels you've chosen in the Label box.

4. Add the address (if you haven't already selected one):
   - To use a recently used address, choose it from the Insert Address button's drop-down list.

   - To include an address from an address book, click the Insert Address button and choose the address book from the Show Names From The drop-down list in the Select Name dialog box. If you aren't logged on to e-mail, you will be prompted to choose a messaging profile before the Select Name dialog box is displayed. Then choose the name, either by typing the first characters of the name into the Type Name or Select from List text box or by selecting it from the list box. Click the OK button to insert the name in the Address box of the Envelopes and Labels dialog box.
   - Alternatively, type the name and address into the Address box.

5. In the Print group box, choose whether to print a full page of the same label or a single label.
   - If you choose to print a single label, set the Row and Column numbers that describe its location on the sheet of labels.

6. If you chose to print a full page of the same label, you can click the New Document button to create a new document containing the labels, then print it and save it for future use. Alternatively, click the Print button to print the sheet of labels. (If you chose to print a single label, Word offers only the Print button.)

TIP

If you want to customize your labels, choose the New Document button, then add any formatting that you like. You can also add graphics by using Word's Insert ➤ Picture command.

Chapter 4

TEXT IMPROVEMENT FEATURES

FEATURING

- **Checking spelling and grammar**
- **Using the Thesaurus**
- **Getting a word count**
- **Inserting symbols and special characters**
- **Hyphenating your documents**

Word offers a number of features for checking and improving your writing. You can check your spelling and grammar at times of your own choosing, or you can have Word attempt to check both automatically as you write. To help you escape the confusion of the English language, Word also provides a Thesaurus for finding synonyms, antonyms, and words generally related to the word you start with. You can use the word count feature to make sure your article or paper is a suitable length, and Word's hyphenation feature to make sure that your prose is laid out attractively.

Checking Spelling and Grammar

In Word 97, you can have the Spelling and Grammar checker check your grammar and spelling either together or independently. Before you start using the Spelling and Grammar checker, you need to be aware of the differing goals and differing success rates of the Spelling checker and the Grammar checker.

The Spelling checker is a great tool for making sure your document contains no embarrassing typos. Bear in mind that the Spelling checker is limited in its goal—it simply tries to match words you type against the lists in its dictionary files, flagging any words it does not recognize and suggesting replacements that seem to be close in spelling. It does not consider the word in context, beyond making sure that you meant to repeat any word that appears straight after itself. Anything more than that is the job of the Grammar checker.

The Grammar checker works by applying grammar rules to your sentences; you can customize the assortment of rules it uses to make it match your writing style a little more closely. The Grammar checker can be helpful for pointing out some problems with your writing—it's particularly hot on passive constructions, and it will try to tell you if you're being politically incorrect—but its suggestions are often unsuitable, and there are many grammatical problems that it cannot identify. If you want to use the Grammar checker, remember that *it does not understand the meaning of your writing*, even though it can identify many of the parts of speech. For example, it likes this sentence:

> Indigenously life beckons diligently sea pre-diet in queasy sand fun for fat delirium.

As far as the Grammar checker is concerned, this is a fine sentence—it has nouns, a verb, prepositions, adverbs, adjectives, and so on, and nothing is obviously out of place. The human reader knows that this sentence is gibberish (with perhaps a nod at William Carlos Williams), but the Grammar checker hasn't a clue.

Diatribe aside, the Grammar checker will occasionally save you from yourself. And you can either have it critique your prose surreptitiously in the background as you write, or switch it off altogether. Read on.

NOTE   Word's AutoCorrect feature offers another form of spell-checking. We'll look at AutoCorrect in detail in Chapter 10.

On-the-Fly Spell-Checking and Grammar-Checking

On-the-fly spell-checking and grammar-checking offers you the chance either to correct each spelling error and grammatical error the moment you make it or to highlight all the spelling errors and grammatical errors in a document and deal with them one by one. This is one of those partially great features that isn't right for everybody. The Spelling checker in particular can be intrusive when you're typing like a maniac trying to finish a project on time and it keeps popping up typos that interrupt your flow. Nonetheless, try enabling these features and see how you do with them. (If you've just installed Word, you'll find the Spelling checker and Grammar checker are enabled by default.)

To enable Word's on-the-fly spell-checking and grammar-checking:

1. Choose Tools ➤ Options to display the Options dialog box.
2. Click the Spelling & Grammar tab to bring it to the front.
3. In the Spelling area, select the Check Spelling as You Type check box.
4. In the Grammar area, select the Check Grammar as You Type check box.
5. Click the OK button to close the Options dialog box.

The Spelling checker will now put a squiggly red line under any word that doesn't match an entry in its dictionary. To spell-check one of these words quickly, right-click in it. Word will display a spelling menu with suggestions for spelling the word (or what it thinks the word is) along with four other options:

- **Ignore All** tells Word to ignore all instances of this word.
- **Add** adds the word to the Word spelling dictionary currently selected (we'll get to this in a minute).
- **AutoCorrect** offers a submenu replicating the suggestions Word displayed at the top of the spelling menu. By choosing one of these, you can quickly create an AutoCorrect entry for this particular typo. We'll look at AutoCorrect in detail in Chapter 10. (If Word has no suggestions for the word it doesn't recognize, it will show no AutoCorrect submenu.)
- **Spelling** fires up a full-fledged spell check (see the next section for details on this too).

Once you have chosen either Add or Ignore All for one instance of a word that the Spelling checker has flagged, Word removes the squiggly red underline from all other instances of that word. (If you have chosen another spelling for a flagged word, either from the main portion of the context menu or the AutoCorrect submenu of the context menu, Word doesn't change all instances of that word.)

If you type the same word twice, Word will flag that, too, and offer you a different menu—Delete Repeated Word, Ignore, and Spelling, as shown here. (In this case, if you choose Spelling, the Spelling dialog box will appear to tell you that you've repeated the word.)

NOTE

As we saw in Chapter 2, the *(no proofing)* language choice (set via the Language dialog box; Tools ➤ Language ➤ Set Language) tells Word not to spell-check the text. If on-the-fly spell checking seems to stop working, check the language formatting of the text in question—it may be set to *(no proofing)*.

The Grammar checker will put a squiggly green line under any word or construction that runs afoul of the rules that the Grammar checker is currently using. To see what

the Grammar checker thinks is wrong with one of these words, right-click it and see what suggestions Word offers on the context menu.

The grammar suggestion may consist of a single word, as it does here. In other instances, Word may suggest a way of rewriting the whole sentence.

TIP

Note how the spelling and grammar changes affect each other: Accepting one proposed spelling change can, in rare cases, affect the spelling of the next word, and often spelling changes will affect the next grammar change, which will in turn affect the rest of the sentence.

The Spelling indicator on the status bar shows the status of spell-checking and grammar-checking. While you're typing (or otherwise inserting text), the icon will show a pen moving across the book; when Word has time to check the text, you'll see a check mark on the right page of the book if everything's fine, and a cross on the page if there's one or more mistakes.

WARNING
The Grammar checker often takes quite a while to identify mistakes, especially if you're running Word on anything less macho than a Pentium 166 or its equivalent, and especially when you're inputting text at high speed. Check the Spelling indicator on the status bar when you take a break, and you may find that the Grammar checker, grumbling along in the background, has taken exception to something you wrote way back in the document.

Static Spell-Checking and Grammar-Checking

If you can't stand Word's on-the-fly spell-checking and grammar-checking, or if you simply want to be sure that you have corrected all the spelling errors in that vital report you've written for your boss before submitting it to her, run Word's regular Spelling and Grammar checker instead.

1. Click the Spelling and Grammar button, choose Tools ➤ Spelling and Grammar, or press F7 to start the Spelling and Grammar checker. You'll see Word working through the document or selection sentence by sentence, highlighting each sentence as it goes.

NOTE
If you have selected any text (or a picture), Word assumes that you want to check it. After Word has finished checking the selected text (or picture—which it usually finds to be correctly spelled), it then displays a message box asking if you want to check the rest of the document. If you have not selected anything, Word will automatically start checking from the beginning of the document.

- If Word does not find any words that it does not recognize, it will display either a message saying that the spelling and grammar check is complete or the Readability Statistics dialog box, which we'll examine in a minute.

3. As soon as Word encounters either a word that does not match an entry in its dictionary, or what it considers a grammatical error, it displays the Spelling and Grammar dialog box. Figure 4.1 shows how Word responds to a spelling error: The Not in Dictionary box shows the offending word in its sentence, and the Suggestions box shows Word's best guess at the word highlighted, with less convincing suggestions below it.

NOTE   Again, text with the *(no proofing)* language formatting will not be checked by the Spelling and Grammar checker.

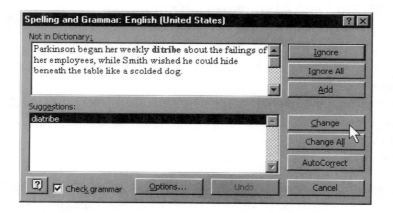

FIGURE 4.1:
The Spelling and Grammar dialog box tackles a spelling problem.

4. You now have several choices:
- If you think this is the only instance of a particular spelling in a document, click the Ignore button to ignore this instance of the apparent misspelling.
- Click the Ignore All button to have Word skip all instances of this word. This is particularly useful for names or technical terms (or foreign words) that will appear in only one document and which you don't want to add to your custom dictionaries.
- Click the Change button to change this instance of the word marked in the Not in Dictionary box to the word selected in the Suggestions list. (If Word has not suggested a different spelling for the word, the Change button will be dimmed.)

- Accept the word selected in the Suggestions list (or choose another of the suggested words) and click the Change All button to change all instances of the marked word in the Not in Dictionary box to the word you've chosen. (Again, the Change All button will be dimmed if Word has not suggested any alternative spellings or words.) Use Change All when you're sure about the correct spelling of a word.
- Click the Add button to add the word marked in the Not in Dictionary box to the custom dictionary currently selected. Once you've added the word to the dictionary, Word will not flag it again. (We'll look at selecting dictionaries in a minute.)
- If Word has found a typo you feel you're likely to repeat, click the AutoCorrect button to add the marked word in the Not in Dictionary box and the chosen suggestion to the list of AutoCorrect entries.
- Click the Undo button to undo the last spell-checking change you made.
- Click the Cancel button or Close button to stop the spell check.

5. When the Spelling and Grammar checker encounters a grammar problem, you'll see a Spelling and Grammar dialog box like the one shown in Figure 4.2: The upper box displays the type of grammatical rule the guilty sentence has supposedly violated, and the Suggestions box contains purported remedies. Your choices here are correspondingly fewer:

- Click the Ignore button to ignore the ostensible problem Word has raised.
- Click the Ignore All button to ignore all instances of this ostensible problem. This is the quickest way to establish your authority when you and Word disagree on trivialities such as subject-verb agreement. (The alternative, as we'll see in a minute, is to turn off Grammar rules that irritate you.)
- Click the Next Sentence button to ignore not only this problem but also any others that Word may claim this sentence has.
- Choose a suggestion from the Suggestions list box or change the text on your own, and click the Change button to implement the change.
- Clear the Check Grammar check box at the bottom of the Spelling and Grammar dialog box to proceed with the spelling check without checking any more grammar.
- Click the Cancel button or Close button to stop the spelling and grammar check.

When you've dealt with all the objections that the Spelling checker and Grammar checker have raised about your document (or the section they just checked), Word may display the Readability Statistics dialog box (see Figure 4.3), which gives you the following information:

- Word, character, paragraph, and sentence count

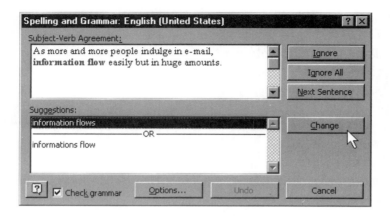

FIGURE 4.2:
The Spelling and Grammar dialog box tackles a grammar problem.

- Average number of sentences per paragraph, words per sentence, and characters per word
- Three types of readability statistics

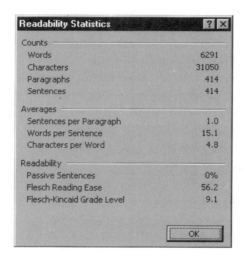

FIGURE 4.3:
Word produces the Readability Statistics dialog box at the end of a grammar check. If you don't like seeing them, clear the Show Readability Statistics check box in the Grammar area of the Spelling & Grammar tab of the Options dialog box (Tools ➤ Options).

Whether or not the Grammar checker displays its spurious readability statistics depends on the Show Readability Statistics check box on the Spelling & Grammar tab of the Options dialog box. To stop the Grammar checker from running, clear the Check Grammar with Spelling check box on the Spelling and Grammar tab.

> **TIP**
>
> Sadly, Word no longer uses the wonderfully named Gunning Fog Index for quantifying the unreadability of your documents. The Gunning Fog appeals (to me, at least) because it bravely measures *unreadability* rather than readability, so you can amuse yourself constructing sentences that are so bad the Index goes above body temperature in Fahrenheit. For intimate details on Flesch Reading Ease (which measures on a scale of 1 to 100 (with 1 being hardest and 100 being easiest) how easy a document is to comprehend) and Flesch-Kincaid Grade Level (the grade level to which your hapless reader needs to have studied to be able to puzzle out your prose), consult the Word Help files. Remember, though, that these are statistical computations of readability; to get a true measurement, have a human read your work instead.

Working with Dictionaries

Word comes with a built-in dictionary of words that it uses for spell-checking. You can't change this dictionary—to save you from yourself, perhaps—but you can create and use custom dictionaries to supplement Word's main dictionary. You can open and close these as needed for the particular documents you're working on; however, the more dictionaries you have open, the slower Word's spell-checking will be, so it pays to think ahead and coordinate your efforts a little.

The Default Custom Dictionary

Word starts off with a default custom dictionary named Custom.dic, which you'll usually find in the \Windows\MSApps\Proof\ folder for Windows 95. Whenever you run the Spelling and Grammar checker, Word adds any words that you add to your custom dictionary by using the Add command during a spelling check to the Custom.dic dictionary—unless you tell it otherwise by selecting another dictionary, which we'll look at in a moment.

TIP

When adding words to your custom dictionary, use lowercase letters unless the words require special capitalization. If you enter a word in lowercase, Word will recognize it when you type it in uppercase or with an initial capital letter, but if you enter a word with an initial capital letter, Word will not recognize it if you type it using all lowercase letters.

Creating a Custom Dictionary

To create a new custom dictionary—for example, for foreign words you use in your English documents (as opposed to foreign words you use in your foreign language documents), or for technical terms that you don't want to keep in Custom.dic—here's what to do:

1. Choose Tools ➤ Options to display the Options dialog box, and then click the Spelling & Grammar tab. (If you're in the middle of spell-checking, click the Options button in the Spelling dialog box instead.)
2. Click the Dictionaries button to display the Custom Dictionaries dialog box (see Figure 4.4).

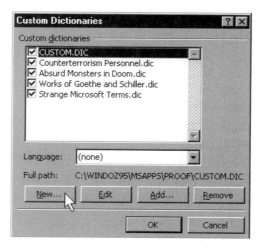

FIGURE 4.4:
In the Custom Dictionaries dialog box, click the New button to create a new dictionary.

3. Click the New button to open the Create Custom Dictionary dialog box (see Figure 4.5).

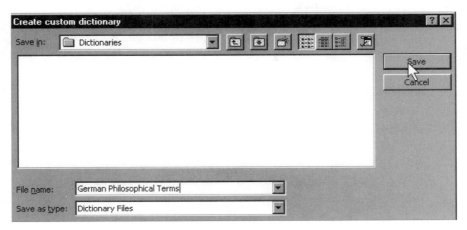

FIGURE 4.5: In the Create Custom Dictionary dialog box, enter the name of the dictionary you want to create, and then click the Save button. As shown here, you can keep dictionaries in locations other than the default location Word suggests.

4. Enter a name for the dictionary in the File Name text box, and then click the Save button to create the dictionary and close the Create Custom Dictionary dialog box. Word will return you to the Custom Dictionaries dialog box, where you will see the new dictionary in the Custom Dictionaries list box.

5. If you want to specify a different language for the new custom dictionary, select it in the Custom Dictionaries list box and choose a language from the Language drop-down list.

6. Make sure that the check box for the new dictionary is selected , then click the OK button to close the Custom Dictionaries dialog box and return to the Options dialog box.

7. If you want to add new terms to the new dictionary rather than to the currently selected dictionary, select the new dictionary in the Custom Dictionary drop-down list.

8. Click the OK button to close the Options dialog box.

Adding Custom Dictionaries from Other Folders

If you have custom dictionaries stored in folders other than the \Proof\ folder, you may need to tell Word where they are.

To add a custom dictionary:

1. Choose Tools ➤ Options to display the Options dialog box, then click the Spelling & Grammar tab. (If you're in the middle of spell-checking, click the Options button in the Spelling and Grammar dialog box instead.)
2. Click the Dictionaries button to display the Custom Dictionaries dialog box.
3. Click the Add button to display the Add Custom Dictionary dialog box.
4. Navigate to the folder containing the custom dictionary you want to add using standard Windows navigation techniques.
5. Select the dictionary to add, then click the OK button. Word will add the dictionary to the list of custom dictionaries and then return you to the Custom Dictionaries dialog box.
6. Make sure the check box for the new dictionary in the Custom Dictionaries list box is selected, then click the OK button to close the Custom Dictionaries dialog box.
7. If you want to add new terms to the new dictionary rather than to the currently selected dictionary, select the new dictionary in the Custom Dictionary drop-down list.
8. Click the OK button to close the Options dialog box.

NOTE

To remove a custom dictionary from the Custom Dictionaries list in the Custom Dictionaries dialog box, select the dictionary you want to remove and then click the Remove button. (This option just removes the dictionary from the list—it does not delete the file.)

Editing a Custom Dictionary

One way of adding the words you need to your custom dictionaries is by clicking the Add button whenever you run into one of them during a spell check. However, Word also lets you open and edit your custom dictionaries. This is particularly useful when you have added a misspelled word to a dictionary, and the Spelling checker is now merrily accepting a mistake in every document you write.

To edit a custom dictionary:

1. Choose Tools ➤ Options to display the Options dialog box, then click the Spelling & Grammar tab.
2. Click the Dictionaries button to display the Custom Dictionaries dialog box.

3. In the Custom Dictionaries list box, choose the dictionary you want to edit and click the Edit button. Word will display a warning telling you that it is about to turn automatic spell-checking off; click the OK button, and Word will open the dictionary as a Word file.

4. Edit the dictionary as you would any other document, making sure you have only one word per line.

5. Choose File ➤ Save to save the dictionary.

6. Choose File ➤ Close to close the dictionary and return to your document.

7. Choose Tools ➤ Options to display the Options dialog box, and turn automatic spell-checking back on by selecting the Check Spelling As You Type check box on the Spelling & Grammar tab. Click OK to close the Options dialog box.

Customizing the Grammar Check

If you find the Grammar checker helpful but think it offers some suggestions that you could do without, try customizing it to use only those rules that you need. You can either select one of the Grammar checker's existing sets of rules or edit a set of rules and turn off those you don't want to use.

To choose a set of rules for the Grammar checker:

1. Choose Tools ➤ Options to display the Options dialog box, then click the Spelling & Grammar tab.

2. In the Grammar area, choose the style of writing you're aiming for from the Writing Style drop-down list: Casual, Standard, Formal, Technical, or Custom.

3. To customize the rules, click the Settings button to display the Grammar Settings dialog box (see Figure 4.6).
   - In the Grammar and Style Options list box, select the check boxes for the items you want to have the Grammar checker apply to your text.
   - In the Require area, select whether Word should check for Comma before Last List Item (also known as *serial comma*), Punctuation with Quotes, and Spaces between Sentences.

4. Click the OK button to apply your choices and close the Grammar Settings dialog box.

5. Click the OK button in the Options dialog box to close it.

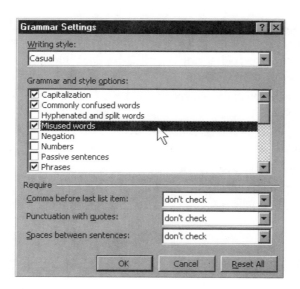

FIGURE 4.6:
In the Grammar Settings dialog box, customize the set of rules that you want the Grammar checker to apply when checking your document.

Using the Thesaurus

If you've ever had a word right on the tip of your tongue but just out of your grasp, Word's Thesaurus will prove a welcome tool. The Thesaurus gives you a hand in unlocking the power and richness of the English language by offering synonyms (words with the same meaning) and antonyms (words with the opposite meaning) of the word or phrase you selected.

To use the Thesaurus:

1. Select the word or phrase you want to look up, or just place the insertion point within the word.

2. Choose Tools ➤ Language ➤ Thesaurus or press Shift+F7 to start the Thesaurus. You'll see the Thesaurus dialog box (see Figure 4.7) with the word you chose displayed in the Looked Up box.

3. In the Meanings box, highlight the word that is closest in meaning to the one you're searching for.

   • If Word finds any antonyms for the word in the Looked Up box, you'll see the word Antonyms at the bottom of the list. Select it to see the list of antonyms.

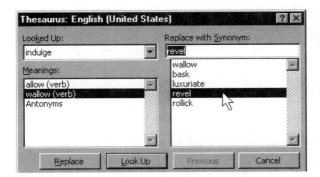

FIGURE 4.7:
The Thesaurus dialog box provides you with a way of digging the depths of the English language for the precise word you need. Here we are looking at the possibilities for "indulge."

- If Word finds any related words that aren't actually synonyms, it will offer the choice Related Words in the Meanings list box (sometimes Word finds synonyms *and* related words. Click Related Words to see a list of related words in the Replace with Related Word list box (which is the Related Words version of the Replace with Synonym list box), and then choose one of those words.
- If Word doesn't find any words it can identify with the word you looked up, the Looked Up box will become the Not Found box, and the Meanings list box will become the Alphabetical List list box. In this list box, you will find a listing of words closest in spelling to the original word. Double-click the word you want in the Alphabetical List list box to display its synonyms in the Replace with Synonym box, or click the Cancel button and select a different word to look up.

> **TIP**
>
> The Thesaurus isn't much good at the declension of nouns or the conjugation of verbs—in most cases, you'll do better to look up a singular noun rather than a plural one (*case* rather than *cases*, for example) and the basic form of a verb rather than the past tense or the present or past participle. Going for the root word will also get you results more quickly—for example, if you look up *charm*, you'll see far more possibilities than if you look up *charming*.

4. Once you've found the meaning you want in the Meanings list box, choose the most appropriate synonym (or antonym or related word) from the Replace with Synonym (or Replace with Antonym or Replace with Related Word) list box. You can then:
   - Click the Replace button to replace the word you looked up in text with the synonym, antonym, or related word.

- Click the Look Up button to look up the meanings and synonyms for the synonym (or antonym or related word).
- Click the Previous button to go back a step in your pursuit of the right word; this restores the previous word to the Looked Up box.
- Click the Cancel button to cancel the search and return to your document.

Getting a Word Count

To get a quick count of the words in your document—not to mention the number of pages, characters, paragraphs, and lines—choose Tools ➤ Word Count. Word will calculate the numbers and display them in the Word Count dialog box (see Figure 4.8).

- To include footnotes and endnotes in the count, select the Include Footnotes and Endnotes check box in the Word Count dialog box. If you're getting the word count for a selection, this check box will be dimmed and unavailable.

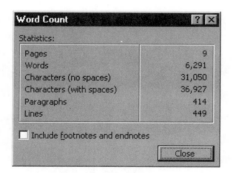

FIGURE 4.8:
Use Tools ➤ Word Count to find out how many words your document contains.

> **TIP**
>
> For a word count of just a part of your document, select that part first. Use Outline View to quickly select one or more heading sections of a document.

Inserting Symbols and Special Characters

Word offers enough symbols and special characters for you to typeset almost any document. Symbols can be any character from multiplication or division signs to the fancy ➤ arrow Sybex uses to indicate menu commands; special characters include em dashes (—) and en dashes (–), trademark symbols (™), and the like—symbols that Microsoft thinks you might want to insert more frequently and with less effort than the symbols relegated to the Symbols tab.

To insert a symbol or special character at the insertion point:

1. Choose Insert ➤ Symbol to display the Symbol dialog box (see Figure 4.9).

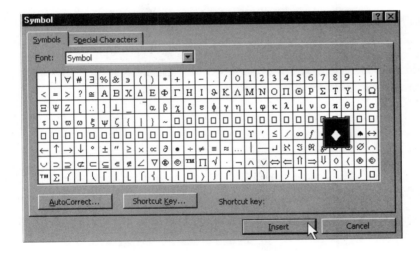

FIGURE 4.9:
In the Symbol dialog box, choose the symbol or special character to insert, and then click the Insert button.

2. To insert a symbol, click the Symbols tab to bring it to the front of the dialog box if it isn't already there, and then choose the symbol to insert from the box.
   - Use the Font drop-down list to pick the font you want to see in the dialog box.
   - To enlarge a character so you can see it more clearly, click it once. An enlarged version of it will pop out at you. You can then move the zoom box around the Symbols dialog box by using ↑, ↓, ←, and →, or by clicking it and dragging with the mouse.

| NOTE | Word will display a shortcut key for the symbol (if there is one) to the right of the Shortcut Key button. If you're often inserting a particular symbol, you can try using the shortcut key instead—or you can create a shortcut key of your own, as we'll see in the next section. You can also create an AutoCorrect entry, which can be a handy way of inserting symbols in text. We'll look at how to do this in Chapter 10. |

3. To insert a special character, click the Special Characters tab to bring it to the front (unless it's already there). Choose the character to insert from the list box (see Figure 4.10).

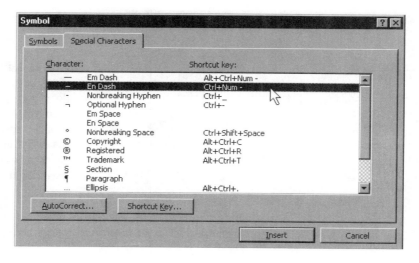

FIGURE 4.10: Choose a special character from the Special Characters tab of the Symbol dialog box, and then click the Insert button.

4. To insert the symbol or special character, click the Insert button. Word will insert the character, and the Cancel button will change to a Close button.
   • You can also insert a symbol or special character by double-clicking it.
5. To insert more symbols or special characters, repeat steps 2 through 4.
6. Click the Close button to close the Symbol dialog box.

Creating a Keyboard Shortcut for a Symbol or Special Character

If you find yourself inserting a particular symbol or special character frequently, you can create a shortcut key combination for placing it more quickly.

To create your own shortcut key combination:

1. Choose Insert ➤ Symbol to display the Symbol dialog box.

2. Choose the symbol or special character you want on the Symbols or Special Characters tab, respectively.

3. Click the Shortcut Key button to display the Customize Keyboard dialog box (see Figure 4.11). The symbol or special character you chose will appear in the Commands box.

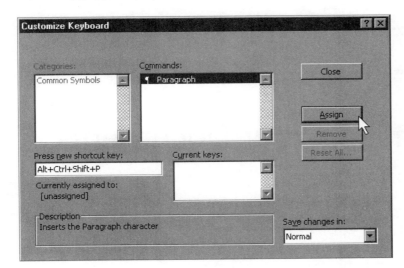

FIGURE 4.11:
Choose a shortcut key combination for a frequently used symbol or special character in the Customize Keyboard dialog box.

4. Click in the Press New Shortcut Key text box, then enter the new shortcut key combination for the symbol or character. A key combination can consist of any of the following:

   • Alt plus a regular key not used for a menu access key
   • Ctrl plus a regular key
   • Ctrl+Alt plus a regular key or function key
   • Shift plus a function key
   • Ctrl+Shift plus a regular key or function key
   • Alt+Shift plus a regular key or function key
   • Ctrl+Alt+Shift plus a regular key or function key

   Because this last option involves using four fingers (or thumbs), you may want to reserve this either for seldom used commands or for pianists.

5. Look at the Currently Assigned To area below the Press New Shortcut Key text box to see if that key combination is already assigned. (If it is and you don't want to overwrite it, press Backspace to clear the Press New Shortcut Key box, and then choose another combination.)

6. Click the Assign button to assign the shortcut and then click the Close button to return to the Symbol dialog box.

7. Create another shortcut if you like, or choose Close to close the Symbol dialog box.

You can now press the shortcut key combination to insert the character or symbol.

> **NOTE** Many of the symbols and special characters already have shortcut keys assigned (these are listed in the Symbol dialog box, as explained in the previous section), but you can replace these with more convenient keyboard shortcuts of your own if you prefer.

Hyphenating Your Documents

Hyphenation is another tedious task that Word is more than happy to take on. If you don't trust its automatic hyphenation, you can hyphenate manually with some help from Word.

First, though, you need to know the three types of hyphens that Word offers:

- Regular hyphens, such as you might use in a phrase like "up-to-date." You enter these by pressing the - (hyphen) key.
- *Optional* hyphens, which are hyphens that appear only if they're needed to break a word at the end of a line. You enter optional hyphens by pressing Ctrl+- (Ctrl+hyphen). Word uses optional hyphens in automatic hyphenation, so that unnecessary hyphens do not print if you adjust the document. You can also insert optional hyphens manually to indicate words or phrases that Word can break if they're at the end of a line.
- *Nonbreaking* hyphens, which are hyphens that you use to tell Word not to break a hyphenated phrase. For example, if you want to make sure Word does not break **ne'er-do-well** over two lines, you could enter nonbreaking hyphens instead of regular hyphens by pressing Ctrl+Shift+- (Ctrl+Shift+hyphen). Nonbreaking hyphens look like regular hyphens unless you display nonprinting characters (by clicking the Show/Hide ¶ button on the Standard toolbar), in which case they look like em dashes (—).

You'll usually insert optional hyphens and nonbreaking hyphens while creating your documents to assist Word later in its automatic hyphenation of the document.

Hyphenating Automatically

To hyphenate a document automatically and set automatic hyphenation:

1. Choose Tools ➤ Language ➤ Hyphenation to display the Hyphenation dialog box (see Figure 4.12).
2. Select the Automatically Hyphenate Document check box.
3. Choose options for hyphenation:
   - Hyphenate Words in CAPS lets Word hyphenate words written in all capitals. Turn this off if your document contains technical terms in capitals that you don't want to have broken.

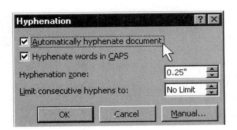

FIGURE 4.12:
Choose the options for hyphenation in the Hyphenation dialog box.

   - Adjust the setting in the Hyphenation Zone box if necessary. This is the width of the area at the right margin where Word will hyphenate. For a less ragged right margin, specify a smaller setting in the Hyphenation Zone box; bear in mind that this will produce more hyphenated words.
   - In the Limit Consecutive Hyphens To box, set an upper limit for the number of consecutive lines that can end in hyphens. Formal typesetting authorities recommend two or at most three lines ending in hyphens (because it can be confusing to the reader's eye); if you don't care how many lines in a row end in hyphens, choose No Limit.
4. Click the OK button to close the Hyphenation dialog box and hyphenate your document.

NOTE   Once you've switched on automatic hyphenation for a document, Word will continue to hyphenate it as necessary while you change it.

Hyphenating Manually

To hyphenate a document (or selected part of a document) manually:

1. Choose Tools ➤ Language ➤ Hyphenation to display the Hyphenation dialog box.
2. Choose the options for hyphenation as described in step 3 of the previous section.
3. Click the Manual button to start hyphenating the document or selection. When Word finds a word in the hyphenation zone that it can hyphenate, it will display the Manual Hyphenation dialog box

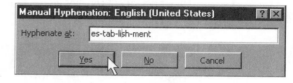

(shown here) with its suggested hyphenation for the word.
4. Decide on hyphenation for the word:
   - To accept Word's suggested hyphenation, click the Yes button.
   - To adjust Word's suggested hyphenation, click any other hyphen in the word, or click to place the insertion point between the appropriate letters. Then click the Yes button.
   - To reject Word's suggested hyphenation and not hyphenate the word, click the No button.
   - To stop hyphenation, click the Cancel button.
5. Word will then display the next word needing hyphenation (unless you chose Cancel). Repeat step 4 until you've finished hyphenating the document or selection. If you were hyphenating just a selection, Word will ask if you want to hyphenate the rest of the document; if you were hyphenating the whole document, Word will display a message box telling you that hyphenation has been completed.

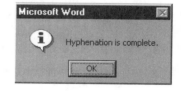

6. Click OK to close the message box and return to your document.

Chapter 5

WORKING WITH HEADERS AND FOOTERS

FEATURING

- **Creating simple headers and footers**
- **Inserting the date and time in headers and footers**
- **Formatting headers and footers**
- **Creating complex headers and footers**

Headers and footers give you an easy way to repeat identifying information on each page of your document. For example, in a header (text placed at the top of each page), you might include the title of a document and the author, while in a footer (text placed at the bottom of each page) you might include the file name, the date, and the page number out of the total number of pages in the document (e.g., *Page 1 of 9*).

You can repeat the same header and footer throughout all the pages of your document, or you can vary them from page to page. For example, if a proposal has two different authors, you might want to identify in the header which author wrote a particular part of the proposal; or if you want to identify in the header the different part titles, you can easily arrange that, too. You can also arrange for odd pages to have different headers and footers from those on even pages, or for the first page in a document to have a different header and footer than subsequent pages.

Setting Headers and Footers

To include a header in your document:

1. Choose View ➤ Header and Footer. Word will display the page in Page Layout view and will display the Header and Footer toolbar (see Figure 5.1).

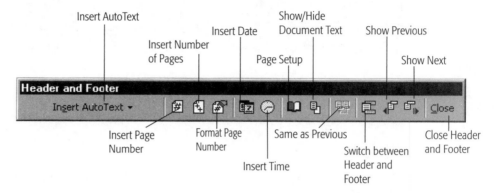

FIGURE 5.1: The Header and Footer toolbar offers 13 buttons that help you produce headers and footers quickly and easily, including a Close Header and Footer button to get you out of the header or footer.

> **NOTE** You can work with headers and footers only in Page Layout view and Print Preview. If you choose View ➤ Header and Footer from Normal view, Online Layout view, or Outline view, Word will switch you to Page Layout view. When you leave the header or footer area, Word will return you to the view you were in before.

2. Enter the text (and graphics, if you like) for the header in the Header area at the top of the page. Use the buttons on the Header and Footer toolbar to speed your work:

   • **Insert AutoText** provides a drop-down menu of canned header and footer text, including the file name and path and *page X of Y* (e.g., Page 3 of 34).

- **Insert Page Number** inserts a code for the current page number at the insertion point.
- **Insert Number of Pages** inserts a code for the number of pages in the document.
- **Format Page Number** displays the Page Number Format dialog box (see Figure 5.2). In the Number Format drop-down list, choose the type of numbering you want: 1, 2, 3; a, b, c; and so on. If you want to include chapter numbers in the page numbering, select the Include Chapter Number check box, then in the Chapter Starts with Style drop-down list, choose the Heading style with which each chapter in the document starts. In the Use Separator drop-down list, choose a separator character for the numbering. Finally, in the Page Numbering area, choose whether to continue the page numbering from the previous section of the document (if there is a previous section) or to start at a number of your choosing. Click the OK button when you've made your selections.

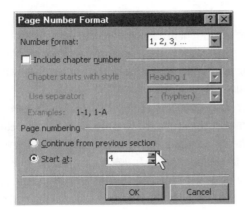

FIGURE 5.2:
In the Page Number Format dialog box, choose formatting and numbering options for the page numbers.

- **Insert Date** inserts a code for the current date in the document.
- **Insert Time** inserts a code for the current time in the document.
- **Page Setup** displays the Page Setup dialog box with the Layout tab at the front.
- **Show/Hide Document Text** displays and hides the document text. Its purpose is a little esoteric: You probably won't want to hide your document's text unless you're trying to place a header or footer behind the text. For example, you might want to add a watermark behind the text on a business letter or a brochure.

WARNING Unwittingly clicking the Show/Hide Document Text button can lead you to think you've lost all the text in your document. If your text suddenly disappears under suspicious circumstances, check to see if the Show/Hide Document Text button is selected. If it is, restore the display of the document text by clicking the Show/Hide Document Text button again. If the Show/Hide Document Text button isn't the culprit and your text has really vanished, try undoing the last actions by choosing Edit ➤ Undo or pressing Ctrl+Z, or try closing the document without saving changes.

- **Same as Previous** makes the current header or footer the same as the header or footer in the previous section (if there is a previous section; we'll get into this in a minute) or page (if you're using a different header and footer on the first page). If there is no previous section, this button will not be available.
- **Switch between Header and Footer** moves the insertion point between header and footer. Alternatively, you can use the up and down arrow keys to move between the two.
- **Show Previous** moves the insertion point to the header or footer in the previous section (if there is a previous section) or page (if you're using different headers and footers on the first page, or different headers and footers for odd and even pages).
- **Show Next** moves the insertion point to the header or footer in the next section (if there is a previous section) or page (if you're using a different header and footer on the first page).
- **Close Header and Footer** hides the Header and Footer toolbar, closes the header and footer panes, and returns you to whichever view you were using before.

3. To return to your document, click the Close Header and Footer button, or choose View ➤ Header and Footer again. You can also double-click anywhere in the main document as long as the Show/Hide Document Text button is not selected.

Formatting Headers and Footers

Despite their special position on the page, headers and footers contain regular Word elements (text, graphics, text boxes, and so on), and you work with them as described in the previous chapters.

By default, Word starts you off with the Header style in the header area and the Footer style in the Footer area. You can modify these styles (as described earlier in this chapter) by choosing other styles (including Header First, Header Even, and Header Odd—which Word provides in some templates) from the Styles drop-down list on the Formatting toolbar (or by choosing Format ➤ Style and using the Styles dialog box), or by applying extra formatting.

> **TIP**
>
> Headers and footers aren't restricted to the header and footer areas that appear on your screen. You can use headers and footers to place repeating text anywhere on your page. While in the header or footer area, you can insert a text box at a suitable location on the page, then insert text, graphics, and so on inside the text box (as described in Chapter 1).

Producing Different Headers and Footers for Different Sections

Often you'll want different headers and footers on different pages of your documents. Word gives you three options:

- A header and footer on the first page of a document that is different from the header and footer on subsequent pages
- A header and footer on odd pages that is different from the header and footer on even pages (combined, if you like, with a header and footer on the first page that is different from the header and footer on subsequent pages)
- A different header and footer for different sections (combined, if you like, with the two previous options)

Different First-Page Headers and Footers

To produce a header and footer on the first page of a document that is different from the header and footer on subsequent pages:

1. Choose File ➤ Page Setup to display the Page Setup dialog box, then click the Layout tab to bring it to the front (see Figure 5.3).

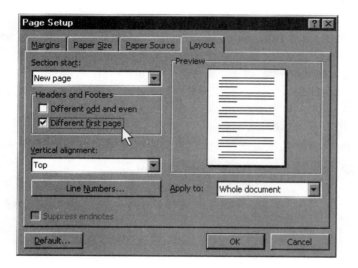

FIGURE 5.3:
Specify options for your headers and footers on the Layout tab of the Page Setup dialog box.

2. In the Headers and Footers group box, select the Different First Page check box.
3. Click the OK button to close the Page Setup dialog box.

After setting up your header and footer for the first page of the document, move to the second page and set up the header and footer for that page and subsequent pages.

Different Headers and Footers on Odd and Even Pages

To create a header and footer on odd pages that is different from the header and footer on even pages, select the Different Odd and Even check box in the Headers and Footers box on the Layout tab of the Page Setup dialog box (File ➤ Page Setup). Move the insertion point to an odd page and set its header and footer, then move to an even page and set its header and footer.

Different Headers and Footers in Different Sections

To set different headers and footers in different sections of a document, create the document, then divide it into sections as described in *Section Formatting* in Chapter 2. To adjust the header or footer for any section, click in that section, then choose View ➤ Header and Footer to display the Header area of the document.

By default, when a document consists of more than one section, Word sets the header and footer for each section after the first to be the same as the header and footer in the previous section; so the Same as Previous button on the Header and Footer toolbar will appear pushed in, and the legend Same as Previous will appear at the top right corner of the header or footer area. To change this, click the Same as Previous button on the Header and Footer toolbar, and then enter the new header or footer in the header or footer area.

To move through the headers or footers in the various sections of your document, click the Show Previous and Show Next buttons on the Header and Footer toolbar.

Chapter **6**

USING FIND AND REPLACE

FEATURING

- **Finding and replacing text**
- **Using Find and Replace to format text**
- **Using special characters and wildcards for powerful searches**
- **Using advanced Find and Replace features**

Word's Find and Replace features are powerful tools for changing your documents rapidly. At their simplest, the Find and Replace features let you search for any *string* of text (a letter, several letters, a word, or a phrase) and replace either chosen instances or all instances of that string. For example, you could replace all instances of *dangerous* with *unwise*, or you could replace selected instances of *this fearful lunatic* with *the Vice President of Communications*. You can also use Find independently of Replace to locate strategic parts of your document or to get to specific words in order to change the text around them.

Beyond the simple uses of Find and Replace, you can search for special characters (such as tabs or paragraph marks), for special operators (such as a digit, a character, or a range of characters), for particular formatting (such as double-underline, bold, or italic in Engravers Gothic font), or for a particular Word style (such as Heading 9 or Body Text). You can search for text in a particular language, for paragraphs with particular tab formatting, or for text that sounds like other text. You can even combine many of these elements to conduct searches of truly fiendish complexity that will confound your colleagues and impress your friends.

In this chapter, we'll start with the basics and move rapidly to more complicated Find and Replace operations.

Finding Text

Word offers a large number of features for finding text. You can search for text without worrying about its formatting; you can search for text with particular formatting, such as bold, double underline, or 44-point Allegro font; or you can search for a particular style.

> **NOTE** You can also combine these Find operations with Replace operations; we'll get to this a little later in the chapter in the sections titled *Finding and Replacing Text*, *Finding and Replacing Formatting*, and *Finding and Replacing Styles*.

To find text:

1. Choose Edit ➤ Find to display the Find and Replace dialog box (see Figure 6.1). If you see only the top half of the dialog box shown here, click the More button to display the rest of the dialog box.

2. In the Find What box, enter the text you're looking for.
   - You can use *wildcard* characters to find a variety of characters. We'll get into this in a moment in the section *Finding Special Characters and Using Wildcards*.
   - Word stores the Find operations from the current session in a drop-down list that you can access by clicking the arrow at the right-hand end of the Find What box.

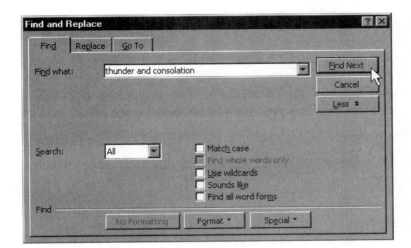

FIGURE 6.1:
The Find and Replace dialog box gives you a quick way to access any combination of characters or formatting in your document. If you're seeing a smaller version of the Find and Replace dialog box, click the More button to expand it.

3. Choose the direction to search from the Search drop-down list: Down, Up, or All. If you choose Down or Up, Word will prompt you to continue when it reaches the end or beginning of the document (unless you started Find at the beginning or end of the document).

4. Choose the options you want from the column of check boxes. Each option you choose will be listed under the Find What box.

- Match Case makes Word use the capitalization of the word in the Find What box as a search constraint. For example, with Match Case selected and **laziness** entered in the Find What box, Word will ignore instances of *Laziness* or *LAZINESS* in the document and find only *laziness*.
- Find Whole Words Only makes Word look only for the exact word entered in the Find What box and not for the word when it is part of another word. For example, by selecting the Find Whole Words Only check box, you could find *and* without finding *land*, *random*, *mandible*, and so on. Find Whole Words Only is not available if you type a space in the Find What box.
- Use Wildcards provides special search options that we'll look at in the section *Finding Special Characters and Using Wildcards* later in this chapter.
- Sounds Like finds words that, according to Word, sound like those in the Find What box. Your mileage may vary depending on your own pronunciation. For example, if you check the Sounds Like check box and enter **meddle** in the Find What box, Word will find both *middle* and *muddle*, but it won't find rhyming words, such as *peddle* and *pedal*.

- Find All Word Forms attempts to find all forms of the verb or noun in the Find What box. This is particularly useful with Replace operations: Word can change *break, broken, breaking,* and *breaks* to *fix, fixed, fixing,* and *fixes.* Enter the basic form of the words in the Find What and the Replace With boxes on the Replace tab of the Find and Replace dialog box—in this example, use *break* and *fix.*

WARNING Find All Word Forms is an ambitious feature prone to random behavior if you use it unwisely. To give Microsoft credit, Word will warn you that choosing Replace All with Find All Word Forms selected may not be advisable—it's likely to find (and change) more than you bargained for. If you use it, use it carefully, and be especially careful with words such as *lead* because the metal *lead* will likely be misinterpreted as the verb *to lead.*

5. Make sure no formatting information appears in the box under the Find What text box. If the No Formatting button at the bottom of the dialog box is active (not dimmed), that means Word will look for words only with the selected formatting; click the button to remove the formatting. If the No Formatting button is dimmed, you're OK.

6. Click the Find Next button to find the next instance of your chosen text. If Word finds the text, it will stop; otherwise, it will tell you that it was unable to find the text.

7. Click the Find Next button again to keep searching, or click the Cancel button to close the Find dialog box.

TIP Word's Find feature is particularly useful in macros, which we'll look at in Chapter 15. With Find, you can seek out specific parts of form documents, and once you've located them, you can format them, eviscerate them, or even create new documents from them. Skip ahead to Chapter 15 if such ideas entertain you.

Once you perform a Find operation (or a Find and Replace operation), Word sets the Object Browser to browse by the item you last found. You'll see that the Next Page and Previous Page buttons at the foot of the vertical scroll bar turn from black to blue, and if you move the mouse pointer over them, you'll see that the ScreenTips identify them as Next Find/Go To and Previous Find/Go To, respectively. You can then click these buttons to move to the next or previous instance of the item you last found; you can also press Ctrl+PageDown or Ctrl+PageUp for the same effect.

To reset the Object Browser to browse by page, click the Select Browse Object button and choose the Browse by Page icon from the pop-up panel, as shown here. (To switch back to Browse by Find after that, you can click the Select Browse Object button again and choose the Browse by Find icon—the binoculars—from the pop-up panel.)

Finding Special Characters and Using Wildcards

Often, you'll want to search for something more complex than plain text—perhaps you'll need to search for an em dash (—), or a paragraph mark, or any number—or you may want to search for words beginning with a specific character, or for words that begin with a certain range of letters. For the first three of these, you'll need to use Word's special characters; for the last two, Word's special search operators will do the trick.

> **TIP**
>
> **The special characters and wildcards are complex to use, but they give you great searching power—if you need it. If you don't, skip this section for now and return to it if and when you need to perform complex searches.**

Special Characters

To find a special character, such as a paragraph mark, a tab character, or a graphic, click the Special button on the Find dialog box and choose the character from the drop-down list that appears (see Figure 6.2).

You can combine special characters with regular text to make your Find operations more effective. For example, the special character for a paragraph mark is ^p; to find every instance where *Joanne* appears at the beginning of a paragraph, you could search for **^pJoanne**.

It's usually easiest to enter special characters from the Special drop-down list, but you can also enter them manually for speed's sake. Here's the full list of characters and what they find:

Character	Finds
^?	Any one character
*	A string of characters. Select the Use Wildcards check box when you use this. (It's actually a wildcard rather than a special character, but it's simpler to use than the other wildcards)
^p	A paragraph mark
^t	A tab
^a	A comment mark
^#	Any digit
^$	Any letter
^^	A caret (^)
^n	A column break
^+	An em dash (—)
^=	An en dash (–)
^e	An endnote mark
^d	A field
^f	A footnote mark
^g	A graphic
^l	A manual line break
^m	A manual page break
^~	A nonbreaking hyphen
^s	A nonbreaking space
^-	An optional hyphen
^b	A section break
^w	A white space

Of these, you'll probably find yourself using ^? and * the most. For example, you could use **sh^?p** to find *ship* or *shop* and **f*d** to find *fad*, *fatherhood*, and *flustered—* not to mention *after the tragic death of Don Quixote*.

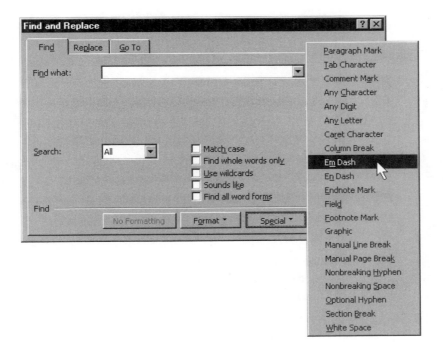

FIGURE 6.2: You can find special characters, such as page breaks or endnote marks, by using the Special drop-down list in the Find dialog box.

WARNING

As you can see from the Don Quixote example, you need to be a little careful when using the * special character, particularly with only one identifying letter on either side of it. For a halfway realistic example of how you might actually use * in a search, see the section *Advanced Find and Replace* at the end of this chapter.

Using Wildcards

Word's *wildcards* go one stage beyond the special characters. You can search for one out of several specified characters, any character in a range, any character except the given one, and even a string of characters at the beginning or end of a word only. To enter these operators, select the Use Wildcards check box, and then click the Special button to display the drop-down list (see Figure 6.3).

Here is the list of wildcards and what they find:

Wildcard	Finds	Examples
[ ]	Any one of the given characters	s[iou]n finds *sin*, *son*, and *sun*.
[-]	Any one character in the range	[g-x]ote finds *note*, *mote*, *rote*, and *tote*. Enter the ranges in alphabetical order.
[!]	Any one character except the characters inside the brackets	[!f][!a]therhood finds *motherhood* but not *fatherhood*.
[!x-z]	Any one character except characters in the range inside the brackets	a[!b-l]e finds *ape*, *are*, and *ate*, but not *ace*, *age*, or *ale*.
{x}	Exactly *x* number of occurrences of the previous character or expression	we{2}d finds *weed* but not *wed*, because *weed* has two e's.
{x,}	At least *x* occurrences of the previous character or expression	we{1,}d finds *weed* and *wed*, because both words have at least one e.
{x,y}	From *x* to *y* occurrences of the previous character or expression	40{2,4} finds *400*, *4000*, and *40000*, because each has between two and four zeroes; it won't find *40*, because it has only one zero.
@	One or more occurrences of the previous character or expression	o@h! finds *oh!* and *ooh!*, which both contain one or more os followed by an h.
<	The following search string (in parentheses) at the beginning of a word	<(work) finds *working* and *workaholic*, but not *groundwork*.
>	The preceding search string (in parentheses) at the end of a word	(sin)> finds *basin* and *moccasin*, but not *sinful*.

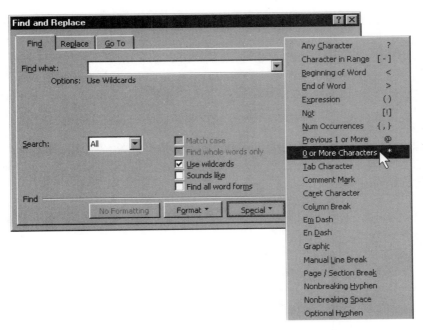

FIGURE 6.3:
To search for wildcards, select the Use Wildcards check box and then choose the wildcards from the Special drop-down list.

Finding and Replacing Text

To find and replace text:

1. Choose Edit ➤ Replace to display the Replace tab of the Find and Replace dialog box (see Figure 6.4).

    • If you're already working on the Find tab of the Find and Replace dialog box, click the Replace tab.

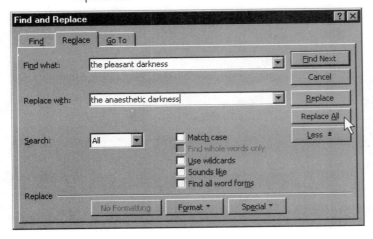

FIGURE 6.4:
The Replace tab of the Find and Replace dialog box

2. In the Find What box, enter the text to find.To find text you've searched for before in the current session, click the arrow at the right-hand end of the Find What box and choose the text from the drop-down list.

3. In the Replace With box, enter the text you want to replace the found text with. To reuse replacement text from the current session, click the arrow at the right-hand end of the Replace With box and choose the text from the drop-down list.

4. Choose a search direction from the Search drop-down list: All, Down, or Up.

5. Choose Replace options such as Match Case and Find Whole Words Only as appropriate (see the section *Finding Text* earlier in this chapter for an explanation of these options).

6. Start the Replace operation by clicking the Find Next button, the Replace button, or the Replace All button:

   - The Find Next button and Replace button will find the next instance of the text in the Find What box. Once you've found it, click the Find Next button to skip to the next occurrence of the text without replacing it with the contents of the Replace With box, or click the Replace button to replace the text with the contents of the Replace With box and have Word find the next instance of the Find What text.

   - The Replace All button will replace all instances of the text in the Find What box with the text in the Replace With box. If you've chosen Up or Down in the Search drop-down list and started the search anywhere other than the end or the beginning of the document (respectively), Word will prompt you to continue when it reaches the beginning or end of the document.

7. When you've finished your Replace operation, click the Close button to close the Replace dialog box (this button will be the Cancel button if you haven't made any replacements).

TIP

When replacing simple text, make sure that Word is displaying no formatting information below the Find What box and Replace With boxes—otherwise Word will find only instances of the text that have the appropriate formatting information (bold, italic, Book Antiqua font, Heading 4 style, and so on), or it will replace the text in the Find What box with inappropriately formatted text from the Replace With box. To remove formatting information from the Find What box and Replace With box, click in the appropriate box and then click the No Formatting button.

Finding and Replacing Formatting

There's no need to use text for Replace operations in Word—you can simply find one kind of formatting and replace it with another. For example, say you received an article for your newsletter in which the author had used boldface rather than italic for emphasizing words she intended to explain. To convert these words from bold to italic, you could replace all Bold text with text with No Bold, Italic formatting.

This replacing function sounds suspiciously utopian, but it works well. Alternatively, you can replace particular strings of text that have one kind of formatting with the same strings of text that have different kinds of formatting; or you can replace formatted strings of text with other formatted strings of text.

To replace one kind of formatting with another kind of formatting:

1. Choose Edit ➤ Replace to display the Find and Replace dialog box.

2. With the insertion point in the Find What box, click the Format button and choose Font, Paragraph, Tabs, or Language from the drop-down list. Word will display the Find Font, Find Paragraph, Find Tabs, or Find Language dialog box. These are versions of the Font, Paragraph, Tabs, and Language dialog boxes discussed in Chapter 2.

3. Choose the formatting you want Word to find, then click the OK button to return to the Find and Replace dialog box. Word will display the

   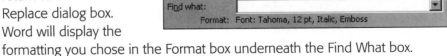

   formatting you chose in the Format box underneath the Find What box.

4. Add further formatting to the mix by repeating steps 2 and 3 with font, paragraph, tab, or language formatting.

5. With the insertion point in the Replace With box, click the Format button and choose Font, Paragraph, Tabs, or Language from the drop-down list. Word will display the Replace Font, Replace Paragraph, Replace Tabs, or Replace Language dialog box. Again, these are versions of the regular Font, Paragraph, Tabs, and Language dialog boxes discussed in Chapter 2.

6. Choose the replacement formatting, then click the OK button to return to the Find and Replace dialog box. Word will display this formatting in the Format box under the Replace With box.

7. Again, add further font, paragraph, tab, or language formatting, this time by repeating steps 5 and 6.

8. Start the search by clicking the Find Next, Replace, or Replace All buttons.

TIP

Without any text entered in the Find What box and Replace With box, Word will replace all instances of the formatting you chose. For example, you could replace all boldface with italic, no boldface. You can also enter text in the Find What box and nothing in the Replace With box to have Word remove that text and put different formatting where it was—or vice versa, entering formatting in the Find What box and replacement text in the Replace With box. (This seems a bizarre concept until you find out how useful it is. We'll look at an example of this in the *Advanced Find and Replace* section at the end of this chapter.) Or you can enter replacement text in both the Find What box and in the Replace With box and replace both the text and the formatting at once. For example, you could replace all boldfaced instances of the word *break* with italicized (without boldface) instances of the word *fix*.

Finding and Replacing Styles

To replace one style with another:

1. Choose Edit ➤ Replace to display the Find and Replace dialog box.
2. Make sure that the Format boxes under the Find What box and the Replace With box don't contain any formatting information. To clear formatting information from the boxes, click in the appropriate box and then click the No Formatting button.
3. With the insertion point in the Find What box, click the Format button and choose Style from the drop-down list. Word will display the Find Style dialog box (see Figure 6.5).
4. Choose the style you want to find from the Find What Style list, then click the OK button to return to the Find and Replace dialog box. The area underneath the Find What box will display the style you chose.
5. Click in the Replace With box (or press Tab to move the insertion point there), then click the Format button and choose Style once more. Word will display the Replace Style dialog box, which is almost identical to the Find Style dialog box.

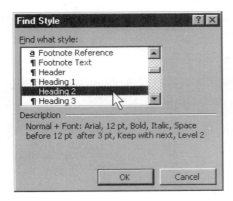

FIGURE 6.5:
In the Find Style dialog box, choose the style you want Word to find.

6. Choose the replacement style from the Replace With Style list, and then click the OK button to return to the Find and Replace dialog box. The area underneath the Replace With box will display the style you chose.

7. Choose a search direction from the Search drop-down list if necessary.

8. Start the search by clicking the Find Next, Replace, or Replace All buttons.

> **TIP**
>
> To replace words or characters in one style with words or characters in another style, choose the styles as described above and then enter the appropriate text in the Find What box and the Replace With box.

Advanced Find and Replace

Once you've mastered them, Find and Replace can seem mundane and unexciting, and it's easy to forget how useful they can be. For example, by simply switching macro recording on and then performing a series of Find and Replace operations, you can completely reformat a document. For example, from a report exported from your local friendly mainframe or minicomputer, you could create something you wouldn't be ashamed to present to your boss a week before your yearly review. Then you can simply run the macro week after week, saving more time than sliced bread and instant coffee combined.

While consistency may be the hobgoblin of small minds, you can use it to your advantage in setting up macros to run automated Find and Replace routines that take the drudgery out of routine tasks.

NOTE Chapter 15 deals with macros. Turn to it for a painless introduction to programming Word to do your bidding.

For example, if you often need to reformat information you receive in text format (e.g., .txt files or information people helpfully dump into e-mail messages instead of sending them as attachments), you may find the vigor of Word's AutoFormat feature (which we looked at briefly in Chapter 2) distressing, and therefore prefer to develop a custom alternative.

Consider the following brief excerpt from a text file, in which the ellipses indicate more of the same:

```
Status Report from Pensacola Office¶
¶
¶
  Here are the highlights from this week:¶
¶
  o Sales increase of $4000¶

  o New personnel manager hired¶
...
¶
1. Sales Increase¶
=========================================================
¶
¶
  This week's surge in sales was driven by a¶
  breakthrough in accounts in the farming area.¶
...
¶
2. New Personnel Manager¶
=========================================================¶
¶
```

As you can see, this report contains several issues:

- You need to remove the extra paragraphs used for spacing.
- You need to remove the paragraphs that are, in fact, just line breaks.
- You need to replace the text-based formatting with Word formatting. For example, you need to replace the lines of equals signs used to denote the subheadings with Word styles to mark the headings themselves.

You could approach reformatting a report such as this as follows:

1. Select the whole document and apply Body Text style (or your favorite text style) to give yourself a base to build on.
2. Tag the subheadings by replacing **={2,}** (two or more equals signs) with **Heading2** or another unique text string. Select the Use Wildcards check box to do this.
3. Tag the bulleted lists by replacing two spaces, an **o**, and another space with **BulletedList** or another unique text string. Clear the Use Wildcards check box for this replace.
4. Replace **^p^p** (two paragraph marks together; i.e., a real paragraph, as opposed to a line break) with **!realpara!** or some other phrase you can be sure won't appear in the rest of the text.
5. Replace **^p** (the remaining paragraph marks, which are really plain old line breaks) with a space.
6. Replace two spaces with one space (to get rid of any extra spaces inserted in the previous step).
7. Replace **!realpara!** with **^p** to restore all of the real paragraph breaks that the document should contain.
8. Replace the **BulletedList** text string with List Bullet style to create a bulleted list.
9. Replace the **BulletedList** text string with nothing to remove it from the document now that the style is safely applied.
10. Replace **Heading2** with the Heading 2 style to apply the style to the subheadings and the text string paragraphs that were originally the lines of equals signs.
11. Replace the **Heading2** text string with nothing to remove it from the document now that the style is safely applied.
12. Apply Heading 1 style to the first paragraph.

A 12-step program like this takes a while to slog through by hand, but for a long report it's massively easier than manually formatting paragraph by paragraph—and when you create a macro to run the whole procedure for you, you can perform the whole operation at the touch of a button.

Chapter 7

COLUMNS AND TABLES

- **Creating, formatting, and deleting columns**
- **Creating and inserting tables**
- **Navigating and editing in tables**
- **Formatting tables**
- **Converting tables to text**

In this chapter, we'll look at two ways of creating multicolumn documents in Word without using large numbers of tabs. Word's *columns* provide a quick way of creating newspaper-style columns of text, while *tables* are for laying out text in columns made up of rows of cells.

Columns

To create columns in a document, you can either convert existing text to columns, or you can create columns and then enter the text in them.

Word uses sections (discussed in Chapter 2) to separate text formatted in different numbers of columns from the rest of the document. If the whole of a document contains the same number of columns, Word doesn't need section breaks, but if the document contains one-column and two-column text, Word will divide the text with section breaks; likewise, two-column text will be separated from three-column text, three-column text from four-column text from two-column text, and so on, as shown in Figure 7.1.

Anytown·Mine·to·Close·Next·Year¶

by·Molly·Hindhaugh¶··Section Break (Continuous)··········

The·rural·community·of· Anytown·was·thrown·into· shock·yesterday·by·the·news· that·its·renowned·copper· mine·will·close·next·year,· five·years·earlier·than·had· been·anticipated.¶

In·a·wide-reaching·imple- mentation·of·the·budget·cuts· agreed·on·at·last·week's·Council· meeting,·Anytown·plans·to· close·the·mine·without·further· investigation·of·opportunities·to· extend·its·life.¶

Anytown·Copper·Works·currently· employs·369·people,·all·of·whose· livelihoods·depend·on·the·copper· mine.·While·the·Copper·Works·may· be·able·to·continue·operating·under· special·circumstances·agreed·upon·by· *(continued·on·page·4·col.·5)*¶·········

Local·Boy·Saves·Dog¶

by·our·Special·Correspondent¶··Section Break (Continuous)··········

By·diving·into·a·roaring·stream·swollen·with· the·runoff·from·spring·downpours·to·rescue·a· sheepdog·swept·off·a·bridge,·Mark·Frazer· claimed·the·respect·of·the·Anytown·community· on·Monday.¶

Mark,·13,·played·down·his·feat·with·the·modesty· that·has·made·him·a·favorite·among·his·schoolmates·at· Anytown·Junior·School.¶

"I·just·saw·the·dog·and·did·it·without·thinking,"·he· explained.¶··········Section Break (Continuous)··········

FIGURE 7.1:   Word uses section breaks to separate the sections of text that have different numbers of columns from each other.

NOTE   Word displays column layouts only in Page Layout view and in Print Preview. In Normal view, Online Layout view, and Outline view, Word won't indicate how the columns in your document will look.

Creating Columns Quickly with the Columns Button

To create columns quickly without worrying about formatting details:

1. To create columns from existing text, select it. To create columns in only one part of your document, select that part.

2. Click the Columns button on the Standard toolbar and drag down and to the right over the grid that appears to indicate how many columns you want. Release the mouse button, and Word will create the columns.

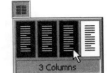

Creating Columns with the Columns Dialog Box

For more control over the columns you create, use the Columns dialog box instead of the Columns button:

1. To create columns from existing text, first select the text. To create columns in only one part of your document, select that part.

2. Choose Format ➤ Columns to display the Columns dialog box (see Figure 7.2).

3. Choose the number of columns you want to create, either by clicking one of the buttons in the Presets list or by entering a number in the Number of Columns box. (These settings affect each other.) Watch the Preview box as you choose the settings for your columns.

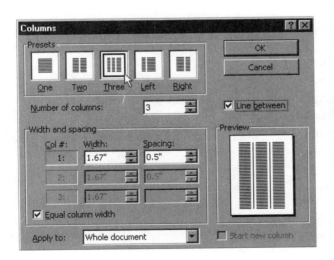

FIGURE 7.2:
The Columns dialog box gives you fine control over the number of and formatting of columns.

4. If need be, adjust the column width and spacing in the Width and Spacing group box.
   - If you chose two or more columns and want to produce columns of varying widths, clear the Equal Column Width check box.
   - In the Width box for each column, enter the column width you want. In the Spacing box, enter the amount of space you want between this column and the column to its right.
5. To add a line between each column on your page, select the Line Between check box.
6. Click the OK button to close the Columns dialog box and create the columns with the settings you chose.

Changing the Number of Columns

Once you've created columns in a document, you can change the number of columns by selecting the relevant text and using either the Columns button or the Columns dialog box:

- Click the Columns button on the Standard toolbar and drag the grid that appears until you've selected the number of columns you want.
- Choose Format ➤ Columns to make adjustments to the columns as described in the previous section, *Creating Columns with the Columns Dialog Box*.

Starting a New Column

To start a new column at the top of the page:

1. Place the insertion point at the beginning of the text that will start the new column.
2. Choose Format ➤ Columns to display the Columns dialog box.
3. In the Apply To drop-down list, choose This Point Forward.
4. Select the Start New Column check box.
5. Click the OK button to close the Columns dialog box. Word will create a new column from the insertion point forward.

Removing Columns from Text

The way Word thinks, you don't so much remove columns from text as adjust the number of columns. For example, to "remove" two-column formatting from text, you change the text to a single-column layout.

The easiest way to switch back to a single-column layout is to click the Columns button on the Formatting toolbar and drag through the resulting grid to select the one-column bar, then release the mouse button. Alternatively, choose Format ➤ Columns to display the Columns dialog box, choose One from the Presets group box, and then click the OK button.

> **TIP**
>
> To switch only part of a document back to a single-column format, select that part before clicking the Columns button or choosing One in the Presets group box of the Columns dialog box. To switch an entire section, place the insertion point anywhere within that section.

Tables

Word's tables give you a way to present complex information in vertical columns and horizontal rows of cells. Cells can contain text—a single paragraph or multiple paragraphs—or graphics.

You can create a table from existing text, or you can create a table first and then enter text into it. Once you've created a table, you can add further columns or rows, or merge several cells in the same row to make one cell.

To embellish your tables, you can use borders, along with font formatting (bold, italic, underline, highlight, and so on), paragraph formatting (indents, line spacing, and so on), and style formatting—not to mention Word's Table AutoFormat feature.

Word provides the Tables and Borders toolbar (see Figure 7.3) for working with tables. Here's what the buttons on the Tables and Borders toolbar do:

- The Draw Table button turns the mouse pointer into a pen that you can click and drag to draw table cells in a document. Click the button again to restore the mouse pointer.
- The Eraser button turns the mouse pointer into an eraser that you can drag to erase the borders of cells. Click the button again to restore the mouse pointer.
- The Line Style button displays a drop-down list of available line styles. Select one for the cells you're about to draw.
- The Line Weight button displays a drop-down list of available line weights for the current line style.
- The Border Color button displays a palette of available border colors.

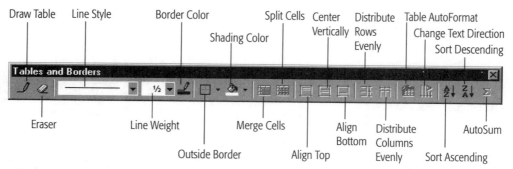

FIGURE 7.3: The Tables and Borders toolbar

- The Border button applies the current border to the selection or to tables or cells you draw. To change the current border, click the drop-down list button and choose a type of border from the palette.
- The Shading Color button applies the current shading color to the selection. To change the current shading color, click the drop-down list button and choose a color from the palette.
- The Merge Cells button merges the contents of selected cells.
- The Split Cells button displays the Split Cells dialog box for splitting the selected cell into two or more cells.
- The Align Top button, the Center Vertically button, and the Align Bottom button control the vertical alignment of selected cells.
- The Distribute Rows Evenly button and the Distribute Columns Evenly button adjust row height and column width, respectively, to equal the tallest cell in the row or the widest cell in the column.
- The Table AutoFormat button displays the Table AutoFormat dialog box. We'll look at autoformatting later in the chapter.
- The Change Text Direction button rotates the text in the selected cell in 90-degree jumps.
- The Sort Ascending button and the Sort Descending button are for quick sorting.
- The AutoSum button inserts a formula for adding the contents of a row or column.

Drawing a Table with the Draw Table Button

For a quick table of your own design, use the Draw Table feature:

1. Display the Tables and Borders toolbar if it's not displayed. (Click on the menu bar or on any displayed toolbar, and choose Tables and Borders from the drop-down list of toolbars.)

2. Verify the settings in the Line Style and Line Weight drop-down lists and the color on the Line Color button to make sure they're suitable for the table you want to draw.

3. Click the Draw Table button on the Tables and Borders toolbar. (Display the Tables and Borders toolbar if it's not displayed.) The mouse pointer will turn into a pen.

4. Click and drag in the document to create the shape for the table.

5. Click and drag across the table to create rows and columns. Word will adjust the row height to make the rows the same height. Click on the Draw Table button again when you need to restore the normal mouse pointer to work in the table.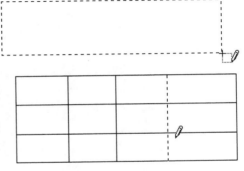

6. To remove extra lines, click the Eraser button and drag the eraser pointer over the line you want to remove. Click the Eraser button again to restore the normal mouse pointer.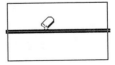

Inserting a Table Quickly with the Insert Table Button

The easiest way to insert a table is to click the Insert Table button on the Standard toolbar. Drag the mouse pointer down and to the right over the grid that appears to select the table layout configuration (number of rows and columns) you want to create, and then release the mouse button. Word will create the table and apply borders to it.

> **TIP**
>
> To create the table from existing text, select the text before clicking the Insert Table button. Word will not display the grid when you click the button, but will convert the text to an appropriately configured table. For example, if you have three columns laid out with tabs, Word will create a three-column table when you click the Insert Table button.

Inserting a Table with the Insert Table Command

You can also insert a table by choosing Table ➤ Insert Table and then choosing the details of the table in the Number of Columns, Number of Rows, and Column Width boxes in the Insert Table dialog box (see Figure 7.4).

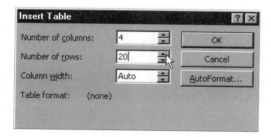

FIGURE 7.4:
In the Insert Table dialog box, set up the table you want to create.

Using Table Autoformatting

Formatting your tables can be a slow business, so Word offers a Table AutoFormat feature that can speed up the process. To create a new table and autoformat it, choose Table ➤ Insert Table and click the AutoFormat button in the Insert Table dialog box. Word will display the Table AutoFormat dialog box (see Figure 7.5).

Use the Formats list box and the adjacent Preview box to choose the format that suits your table best. You'll find that some of the formats (for example, Elegant and Professional) fail to live up to their names, but others (such as 3D Effects 2) are in-offensive and borderline pleasing.

In the Formats to Apply area, choose whether you want Word to apply Borders, Shading, Font, and Color formatting to the table by selecting or clearing the check boxes. Watch the Preview box to see the effects of your changes. The most important of these formatting options is AutoFit, which causes Word to adjust the column width to suit the text in your table rather than blindly allotting a standard (and most likely inappropriate) width to each column.

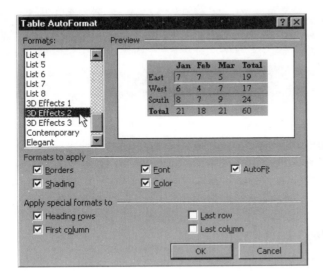

FIGURE 7.5:
The Table AutoFormat dialog box offers quick access to a veritable plethora of predefined table formats and options to customize tables.

TIP

If you're not quite sure what shape and layout your table will take on as you create it, you can also apply autoformatting after creating the table—just click inside the table and click the Table AutoFormat button on the Tables and Borders toolbar, or right-click in the table and choose Table AutoFormat from the context menu, or choose Table ➤ Table AutoFormat from the menu bar. Alternatively, you can format the table manually, as we'll see in *Formatting a Table* later in this chapter.

In the Apply Special Formats To area, check the boxes to choose which rows and columns you want Word to apply special formatting to: Heading Rows, First Column, Last Row, and Last Column. The last two choices are good for emphasizing totals or conclusions.

TIP

By clearing all the check boxes in the Formats to Apply group box and the Apply Special Formats To group box, you can render all the formats the same. (I mention this as a curiosity, not as a recommendation—AutoFormat assumes you want to apply *some* formatting, not none at all. You *can* use this ability to clear formats from a table, but it's easier to select None in the Formats list box.)

Once you've made your choices, click the OK button. If you're creating a table, Word will return you to the Insert Table dialog box, where you again click OK to dismiss the dialog box and create the table with the formatting you've chosen; if you're running AutoFormat on a table already created, Word will apply the formatting you chose to the table.

Converting Existing Text to a Table

If you've already got the material for a table in a Word document, but it's laid out with tabs, paragraphs, commas, or the like, you can quickly convert it to a table.

1. First, select the text.
2. Choose Table ➤ Convert Text to Table. Word will display the Convert Text to Table dialog box (see Figure 7.6) with its best guess about how you want to separate the text into table cells.
    - If the selected text consists of apparently regular paragraphs of text, Word will suggest separating it at the paragraph marks—each paragraph will then go into a separate cell.
    - If the selected text appears to contain tabbed columns, Word will suggest separating it at each tab, so that each tabbed column will become a table column.
    - If the selected text appears to have commas at regular intervals in each paragraph—as in a list of names and addresses, for example—Word will suggest separating the text at each comma. This is good for database-output information (such as names and addresses) separated by commas.
    - If the selected text appears to be divided by other characters (such as hyphens), Word will suggest dividing it at each hyphen).
3. If necessary, change the setting in the Separate Text At box. This may change the number of columns and rows that Word has suggested. If you choose Other, enter the separator character in the Other box. This can be any character or any letter.

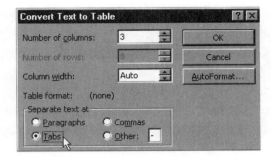

FIGURE 7.6:
In the Convert Text to Table dialog box, choose the options for converting existing text into a Word table.

4. If necessary, manually adjust the number of columns and rows by entering the appropriate number in the Number of Columns. (For example, you might want to add an extra column at the end of the table and enter text in it later.) The setting in the Number of Columns box automatically adjusts the setting in the Number of Rows box to match the possible configurations of the table based on the setting in the Separate Text At group box.

5. Adjust the setting in the Column Width box if you want to. Auto usually does a reasonable job, and you can adjust the column widths later if you need to.

6. Click the OK button to convert the text to a table, or click the AutoFormat button to have Word walk you through formatting the table. After formatting, Word will return you to the Convert Text to Table dialog box; click the OK button to close it and create the table.

Selecting Parts of a Table

When manipulating your tables, first you need to select the parts you want to manipulate. While you can just click and drag with the mouse (or use the keyboard or the Shift-click technique discussed in Chapter 1), Word also offers shortcuts for selecting parts of tables.

Here's how to select parts of tables:

- To select one cell, move the mouse pointer into the thin cell-selection bar at the left edge of the cell. You'll know when it's in the right place because the insertion point will change to an arrow pointing north-northeast. Then click once to select the cell (including its end-of-cell marker).
- To select a row, move the mouse pointer into the table-selection bar to the left of the row, and then click. Alternatively, double-click in the cell selection bar at the left edge of any cell in the row.
- To select multiple rows, click in the table selection bar and drag up or down.

> **TIP**
>
> One of the keys to understanding how Word selects cells is the hidden end-of-cell marker that each cell contains. Once you drag past this to another cell, you've selected both that cell and the other. The end-of-cell marker is a little circle with pointy corners, inescapably reminiscent of the original *Space Invaders* that transformed school life in the late 1970s. To display end-of-cell markers, choose Tools ➤ Options and select the Paragraphs check box in the Nonprinting Characters area on the View tab in the Options dialog box, or click the Show/Hide ¶ button on the Standard toolbar.

- To select a column, Alt-click in it. Alternatively, move the mouse pointer to just above the top-most row of the column, where it will turn into a little black arrow pointing straight down, and then click.
- To select multiple columns, click just above the top-most row of any column and drag left or right.
- To select the whole table, Alt–double-click anywhere in it.

Word also offers menu options for selecting parts of tables. Place the insertion point in the appropriate row or column (or drag through the rows or columns to select cells in multiple rows or columns) and then do the following:

To Select	Choose
A column	Table ➤ Select Column
A row	Table ➤ Select Row
The whole table	Table ➤ Select Table

Navigating in Tables

You can move easily through tables using the mouse, the arrow keys, or the Tab key. ← moves you backward through the contents of a cell, character by character, and then to the end of the previous cell; → moves you forward and then to the start of the next cell; ↑ moves you up through the lines and paragraphs in a cell and then up to the next row; and ↓ moves you down. Tab moves you to the next cell, selecting any contents in the process; Shift+Tab moves you to the previous cell and also selects any contents in the cell.

Editing Text in a Table

Once the insertion point is inside a cell, you can enter and edit text (and other elements) as in any Word document, except for entering tabs, for which you need to press Ctrl+Tab.

Row height adjusts automatically as you add more text to a cell or as you increase the height of the text. You can also adjust the row height manually, as we'll see in a moment.

Adding and Deleting Cells, Rows, and Columns

Often you'll need to change the layout of your table after you create it—for example, you might need to add a column or two, or delete several rows, so that it presents your information most effectively.

> **TIP** Word distinguishes between deleting the *contents* of a cell, row, or column and deleting the cell, row, or column itself. When you delete the contents of a cell, row, or column, the cell, row, or column remains in place; but when you delete the cell, row, or column, both it and its contents disappear. To delete just the contents of a cell, row, or column, select your victim and press the Delete key.

Deleting Cells

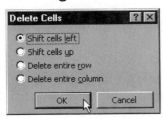

To delete cells and their contents from a table, select the cells, right-click and choose Delete Cells from the context menu, or choose Table ➤ Delete Cells. If your selection includes an entire row or an entire column, this command will be displayed as Delete Rows or Delete Columns (see the *Deleting Rows* and *Deleting Columns* sections a little later). Otherwise, Word will display the Delete Cells dialog box. This dialog box offers to move the remaining cells up or to the left to fill the space left by the cells you're deleting. It also offers to delete the entire row or column that the selected cells occupy. Make your choice and then click the OK button.

Adding Cells

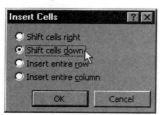

To add cells to a table, select the cells above which, or to the right of which, you want to insert the new cells, then right-click and choose Insert Cells from the context menu or Table ➤ Insert Cells. If your selection includes an entire row or entire column, this command will be displayed as Insert Rows or Insert Columns (see the *Adding Rows* and *Adding Columns* sections a little later), and Word will automatically add the row or column. Otherwise, in the Insert Cells dialog box, choose Shift Cells Right or Shift Cells Down (or choose Insert Entire Row or Insert Entire Column to specify how the selected cells should move, then click the OK button.)

Adding Rows

 **To add a row to the end of a table instantly, position the insertion point in the last cell (the lower-right cell) of the table and press Tab.**

To add a row to a table, click in the row above which you want to add the new row, then right-click and choose Insert Rows from the context menu, or choose Table ➤ Insert Rows.

- To insert multiple rows, select the same number of existing rows, then right-click and choose Insert Rows from the context menu or choose Table ➤ Insert Rows. For example, to add three rows, select three rows. The new rows will appear above the rows you selected.
- Alternatively, after selecting a cell, or cells in a number of rows, choose Table ➤ Insert Cells, select the Insert Entire Row option in the Insert Cells dialog box and then click OK.

TIP **The Insert Table button on the Standard toolbar changes into an Insert Rows button when the insertion point is inside a table and into an Insert Columns button when you've selected one or more columns in a table.**

Deleting Rows

To delete a row of cells from a table, right-click in the row you want to delete and choose Delete Cells from the context menu, or click in the row and choose Table ➤ Delete Cells. In the Delete Cells dialog box, choose Delete Entire Row and click the OK button.

- To skip the Delete Cells dialog box, select the row. Then either right-click and choose Delete Rows from the context menu or choose Table ➤ Delete Rows.
- To delete multiple rows, select the rows you want to delete, then either right-click and choose Delete Rows from the context menu or choose Table ➤ Delete Rows.

Adding Columns

To add a column to a table, select the column to the left of the new column you want to add, and then right-click and choose Insert Columns from the context menu, or choose Table ➤ Insert Columns.

To insert multiple columns, select the same number of existing columns, and then right-click and choose Insert Columns from the context menu or choose Table ➤ Insert Columns. For example, to add three columns, select three columns. The new columns will appear to the left of the columns you selected.

Deleting Columns

To delete a column of cells from a table, right-click in the column and choose Delete cells from the context menu or choose Table ➤ Delete Cells. In the Delete Cells dialog box, choose Delete Entire Column and click the OK button.

- To skip the Delete Cells dialog box, select the column, then right-click and choose Delete Columns from the context menu, or choose Table ➤ Delete Columns.
- To delete multiple columns, select the columns you want to delete, then right-click and choose Delete Columns from the context menu, or choose Table ➤ Delete Columns.

TIP To delete an entire table, select the table using Table ➤ Select Table, and then choose Table ➤ Delete Rows.

Formatting a Table

As with editing a table, you can use the regular Word formatting features—from the toolbars, the Font and Paragraph dialog boxes, and so on—to format your tables. However, there are a couple of exceptions worth mentioning: alignment and indents.

Setting Alignment in Tables

Alignment in tables is very straightforward once you know that not only can any row of the table be left-aligned, right-aligned, or centered (all relative to the margins set for the page) but also, within those rows, the text in each cell can be left-aligned, right-aligned, centered, or justified, relative to the column it's in. If that's not enough, the contents of any cell can be aligned top or bottom, or centered vertically.

For example, you could center your table horizontally on the page and have the first column left-aligned, the second centered, the third justified, and the fourth right-aligned (though the result would almost certainly look weird). Figure 7.7 shows a table that is more reasonably aligned: The first column is right-aligned to present the numbers in a logical fashion; the second column is right-aligned, and the third left-aligned with the space between the columns reduced to display each first name and last name together while retaining the ability to sort by the last name. The Age column is centered (for aesthetics and this example); and the numbers in the Years of Service column are right-aligned. The table itself is centered on the page.

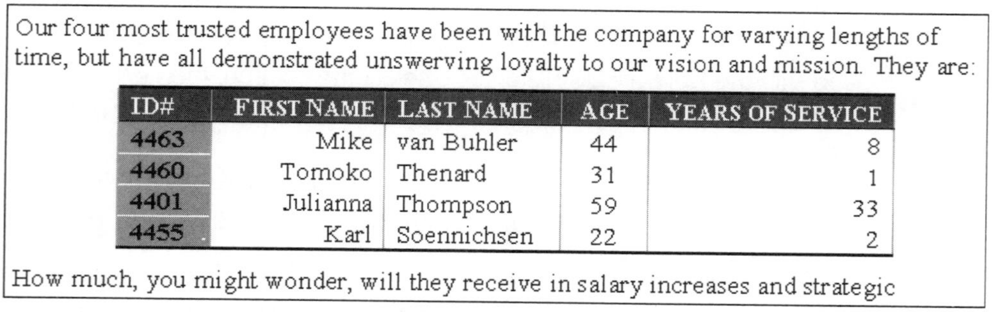

Our four most trusted employees have been with the company for varying lengths of time, but have all demonstrated unswerving loyalty to our vision and mission. They are:

ID#	FIRST NAME	LAST NAME	AGE	YEARS OF SERVICE
4463	Mike	van Buhler	44	8
4460	Tomoko	Thenard	31	1
4401	Julianna	Thompson	59	33
4455	Karl	Soennichsen	22	2

How much, you might wonder, will they receive in salary increases and strategic

FIGURE 7.7: Use the different types of alignment to display your information clearly.

To set alignment within any cell, use the methods discussed in Chapter 2: the alignment buttons on the Formatting toolbar, the keyboard shortcuts, or the Paragraph dialog box.

To set alignment for a row, choose Table ➤ Cell Height and Width and choose Left, Center, or Right in the Alignment area on the Row tab of the Cell Height and Width dialog box (see Figure 7.8).

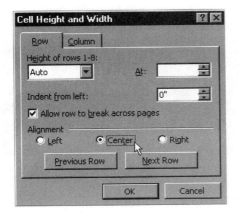

FIGURE 7.8:
Set alignment for a row on the Row tab of the Cell Height and Width dialog box.

To set vertical alignment for a cell, click the Align Top, Center Vertically, or Align Bottom button on the Tables and Borders toolbar. Alternatively, right-click in the table, choose Alignment from the context menu, and select Align Top, Center Vertically, or Align Bottom from the Alignment submenu.

Setting Indents in Tables

As with alignment, you can indent the entire table or the contents within each cell. By understanding the difference, you can position your tables precisely where you want them on the page and lay out the table text using suitable indents.

To set indentation for the text in the current cell, use the methods you learned in Chapter 2—drag the indentation markers on the ruler or change the settings in the Indentation area on the Indents and Spacing tab of the Paragraph dialog box. For example, the numbers in the Years of Service column in the table shown in Figure 7.7 have been indented 0.4" from the right margin of the cell to display them more clearly.

To set indentation for a row, select one or more cells in the row, choose Table ➤ Cell Height and Width, and enter a measurement in the Indent from Left box on the Row tab of the Cell Height and Width dialog box, then click the OK button. If there is no text selected and the insertion point is in the table, the settings you make in the Cell Height and Width dialog box will be applied to all the rows in the table.

Adding Borders and Shading to Your Tables

Adding borders and shading to your tables is a little more complex than you might expect. Because Word lets you add borders and shading to the paragraphs inside the table, to any given cell, or to the whole table, you have to be a little careful about what you select.

> **TIP**
>
> The quickest way to add borders and shading to a table is to use the Table AutoFormat command, discussed earlier in *Using Table Autoformatting*. If you want more information, read on. You can also experiment by using the Border button and Shading button on the Tables and Borders toolbar.

Adding Borders and Shading to the Whole Table

To add borders and shading to the whole table, click anywhere in it but don't select anything, then choose Format ➤ Borders and Shading. Word will display the Borders and Shading dialog box. Make sure the Apply To drop-down list shows Table. Choose the border options you want on the Borders tab and the shading options you want on the Shading tab, then click the OK button.

Adding Borders and Shading to Selected Cells

To add borders and shading to selected cells in a table, select the cells by dragging through them or by using the keyboard. (If you're selecting just one cell, make sure you select its end-of-cell mark as well, so that the whole cell is highlighted, not just part of the text.) Then choose Format ➤ Borders and Shading to display the Borders and Shading dialog box. Make sure the Apply To drop-down list shows Cell rather than Table, Paragraph, or Text. Again, choose the border options you want on the Borders tab and the shading options you want on the Shading tab, and then click the OK button.

Adding Borders and Shading to Paragraphs within Cells

To add borders and shading to paragraphs within a cell, select the text you want to format in the cell but don't select the end-of-cell mark. Then choose Format ➤ Borders and Shading to display the Borders and Shading dialog box. This time, make sure that the Apply To drop-down list shows Text (for less than a paragraph) or Paragraph (for more than one paragraph). Choose the border and shading options you want. If you want to adjust the placement of the borders from the text, click the Options button to display the Border and Shading Options dialog box, then set the placement in the Top, Bottom, Left, and Right boxes in the From Text area and click OK.

Merging Cells

Once you've set up your table, you can create special layout effects by merging cells—converting two or more cells into a single cell. To merge cells, select the cells to merge, then click the Merge Cells button on the Tables and Borders toolbar, or right-click and choose Merge Cells from the context menu, or choose Table ➤ Merge Cells. Word will combine the cells into one, putting the contents of each in a separate paragraph in the merged cell; you can then remove the paragraph marks to reduce them to one paragraph if necessary.

1994	1995	1996	1997	1998	1999	2000
Western Region Results						
44	48	65	67	71	79	100
Eastern Seaboard Results						
11	12	15	22	23	26	43

Merged cells are especially useful for effects such as table spanner heads. In the example shown here, the headings "Western Region Results" and "Eastern Seaboard Results" occupy merged cells that span the whole table:

Changing Column Width

The easiest way to change column width is to move the mouse pointer over a column's right-hand border so that the insertion point changes into a two-headed arrow pointing left and right. Then click and drag the column border to a suitable position. (You can also click in the column division mark in the horizontal ruler and drag that instead.) If there is a column to the right of the border you're dragging, Word will resize it accordingly. If you want to change only the column to the left of the border you're dragging, hold down Shift as you drag. Word will increase or decrease the width of the table to allow for the increase or decrease in the width of the column you adjust.

TIP

Hold down Shift while you drag the column border to affect only the column whose right border you're dragging. Otherwise, Word will change the width of the column to the right of the border you're moving.

To change column width more precisely, position the insertion point in the column you want to change, and then choose Table ➤ Cell Height and Width. In the Cell Height and Width dialog box, click the Column tab to bring it to the front if it isn't already there, and then set the column width in the Width of Column *n* box (see Figure 7.9).

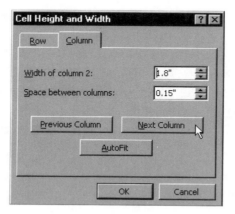

FIGURE 7.9:
Setting the column width on the Column tab of the Cell Height and Width dialog box

- If you like, you can also change the amount of space separating columns by entering a different measurement in the Space between Columns box.
- Use the Previous Column and Next Column buttons to move to different columns and set their width.
- Click the AutoFit button to have Word automatically set a width for the column based on its contents. This will close the Cell Height and Width dialog box.
- Click the OK button to close the Cell Height and Width dialog box.

TIP   To share available space evenly among columns, select the columns (or the whole table) and choose Table ➤ Distribute Columns Evenly.

Changing Row Height

Word sets row height automatically as you add text to (or remove text from) the cells in any row or adjust the height of the contents of the cells. But you can also set the height of a row manually by placing the insertion point in it and choosing Table ➤

Cell Height and Width. Word will display the Cell Height and Width dialog box. If the Row tab isn't foremost, click it.

TIP To make a number of rows the same height as the row that contains the tallest cells, select the rows (or the whole table) and choose Table ➤ Distribute Rows Evenly.

From the Height of Row *n* drop-down list, choose At Least to enter a minimum height for the row, or Exactly to enter a precise height. Then enter the measurement in the At box.

- Use the Previous Row and Next Row buttons to move to the previous or next row and set its height.
- Check the Allow Row to Break Across Pages box if you're working with long cells that you can allow to break over pages.
- Click the OK button to close the Cell Height and Width dialog box.

TIP You can also change row height in Page Layout view by clicking and dragging a row-break mark on the vertical ruler or dragging any horizontal border (except the top one) in a table.

Table Headings

If you're working with tables too long to fit on a single page, you'll probably want to set table headings that repeat automatically on the second page and subsequent pages. To do so, select the row or rows that form the headings, and then choose Table ➤ Headings. Word will place a check mark by the Headings item in the Table menu.

Word will repeat these headings automatically if the table is broken with an automatic page break, but not if you insert a manual page break. Word displays the repeated headings only in Page Layout view and Print Preview, so don't expect to see them in Normal view.

To remove table headings, choose Table ➤ Headings again. Word will remove the check mark from the Headings item in the Table menu.

Table Formulas

If you're using tables for numbers—sales targets, net profits, expense reports, or whatever—you may want to use Word's table formulas, for which you use the Table ➤ Formula command to display the Formula dialog box. These include a variety of mathematical functions, including rounding and averaging, that you may want to get into on your own but which go beyond the scope of this book.

The most useful formula for everyday purposes is the SUM formula. To add the numbers in a row or column of cells, click the AutoSum button on the Tables and Borders toolbar.

> **TIP**
>
> Using table formulas is a bit like building a mini-spreadsheet in Word. If table formulas aren't enough to satisfy you and you need to create a full-fledged spreadsheet in Word, look ahead to Chapter 19, *Office Binders and OLE*, in which we'll look at how you can embed an Excel spreadsheet in a Word document.

Copying and Moving within Tables

To copy or move material within a table, use the methods discussed in Chapter 1—either use the mouse and drag to move the selection (or Ctrl-drag to copy it), or use the Cut, Copy, and Paste commands via the Standard toolbar, the Edit menu, or the keyboard shortcuts.

Converting a Table to Text

Sooner or later you're going to need to convert a table back to text. To do so, simply select the table by choosing Table ➤ Select Table or by Alt–double-clicking inside it, and then choose Table ➤ Convert Table to Text. Word will display the Convert Table to Text dialog box with its best guess (based on the contents of the table) at how it should divide the cells when it converts it: with paragraphs, with tabs, with commas, or with another character of your choice. Correct the Separate Text With setting if it's inappropriate, and then click the OK button.

That's it for tables—except for one of the most useful things that you can do with tables in Word: Sort your information into its most effective order. We'll look at sorting in Chapter 8.

Chapter 8

SORTING INFORMATION

- **Understanding how Word sorts data**
- **Arranging your data suitably for sorting**
- **Sorting your data**
- **Using Word's sorting options**

Once you've created tables of information or even multicolumn lists formatted using tabs, you'll probably need to sort the information.

Word's sorting feature lets you sort data by up to three types of information at once, such as last name, street name, and ZIP code. If that doesn't produce fine enough results, you can then sort the same data again using different types of information, such as first name and age—and then sort it again, if need be.

In this chapter, we'll look first at how Word sorts information, so you can make full use of the sorting feature. Then we'll look at how to arrange information in your documents, so you can sort the data effectively at a moment's notice. Finally, we'll perform a multilevel sort.

How Word Sorts

Word sorts by *records* and *fields*, two familiar words that carry quite different meanings in computing. A *record* will typically make up one of the items you want to sort and will consist of a number of *fields*, each of which contain one piece of the information that makes up a record. For example, in a mailing database containing name and address information, each customer and their associated set of data would form a record; that record would consist of a number of fields, such as the customer's first name, middle initial, last name, street address, city, state, ZIP code, area code, phone number, and so forth. In Word, this record could be entered in a table (with one field per cell) or as a paragraph, with the fields separated by tabs, commas, or a character of your choice.

Next, you need to know what order Word sorts things in. Here are the details:

- Word can sort by letter, by number, or by date (in a variety of date formats).
- Word can sort in ascending order—from A to Z, from 0 to 9, from early dates to later dates—or in descending order (the opposite).
- When sorting alphabetically, Word sorts punctuation marks and symbols (e.g., &, !) first, then numbers, and finally letters. When sorting numerically, Word sorts symbols first, then letters, then punctuation marks, and finally numbers. If two items start with the same letter, Word goes on to the next letter and sorts by that, and so on; if two fields are the same, Word sorts using the next field, and so forth.

Arranging Your Data for Sorting

If you've already entered all the data in your document or table and are raring to go ahead and sort it, skip to the next section, *Performing a Multilevel Sort*. If you're still in the process of entering your data, or haven't yet started, read on.

The first key to successful sorting is to divide up your records into as many fields as you might possibly want to sort by. For example, it's usually best to put first names and last names in separate fields, so that you can sort by either; likewise, you'll usually want to break addresses down into street, city, state, and ZIP code, so that you can sort your data by any one of them. If you need to be able to target customers street by street, you might even break up the street address into the number and the street name, so that you can produce a list of customers on Green Street, say, or Hesperian Avenue.

Use a table for complex data or for data that won't all fit on one line of a tabbed document. (You can carry over tabs from the first line of a paragraph onto the second and subsequent lines, but it's visually confusing and rarely worth the effort when table cells can wrap text and keep it visually clear.)

> **NOTE** Above all, before running any complex sorts, save your data and make a backup of it—or even run a practice sort on a spare copy of the data.

Performing a Multilevel Sort

The following sections cover performing multilevel sorts with paragraph text and with tables. In either case, you can perform a single-level sort by choosing only one sort key in the Sort Text dialog box or the Sort dialog box.

Sorting Text in Paragraphs

When you sort text in paragraphs, Word treats each paragraph as a unit to be sorted unless you tell it to do otherwise. (For instructions on how to sort only part of a number of paragraphs—for example, a section set off by tabs or commas—see the section *Using Sort Options* later in this chapter.)

To sort text in paragraphs:

1. Select the paragraphs you want to sort. (Remember that in Word a paragraph is a paragraph mark and anything between it and the previous paragraph mark.)

First Name	Last Name	Phone Number
Amy	Lignin	808-555-1212
Grant	Pepperidge	314-555-1234
June	Williams	212-555-9753

2. Choose Table ➤ Sort to display the Sort Text dialog box (see Figure 8.1).
3. First, check the My List Has area at the bottom of the dialog box and see if Word has correctly identified any header row (i.e., row of headings) at the top of the text you're sorting. If the text has a header row, make sure the Header Row option button is selected—otherwise Word will treat the header row as text and sort it along with everything else, which is usually less than

desirable. If the text has no header row, make sure that the No Header Row option button is selected.

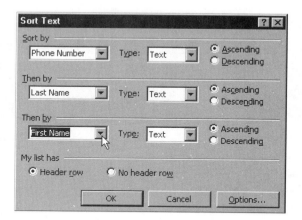

FIGURE 8.1:
Choose options for sorting text in the Sort Text dialog box.

> **TIP**
>
> **Word identifies a header row by the differences in formatting from the rest of the text—a different style, font, font size, bold, italic, and so on. (The header row doesn't have to be a bigger font size or boldfaced—it can be smaller than the other text or have no bold to the other text's bold—just so long as Word can recognize it as different.) Be warned that Word may miss your header row if several paragraphs have different formatting, not just the first paragraph; it may also miss the header row for reasons known only to itself.**

4. In the Sort By group box, choose the field by which to sort the text first.

- If your text has a header row, Word will display the names of the headings (abbreviated if necessary) in the drop-down list to help you identify the sort key you want. If your text has no header row, Word will display Field 1, Field 2, and so on.
- If your text consists of paragraphs with no fields that Word can identify, Word will display Paragraphs in the Sort By box.

5. In the Type box, make sure that Word has chosen the appropriate option: Text, Number, or Date.

6. Next, choose Ascending or Descending for the order in which to sort the text.

7. If necessary, specify a second sort key in the first Then By box. Again, choose the field by which to sort, check the Type, and choose Ascending or Descending.

8. To sort by a third sort key and produce a more useful sort, repeat step 7 for the second Then By box.

9. Click the OK button to perform the sort and close the Sort Text dialog box.

First Name	Last Name	Phone Number
June	Williams	212-555-9753
Grant	Pepperidge	314-555-1234
Amy	Lignin	808-555-1212

Word will leave the paragraphs highlighted, so if you want to run another sort to get your data into an even finer order, simply repeat steps 2–9.

Sorting Text in a Table

As we saw in Chapter 7, Word's tables are ideal for laying out data too complex for tabbed columns. Tables are also great for sorting data to within an inch of its life.

> **TIP**
>
> Word sorts tables by rows, treating each row as a unit, unless you tell it otherwise. For example, if you select only cells in the first two columns of a four-column table and run a sort operation, Word will rearrange the third and fourth columns as well according to the sort criteria you chose for the first two columns. To sort columns without sorting entire rows, see the section titled *Using Sort Options* later in this chapter.

To sort text in a table:

1. Select the part of the table you want to sort. To sort the whole table, just click anywhere inside the table; Word will select the whole table for you automatically when you choose Table ➤ Sort.

2. Choose Table ➤ Sort to display the Sort dialog box (see Figure 8.2).

3. Look at the My List Has area at the bottom of the dialog box and ensure that Word has correctly identified any header row (i.e., row of headings) at the top of the table or of the rows you're sorting. Word omits the header row from the sort, figuring that you'll still want it at the top of the table. If the text has a header row, make sure the Header Row option button has

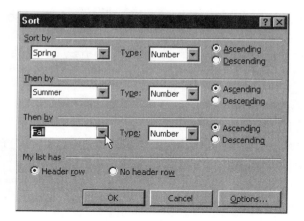

FIGURE 8.2:
Choose options for sorting tables in the Sort dialog box.

been selected—otherwise Word will treat the header row as text and sort it along with everything else. You will need to select at least three rows to persuade Word that the rows have a header row.

- If you've set table headings by using the Table ➤ Headings command, you don't need to worry about the My List Has box—Word knows that the table has headings and dims the options in the My List Has box.

4. In the Sort By group box, choose the column (i.e., the field) by which to sort the rows of cells first.

- If your table (or your selected rows) has a header row, Word will display the names of the headings (abbreviated if necessary) in the drop-down list to help you identify the sort key you want. If your text has no header row, Word will display Column 1, Column 2, and so on.

5. In the Type box, make sure that Word has chosen the appropriate option: Text, Number, or Date.

6. Next, choose Ascending or Descending for the order in which to sort the rows.

7. If necessary, specify a second sort key in the first Then By box. Again, choose the field by which to sort, verify the Type, and choose Ascending or Descending.

8. To sort by a third sort key and produce a finer sort, repeat step 7 for the second Then By box.

9. Click the OK button to perform the sort and close the Sort dialog box.

Word will leave the table (or the selection of rows) highlighted, so if you want to run another sort to get your data into a more precise order, simply repeat steps 2–9.

Using Sort Options

To allow you to direct its sorting capabilities even more precisely, Word offers five sort options in the Sort Options dialog box (see Figure 8.3). Some of these options are available only for particular types of sorts.

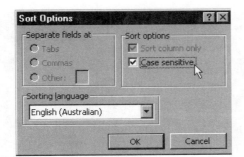

FIGURE 8.3:
The Sort Options dialog box provides ways of refining the sort process even further.

To choose sort options, click the Options button in the Sort Text dialog box or the Sort dialog box.

The Sort Options group box in the Sort Options dialog box offers the following options:

- **Sort Column Only** sorts only the selected columns of a table or the selected columns of characters in regular text or in a tabbed list (selected by Alt-dragging). This option is not available if you've selected entire paragraphs or rows.
- **Case Sensitive** will sort (in ascending order) lowercase before uppercase, sentence case before title case, and title case before all capitals.

The Separate Fields At group box lets you specify which character separates the different fields of text when sorting paragraphs: Tabs, Commas, or Other. Word can usually identify fields separated by tabs or commas, or even with conventional separators such as hyphens, but if your boss has used something unorthodox like em dashes as separators, you'll need to specify that in the Other box.

The Sorting Language group box allows you to specify that your text be sorted in a different language. This will change the sort order to follow the alphabet and sorting rules of that language.

Once you've made your choices in the Sort Options dialog box, click the OK button to return to the Sort Text dialog box or Sort dialog box.

Chapter 9

MAIL MERGE

- **Creating the main document**
- **Creating the data source**
- **Choosing merge options**
- **Merging the data**
- **Using non-Word documents as data sources**

Mail merge strikes terror into the hearts of many office workers. It gained its notoriety quite deservedly in the early days of word processing, when brave souls using WordStar, SuperScripsit, and other pioneering programs fought their way through truly incomprehensible instructions only to produce memorable letters beginning like this:

```
Mr. Dear 861 Laurel Street
Ronald@Geldofsson   #2
```

You have probably received a few such letters in the past, and from what I can see, Publishers Clearing House is still heroically churning them out. But nowadays you can do better than that with far less effort.

Mail merge in today's word processing applications is, by comparison, friendly and fun. With just a little attention to the details of what you're doing, you can whip together merged letters, forms, envelopes, labels, or catalogs. Word's Mail Merge Helper smoothes out many of the potential speed bumps in the process.

> **TIP** You can even use data sources from other applications, for example, data from Excel spreadsheets or from Access tables, with zero complications. We'll look at this towards the end of the chapter.

While Word's Mail Merge Helper lets you carry out merges in a variety of different orders, in this chapter we'll look at the most conventional order of proceeding. Once you see what's what, you can mix and match to produce the variations that suit you best. You'll also find that Mail Merge has a number of different areas, and in some of them, the water gets deep fast—hit a couple of buttons and Word will be expecting you to put together some SQL statements for MS Query to use in torturing a FoxPro database (or worse). In the spirit of cooperation, sadly lacking so far in the 1990s, I'll show you how to avoid such predicaments and steer a path through the pitfalls of mail merge.

Enough mixed metaphors. Let's look first at creating the main document for the merge.

Creating the Main Document

The *main document* is the file that contains the skeleton into which you fit the variable information from the data file. The skeleton consists of the text that stays the same in each of the letters, catalogs, or whatever, and the *merge fields* that receive the information from the data file. The data file is typically a Word table that contains information about the recipients of the form letters or the products you're trying to sell them.

First, if you've got a main document that you want to use, open it and make it the active window.

Choose Tools ➤ Mail Merge to start the merging process. Word will respond by displaying the Mail Merge Helper dialog box (see Figure 9.1).

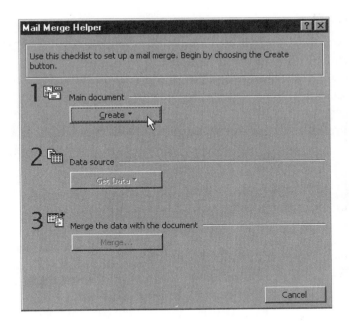

FIGURE 9.1:
The first of many appearances for the Mail Merge Helper dialog box. Click the Create button in the Main Document area to get started.

| TIP | The Mail Merge Helper dialog box displays increasing amounts of information and instructions about the merge as you go through the process. If you get confused about which stage you've reached, and you don't have the Mail Merge Helper dialog box on screen to help you, choose Tools ➤ Mail Merge to display the Mail Merge Helper and scan the information and instructions it's currently displaying. |

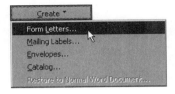

Click the Create button in the Main Document area and choose the type of document you want to create: Form Letters, Mailing Labels, Envelopes, or Catalogs. (For the example, I chose Form Letters because that still seems to be the most popular type of mail merge.)

In the message box that appears, choose whether to use the document in the active document window—the document that was open when you started the Mail Merge Helper—or to create a new main document.

- If you choose to use the active document, Word records its name and path underneath the Create button in the Mail Merge Helper dialog box.
- If you choose to create a new main document, Word opens a new document for you and records its name under the Create button: *Document2* or a similar name.

Specifying the Data Source

The next step is to specify the data source for the mail merge.

Click the Get Data button and choose an option from the drop-down list:

- Create Data Source lets you create a new mail merge data source for this merge project.
- Open Data Source lets you open an existing data source (e.g., the one from your last successful mail merge).
- Use Address Book lets you use an existing electronic address book, such as your Outlook address book (if you're using Microsoft Office) or your MAPI Personal Address Book (which you may be using with Exchange), as data for the merge.
- Header Options is a little more esoteric. We won't go into detail here, but Header Options lets you run a merge in which the data comes from one source and the header information that controls the data comes from another source. This can be useful if you already have a main document with fields defined and a data source with headers that don't match the fields: Instead of changing the headers in the data source (and perhaps thereby rendering it unsuitable for its regular uses), you can choose Header Options, click the Create button, and set up a new set of headers that will bridge the gap between the main document and the data source.

Creating a New Data Source

To create a new data source, click the Get Data button and choose Create Data Source from the drop-down list. Word will display the Create Data Source dialog box (see Figure 9.2).

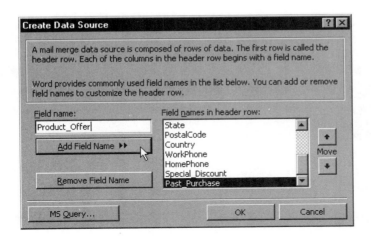

FIGURE 9.2:
Creating a new data source in the Create Data Source dialog box

First, you create the *header row* for the data source—the field names that will head the columns of data and that you will enter into your main document to tell Word where to put the variable information.

Word provides a list of commonly used field names for you to customize: Title, FirstName, LastName, JobTitle, and so on. You'll find these more suitable for some projects than others—for example, for a parts catalog, you'll probably want to customize the list extensively, whereas the list is pretty much on target for a business mailing.

- To add a field name to the list, type it in the Field Name box, then click the Add Field Name button. (The largest number of fields you can have is 31, at which point Word will stop you from adding more.)

TIP

Field names can be up to 40 characters long, but you'll usually do better to keep them as short as possible while making them descriptive—ultra-cryptic names can cause confusion later in the merge process. Names can use both letters and numbers, but each name must start with a letter. You can't include spaces in the names, but you can add underscores instead—Career_Prospects, and so forth—which helps make them readable.

- To remove a field name from the list, select it in the Field Names in Header Row list box and click the Remove Field Name button.

- To rearrange the field names in the list, click a field name and then click the Move buttons to move it up or down the list.

TIP **The list of field names in the Field Names in Header Row list box forms a loop, so you can move the bottom-most field to the top of the list by clicking the down button.**

When you have the list of field names to your liking, click the OK button to close the Create Data Source dialog box and save the data source you're creating.

WARNING **Clicking the MS Query button in the Create Data Source dialog box takes you off into the "Twilight Zone" of Structured Query Language (SQL, pronounced *sequel* by aficionados, in case you're wondering). I suggest not clicking it unless you're experienced in SQL queries and are happy playing with databases.**

Word will now display the Save As dialog box for you to save the data source. Save your document in the usual way.

Once the document is saved, Word will display a message box telling you that the document contains no data—no surprise, as you've just created it—and inviting you to edit it or to edit the main document. For now, choose the Edit Data Source button.

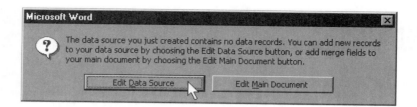

Word will display the Data Form dialog box (see Figure 9.3), which is a custom dialog box built from the field names you entered in the Create Data Source dialog box.

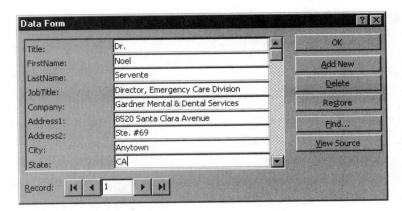

FIGURE 9.3:
In the Data Form dialog box, enter records for the data source you just created.

Add data to the data source: Type information into the fields in the dialog box. Press ↵ or Tab to move between fields.

- Click the Add New button to begin a new record after entering the first one.
- Click the Delete button to delete the current record.
- Click the Restore button to restore the record to its previous condition (the information it contained before any changes you just made onscreen).
- Click the View Source button to see the kind of data source you're working with in Word. (Usually this means that Word will display a table containing the records that you've entered.)
- Click the Record buttons at the bottom of the Data Form dialog box to see your records: the four buttons call up the first record, previous record, next record, and last record respectively, and the Record box lets you type in the record number that you want to move to.

Click the OK button when you've finished adding records to your data source. Word will close the Data Form dialog box and take you to your main document with the Mail Merge toolbar displayed. Skip ahead to *Adding Merge Fields to the Main Document*.

Using an Existing Data File

To use an existing data file for your mail merge, click the Get Data button in the Mail Merge Helper dialog box and choose Open Data Source. Word will display the Open Data Source dialog box (shown in Figure 9.4), which you'll recognize as the Open dialog box in disguise. Navigate to the data source document the usual way, select it, and open it by clicking the Open button.

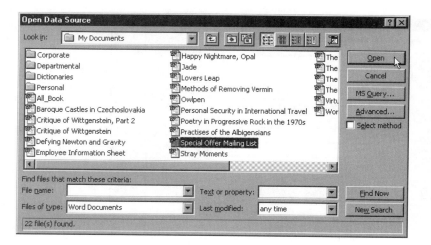

FIGURE 9.4:
Open your existing data source from the Open Data Source dialog box.

Word will now check your purported data source for fields. If it doesn't contain any fields that Word can recognize, Word will display the Header Record Delimiters dialog box for you to indicate how the fields and records are divided (delimited), as shown in Figure 9.5. Pick the delimiter characters in the Field Delimiter and Record Delimiter drop-down lists (you get to choose from paragraphs, tabs, commas, periods, exclamation points, and anything else Word thinks might be a delimiter character in this document), and then click the OK button. (If you opened the wrong file, click the Cancel button to close the Header Record Delimiters dialog box and then click the Get Data button again to reopen the Open Data Source dialog box.)

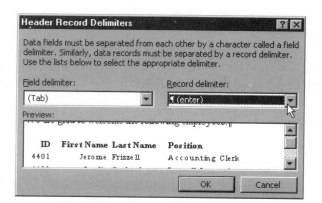

FIGURE 9.5:
If Word displays the Header Record Delimiters dialog box, you may have picked the wrong file by mistake. If not, indicate to Word how the fields and records are divided.

Once Word has established that your data source contains fields, it will check your main document for merge fields. If it finds none—most likely if you're creating a new main document for the merge—it will display a message box inviting you to insert them.

Click the Edit Main Document button and Word will return you to your main document. Now it's time to add merge fields to it. Skip ahead to *Adding Merge Fields to the Main Document*.

Using Your Address Book

To run a mail merge from the data in your electronic address book, click the Get Data button in the Mail Merge Helper dialog box and choose Use Address Book. Word will display the Use Address Book dialog box (see Figure 9.6). From the Choose Address Book list, choose the address book to use and click the OK button.

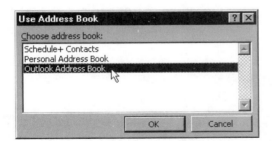

FIGURE 9.6:
Choose the address book you want to use in the Use Address Book dialog box.

Depending on which address book you select, the next few actions will vary. For example, if you choose your Personal Address Book, Word may invite you to choose a profile for the merge. Play along, and shortly after interrogating you about your social security number and your mother's maiden name, Word will announce in its status bar that it's converting the address book. It will then scan the address book for viable information to use for the merge. Once Word is satisfied that you've picked a suitable address book, it will display a message box telling you that it found no merge fields in your main document and inviting you to add some. Click the Edit Main Document button to do so.

Adding Merge Fields to the Main Document

Back in the main document, you'll see that Word has opened a Mail Merge toolbar that provides buttons for inserting merge fields and Word fields into the main document.

If you're starting a main document from scratch, add the merge fields as you write the document. If you started off with the basis of your merge document already written, you just need to add the merge fields to it.

`Insert Merge Field ▾` To insert a merge field, click the Insert Merge Field button and choose the merge field from the drop-down list of merge fields in the data source you created or chose. For example, to enter an address, choose the Title field; Word will insert a field saying **<<Title>>** in the document. Follow that with a space, insert the FirstName

```
«Title» «FirstName» «LastName»
«JobTitle»
«Company»
«Address1», «Address2»
«City», «State» «PostalCode»
```

field and another space, and then insert the LastName field. Press ↵ and start entering the address fields. Remember the spaces and punctuation that the words will need—they're easy to forget when you're faced with a large number of fields.

> **TIP**
>
> The Insert Word Fields button produces a drop-down list of special fields for use in complex merges, such as Ask, If…, Then…, Else…, and Fill-in. These fields provide you with a way to customize your merge documents so that they prompt the user for keyboard input, act in different ways depending on what kind of data they find in merge fields, and so on. They're beyond the scope of this book, but if you do a lot of complex mail merges, you'll no doubt want to learn how to use them.

At this point, you've got the components of the merge in place—a data source with records and a main document with field codes that match the header names in the data source. Next, you can specify options for the merge—filtering and sorting, error checking, and more—or just damn the torpedoes and merge the documents.

 If you need to make adjustments to your data source, click the Edit Data Source button on the Mail Merge toolbar—the right-most button on the toolbar.

If you suddenly realize you've selected the wrong data source, click the Mail Merge Helper button on the Mail Merge toolbar, click the Get Data button in the Mail Merge Helper dialog box, and choose the right data source.

Setting Merge Options

In this section, we'll look quickly at how you can sort and filter merge documents so you can perform a merge without producing documents for every single record in your database. If you don't want to try sorting or filtering, go straight on to the section titled *Merging Your Data*.

Sorting the Records to Be Merged

By filtering your records, you can restrict the scope of your mail merges to just the appropriate part of your data source rather than creating a label, catalog entry, or form letter for every single record. For example, you can filter your records so that you print labels of only your customers in California and Arizona, or so that you send a letter extolling your pine-colored leatherette goblins only to people called Green (first name or last).

You can also use sorting to restrict mail merges. Instead of having Word print out your merge documents in the order in which you entered the records on which they're based in the data source, you can sort them by state and by city to placate the mail room.

To sort your records:

1. Click the Mail Merge Helper button to display the Mail Merge Helper dialog box.
2. Click the Query Options button to open the Query Options dialog box (see Figure 9.7). Click the Sort Records tab to bring it to the front if it isn't already there.
   - You can also get to the Query Options dialog box by clicking the Query Options button in the Merge dialog box.
3. In the Sort By box, choose the first field you want to sort by from the drop-down list, and then choose an Ascending or Descending sort order.

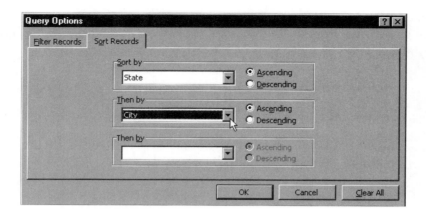

FIGURE 9.7:
On the Sort Records tab of the Query Options dialog box, choose how you want your records sorted.

4. To sort more precisely, choose the second field in the first Then By box. (For example, to sort by city within state, choose State in the Sort By box and City in the first Then By box.) Again, choose Ascending or Descending order.

5. Specify another sort field in the second Then By box if necessary, and choose the order.

6. Click the OK button to close the Query Options dialog box.
   - If you want to filter your sorted data, click the Filter Records tab instead and skip to step 3 in the next section.
   - If you choose the wrong sort fields, click the Clear All button to reset the drop-down lists to no field.

Filtering the Records to Be Merged

To filter the records you'll be merging:

1. Click the Mail Merge Helper button to display the Mail Merge Helper dialog box.

2. Click the Query Options button to open the Query Options dialog box (see Figure 9.8). Click the Filter Records tab to bring it to the front if it isn't already displayed.

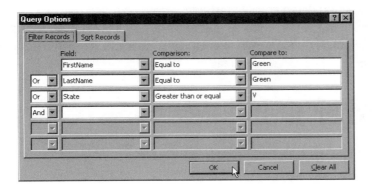

FIGURE 9.8:
On the Filter Records tab of the Query Options dialog box, choose how to filter the records you'll be merging.

3. In the Field drop-down list in the top row, choose the field you want to use as the first filter.

4. In the Comparison drop-down list in the top row, choose the filtering operator to specify how the contents of the field must relate to the contents of the Compare To box: Equal to (match), Not Equal to (not match), Less Than, Greater Than, Less than or Equal, Greater than or Equal, Is Blank (the merge field must be empty), Is Not Blank (the merge field must not be empty).

> **TIP**
>
> For these mathematically inclined comparisons, Word evaluates numbers using the conventional manner (1 is less than 11 and so on) and text using the American National Standards Institute (ANSI) sort order: *ax* comes before *blade* alphabetically, so *ax* is "less than" *blade*. You could also use State Is Greater than or Equal to V to filter records for Vermont, Virginia, Washington, and Wyoming. For fields that mix text and numbers, Word treats the numbers as text characters, which means that 11 will be sorted between 1 and 2 (and so on).

5. In the second and subsequent rows, choose And or Or in the unnamed first column before the Field column to add a finer filter to the filter in the previous row or to apply another filter. For example, you could choose And LastName Is Equal to Green to restrict your merge to Greens in Vermont. Click the Clear All button if you need to reset all the filtering fields.

6. Click the OK button when you've finished defining your filtering criteria. Word will return to the Mail Merge Helper dialog box (unless you got to the Query Options dialog box by clicking the Query Options button in the Merge dialog box, in which case Word will take you there).

Merging Your Data

Now you're all set to merge your data source with your main document. In the Mail Merge Helper dialog box, click the Merge button. Word will display the Merge dialog box (see Figure 9.9).

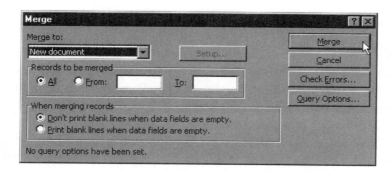

FIGURE 9.9:
In the Merge dialog box, choose whether to merge to a new document, to a printer, or to e-mail.

To merge your data:

1. Choose whether to merge to a new document, to your printer, or to e-mail (if you have Exchange or Outlook installed and correctly configured):

   - If you merge to a new document, Word will divide the resulting documents as it thinks best. For example, it will put page breaks between form letters so that they're ready for printing, whereas mailing labels will share page one.

> **TIP**
> By merging to a new document, you give yourself a chance to check the merged documents for errors—and, if you want, to add personalized notes to particular documents that you didn't want to put into your data source.

   - If you merge to your printer, Word simply prints all the documents and doesn't produce an onscreen copy.

- If you merge to e-mail, click the Setup button to display the strangely named Merge To Setup dialog box (see Figure 9.10). Specify the field that contains the e-mail address in the Data Field with Mail/Fax Address drop-down box, add a subject line for the message in the Mail Message Subject Line text box, and select the Send Document as an Attachment check box if the document contains formatting that will not survive transmission as an e-mail message. (This depends on the sophistication of your e-mail package and of the service provider you're using: If you have basic, text-only e-mail, not even bold or italic will make it through unscathed.) Then click the OK button to close the Merge To Setup dialog box and return to the Merge dialog box.

FIGURE 9.10:
In the Merge To Setup dialog box, specify the merge field that contains the e-mail address and add a subject line for the message.

2. If need be, choose which records to merge in the Records to Be Merged group box. Either accept the default setting of All, or enter record numbers in the From and To boxes.
   - If you're using sorting or filtering, the records will be in a different order from that in which they were entered in the data source.
   - To merge from a specific record to the end of the record set, enter the starting number in the From box and leave the To box blank.
3. In the When Merging Records group box, select the Print Blank Lines When Data Fields Are Empty option button if you need to track gaps in your data. Usually, though, you'll want to leave the Don't Print Blank Lines When Data Fields Are Empty option button selected to produce a better looking result.
4. Click the Check Errors button and verify which option button has been selected in the Checking and Reporting Errors dialog box (shown below). The default choice is Complete the Merge, Pausing to Report Each Error as It Occurs; you can also choose Simulate the Merge and Report Errors in a New Document if you consider the merge potentially problematic; or you can choose Complete the Merge without Pausing. This option reports errors in a new document. Click the OK button when you've made your choice.

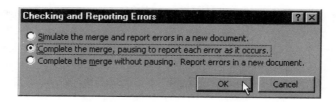

5. Click the Merge button to run the mail merge.

- If you're merging to a new document, Word will display it onscreen. You can then check the merged document for errors before printing, and you can save it if you want to keep it for future use.
- If you're merging to a printer, Word will display the Print dialog box. Choose the page range and number of copies, if necessary, and then click the OK button to print the documents. When Word has finished printing, it will return you to your main document. Word doesn't create the merged document on disk, so you can't save it.
- If you're merging to e-mail, Word will check your MAPI profile settings, and then mail the messages and documents (if you're currently online or connected to the network that handles your e-mail) or place them in your Outbox (if you're not currently online or connected to the network).

Merging Labels and Envelopes

In Chapter 3, we looked at how you can print labels and envelopes with Word. In this section, we won't grind through *all* that information again—we'll just look at the parts that are different when you're running a mail merge to print labels and envelopes.

Merge-Printing Labels

To create labels for a merge-print:

1. Choose Tools ➤ Mail Merge, select Mailing Labels from the Create drop-down list, and then follow the procedures described earlier in this chapter until you've created or selected your data source. Then Word will display a message box telling you it needs to set up your main document; accept by clicking the Set Up Main Document button.
2. Word will then display the Label Options dialog box. Choose your labels as discussed in Chapter 3 and click the OK button.

3. Word will then display the Create Labels dialog box (see Figure 9.11), so you can set up a label format. Click the Insert Merge Field button and choose the fields for the labels from the drop-down list. Word will insert them in the Sample Label box. Include punctuation and spaces, and start new lines as appropriate.

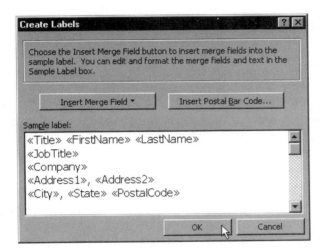

FIGURE 9.11:
In the Create Labels dialog box, set up your labels for merge-printing.

> **TIP**
>
> You can apply formatting to the merge field codes by selecting them and either using keyboard shortcuts (such as Ctrl+B for boldface and Ctrl+I for italic) or right-clicking and choosing Font from the context menu to display the Font dialog box. You can adjust the paragraph layout by right-clicking and choosing Paragraph from the context menu.

4. If you want to include a postal bar code for the address, click the Insert Postal Bar Code button and select the fields from the Merge Field with ZIP Code and Merge Field with Street Address drop-down lists.

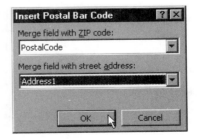

5. Click the OK button to close the Insert Postal Bar Code dialog box. Word will insert a boldfaced line saying **Delivery point bar code will print here!** at the top of the Sample Label box in the Create Labels dialog box.

6. Click the OK button to close the Create Labels dialog box.

Word will create the main document for the labels from the contents of the Sample Label box and will return you to the Mail Merge Helper dialog box. From there, follow the instructions in the section titled *Merging Your Data* to complete the merge.

Merge-Printing Envelopes

To set up envelopes for a merge-print:

1. Choose Tools ➤ Mail Merge, select Envelopes from the Create drop-down list, and then follow the procedures described earlier in this chapter (in *Creating the Main Document* and *Specifying the Data Source*) until you've created or selected your data source. As with labels, Word will display a message box asking you to click the Set Up Main Document button to finish setting up your main document.

2. Click the Set Up Main Document button and Word will display the Envelope Options dialog box that we investigated in Chapter 3.

3. Make your choices in the Envelope Options dialog box, then click the OK button to display the Envelope Address dialog box.

4. Click the Insert Merge Field button and choose the fields for the envelopes from the drop-down list. Word will insert them in the Sample Envelope Address box.

   • Include punctuation and spaces, start new paragraphs where you want them to be, and add any text that you want on each envelope.

   • You can apply formatting to the merge field codes by either using keyboard shortcuts or by right-clicking and choosing Font from the context menu to display the Font dialog box.

   • You can change the paragraph layout by right-clicking and choosing Paragraph from the context menu.

5. To include a postal bar code for the address, click the Insert Postal Bar Code button and select the fields from the Merge Field with ZIP Code and the Merge Field with Street Address drop-down lists.

TIP   You'll see that in the **Insert Postal Bar Code dialog box for envelopes, there's also an FIM-A Courtesy Reply Mail check box that you can select if you want to print a Facing Identification Mark on courtesy reply envelopes.**

6. Click the OK button to close the Insert Postal Bar Code dialog box. Word will insert a boldfaced line saying **Delivery point bar code will print here!** at the top of the Sample Envelope Address box.

7. Click the OK button to close the Envelope Address dialog box.

Word will create the main document for the envelopes from the contents of the Sample Envelope Address box and will return you to the Mail Merge Helper dialog box. From there, follow the instructions in the section titled *Merging Your Data* to complete the merge. If you choose to merge to a printer, line up the envelopes so they are ready for printing.

Using a Data Source Other Than a Word Document

To use a data source other than a Word document for a mail merge, you hardly need to do anything different from the procedures described earlier in this chapter. Word just requires you to specify exactly where the information is coming from, and even that is very straightforward.

Click the Get Data button in the Mail Merge Helper dialog box and choose Open Data Source. In the Open Data Source dialog box, choose the type of file you want to use from the Files of Type drop-down list; navigate to the file and open it in the usual way.

Unless the application that the file was created in is already open, Word will fire up a copy of it in the background (you'll still see Word onscreen) and will open the file in question. What follows next depends on the data source you're opening; if it's an Excel spreadsheet, Word will display a dialog box in which you select the range of cells to use for the merge (see Figure 9.12).

FIGURE 9.12:
When using an Excel spreadsheet as a data source, select a named range or cell range from the Named or Cell Range box to use for the merge.

Once you've done that, Word will put you back into the regular mail merge loop of editing your main document. When the merge is finished, Word will close the other application (unless it was already open, in which case Word will close only the file it opened).

Restoring a Main Document to a Regular Document

If you know you won't need to use your main document again for a mail merge, be reassured that it isn't merged forever—you can easily restore it to a regular Word document.

To restore a main document to a regular document:

1. Open the main document.
2. Choose Tools ➤ Mail Merge to display the Mail Merge Helper dialog box.
3. Click the Create button and choose Restore to Normal Word Document from the drop-down list. Word will break the main document's attachment to its data file and restore it to normal document status.

Chapter 10

USING WORD'S DOCUMENT AUTOMATION FEATURES

FEATURING

- **Using AutoCorrect**
- **Using AutoText**
- **Using automatic bullets and numbering**
- **Using automatic captioning**
- **Using bookmarks to identify parts of your documents**

In addition to its on-the-fly spell-checking and grammar-checking, Word offers four automation features that can greatly increase the speed at which you work with documents. AutoCorrect acts as a monitor for your typing, automatically correcting mistakes and expanding predefined abbreviations; AutoText lets you create abbreviations for boilerplate text you enter frequently in documents. Word also gives you the advantage of automatic bullets and numbering, including heading numbering, along with automatic captioning for figures and tables, and more. Word's bookmarks give you quick access to parts of your documents. We'll look at each of these features in turn in this chapter.

AutoCorrect

AutoCorrect offers five features that help you quickly enter your text in the right format. AutoCorrect works in a similar way to the on-the-fly Spelling checker that we looked at in Chapter 4, but AutoCorrect has far greater potential for improving your working life. Every time you finish typing a word and press the spacebar, press Enter, press Tab, or type any form of punctuation (comma, period, semicolon, colon, quotation marks, exclamation point, question mark, or even a % sign), Word checks it for a multitude of sins and, if it finds it guilty, takes action immediately.

The first four of AutoCorrect's features are straightforward; the fifth is a little more complex:

- **Correct TWo INitial CApitals** stops you from typing an extra capital at the beginning of a word. If you need to type technical terms that need two initial capitals, clear the check box to turn this option off or create AutoCorrect exceptions for them. We'll look at exceptions later in this section.

> **TIP**
>
> If you type three initial capitals in a word, Word will not correct the second and third, figuring you're typing an acronym of some sort. (It will still query the spelling of the word if it doesn't recognize it.)

- **Capitalize First Letter of Sentences** does just that. If you and Word disagree about what constitutes a sentence, turn this option off by clearing the check box.
- **Capitalize Names of Days** does just that.
- **Correct accidental usage of cAPS lOCK key** is a neat feature that works most of the time. If Word thinks you've got the Caps Lock key down and you don't know it, it will turn Caps Lock off and change the offending text from upper- to lowercase and vice versa. Word usually decides that Caps Lock is stuck when you start a new sentence with a lowercase letter and continue with uppercase letters; however, the end of the previous sentence may remain miscased.
- **Replace Text as You Type** is the best of the AutoCorrect features. We'll look at it in detail in the next section.

Replace Text As You Type

The AutoCorrect Replace Text as You Type feature keeps a list of AutoCorrect entries. Each time you finish typing a word, AutoCorrect scans this list for that word. If the word is on the list, Word substitutes the replacement text for the word.

Replace Text as You Type is a great way of fixing typos you make regularly; and in fact, Word ships with a decent list of AutoCorrect entries already configured. If you type **awya** instead of **away** or **disatisfied** instead of **dissatisfied**, Word will automatically fix the typo for you. But AutoCorrect is even more useful for setting up abbreviations for words or phrases that you use frequently in your day-to-day work, saving you not only time and keystrokes but also the effort of memorizing complex spellings or details. For example, suppose you write frequently to your bank manager demanding an explanation of charges to your account: You could set up one AutoCorrect entry containing the address and salutation, another containing your account details, a third containing your ritual complaint, and a fourth containing your name and signature; you would have the bulk of the letter written in a four-fold flurry of keystrokes. (You could also use a template, but that's quibbling.)

You can add AutoCorrect entries to Word's list in two ways—either automatically while running a spelling check, or manually at any time.

Adding AutoCorrect Entries While Spell-Checking

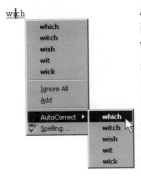

Adding AutoCorrect entries while spell-checking a document is a great way to teach Word the typos you make regularly. When the Spelling checker finds a word it doesn't like, make sure the appropriate replacement word is highlighted in the Suggestions box; if the word selected in the Suggestions box isn't the appropriate one, type in the right word. Then click the AutoCorrect button in the Spelling dialog box. Word will add the word from the Not in Dictionary box to the Replace list in AutoCorrect and the word selected in the Suggestions box to the With list in AutoCorrect. This way, you can build an AutoCorrect list tailored precisely to your typing idiosyncrasies.

As we saw in Chapter 4, you can also add AutoCorrect entries during on-the-fly spell-checks by choosing AutoCorrect from the context menu and selecting the word to which the current typo should be mapped in the submenu that appears.

Adding AutoCorrect Entries Manually

Adding AutoCorrect entries while spell-checking is great for building a list of your personal typos in Word, but of little use for setting up AutoCorrect with abbreviations that will increase your typing speed dramatically. For that, you need to add AutoCorrect entries manually.

To add AutoCorrect entries manually:

1. If the replacement text for the AutoCorrect entry is in the current document, select it.

> **TIP**
>
> To create an AutoCorrect entry that contains formatting—bold, italic, paragraph marks, tabs, and so on—or a graphic, you need to select the formatted text (or the graphic) in a document before opening the AutoCorrect dialog box.

2. Choose Tools ➤ AutoCorrect to display the AutoCorrect dialog box (see Figure 10.1).
3. Make sure that the Replace Text as You Type check box is selected.
4. Enter the typo or abbreviation to replace in the Replace box.

> **TIP**
>
> When choosing the Replace text for an abbreviated AutoCorrect entry, avoid using a regular word that you might type in a document and not want to have replaced. Try reducing the word or phrase to an abbreviation that you'll remember—for example, omit all the vowels and include only the salient consonants.

5. Enter the replacement text in the With box.
   - If you selected text before opening the AutoCorrect dialog box, that text will appear in the With box. If the text needs to retain its formatting, make sure the Formatted Text option button has been selected. (The Formatted Text option button also needs to be selected if your selection contains a paragraph mark or tab—that counts as formatting.)
6. Click the Add button or press Enter to add the AutoCorrect entry to the list.

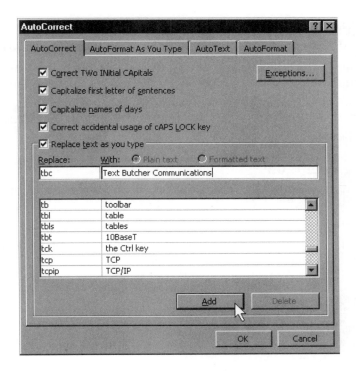

FIGURE 10.1:
The AutoCorrect dialog box

- If Word already has an AutoCorrect entry stored for that Replace text, you'll see a Replace button instead of the Add button. When you press Enter or click this button, Word will display a confirmation dialog box to make sure that you want to replace the current AutoCorrect entry.

7. To add another AutoCorrect entry, repeat steps 3 through 6.

8. To close the AutoCorrect dialog box, click the Close button.

TIP

You can include graphics, text boxes, borders, and so on in AutoCorrect entries; graphics need to be entered in the text of the document, not floating over the text. For example, you can easily include your company's logo in an AutoCorrect entry for the company address for letterhead. Be imaginative and AutoCorrect can save you plenty of time.

Deleting AutoCorrect Entries

To delete an AutoCorrect entry, open the AutoCorrect dialog box (by choosing Tools ➤ AutoCorrect) and select the entry from the scroll list at the bottom of the dialog box. (You can type the first few letters of an entry's Replace designation in the Replace box to scroll to it quickly.) Then click the Delete button.

You can then either delete further AutoCorrect entries or click the OK button to close the AutoCorrect dialog box.

Using AutoCorrect Exceptions

If you've already managed to think up a couple of things that could cause problems with AutoCorrect, hold up a moment: AutoCorrect has an Exceptions feature that you can use to prevent specific items from triggering AutoCorrect corrections.

From the AutoCorrect tab of the AutoCorrect dialog box, click the Exceptions button to display the AutoCorrect Exceptions dialog box (see Figure 10.2).

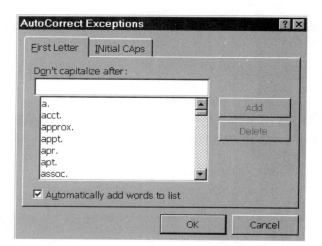

FIGURE 10.2:
In the AutoCorrect Exceptions box, set exceptions to prevent specific terms you use from being corrected automatically.

When Word doesn't recognize an abbreviation, it will think the period that denotes the abbreviation is the end of a sentence instead. On the First Letter tab, you can prevent this from happening by adding to the list of abbreviations any abbreviation that Word does not recognize. Simply type the word into the Don't Capitalize After text box and click the Add button.

When the Automatically Add Words to List check box at the bottom of the First Letter tab is selected, Word will automatically add first-letter exceptions to the list when you use Backspace to undo AutoCorrect's correction of them. For example, say you're writing about syntax and you need to use the abbreviation **prep.** for preposition. If you type **prep. used**, AutoCorrect will change **used** to **Used** because it thinks the period ends a sentence. But if you now use Backspace to delete **Used** and then type in **used** to replace it, Word will create a first-letter exception for **prep.**

To delete a first-letter exception, select it in the Don't Capitalize After list box and click the Delete button.

On the cutely named INitial CAps tab, you can create exceptions for those rare terms that need two initial capitals (for example, IPng, the next-generation Internet Protocol). Enter the text in the Don't Correct text box, then click the Add button.

To delete an initial-cap exception, select it in the Don't Correct list box and click the Delete button.

When the Automatically Add Words to List check box at the bottom of the INitial CAps tab is selected, Word will automatically add words with two initial caps to the list when you use Backspace to undo AutoCorrect's correction of them and then retype them. For example, if you're writing about the next-generation Internet protocol and you type **IPng** and a space, AutoCorrect will change **IPng** to **Ipng**. But if you press Backspace four times (once for the space, once for the **g**, once for the **n**, and once for the **p**, leaving the **I** there) and then type **Png** and a space, Word will create a two–initial-cap exception for **IPng** and will cease and desist from lowercasing the second letter.

AutoText

Word's AutoText feature provides another way to insert frequently used text and graphics in your documents. AutoText has several components that we'll look at in sequence in the following sections.

Creating an AutoText Entry

To create an AutoText entry:

1. Select the text (and/or graphics) from your document for the AutoText entry. Make sure that it contains all the formatting it needs.

 2. Click the Create AutoText button on the AutoText toolbar or press Alt+F3 to display the Create AutoText dialog box (see Figure 10.3).

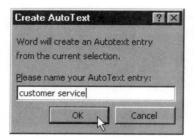

FIGURE 10.3:
In the Create AutoText dialog box, select a name for your AutoText entry and then click the OK button.

3. In the Please Name Your AutoText Entry text box, enter the name you'll use to identify the AutoText entry.
   - If you chose text for the AutoText entry, Word will automatically display the first couple of words from your selection in the Please Name Your AutoText Entry box. Often you'll want to change this and use something catchy that you won't forget.
   - Unlike AutoCorrect entries, AutoText entries can have plain English names that you'll type all the time because AutoText does not automatically replace your typing.
4. Click the OK button to add the AutoText entry to Word's list and close the Create AutoText dialog box.
   - If an AutoText entry with the same name already exists, Word will ask if you want to redefine it. Choose Yes or No; if you choose No, Word will let you choose another name for the AutoText entry; if you choose Yes, Word will replace the existing AutoText entry with the new one.

Inserting an AutoText Entry

You can insert an AutoText entry in several ways:
- by using the AutoText toolbar
- by typing and using the AutoComplete feature
- by typing and choosing the entry manually
- by using the Insert ➤ AutoText menu item

Inserting an AutoText Entry from the AutoText Toolbar

To insert an AutoText entry from the AutoText toolbar, use the Insert AutoText button. This button will bear the name of the style of the current paragraph, such as **Heading 1** or **Body Text**. Click the button to display a list of the AutoText entries associated with the current style.

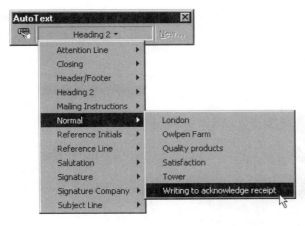

To insert an entry associated with another style or with one of Word's predefined entries, hold down Shift as you click the Insert AutoText button. Word will display a menu of all the AutoText categories that it contains, including its predefined categories (Attention Line, Closing, Header/Footer, and so on) and all the styles that have AutoText entries defined. Select the category you want, then choose the item from the submenu that appears.

Inserting an AutoText Entry by Using the AutoComplete Feature

To insert an AutoText entry quickly using the Auto-Complete feature, start typing the name of the entry. As soon as you've typed four letters of it, or enough of it to distinguish it from any other AutoText entry that starts with the same four letters, AutoComplete will pop up a suggestion box, as shown here. Press Enter or F3 to replace the name of the entry with the full text of the entry; keep typing to ignore the suggestion.

You can turn off the AutoComplete feature as follows:

1. Click the AutoText button or choose Insert ➤ AutoText ➤ AutoText to display the AutoText tab of the AutoCorrect dialog box.
2. Clear the Show AutoComplete Tip for AutoText and Dates check box.
3. Click the OK button to close the AutoCorrect dialog box.

Inserting an AutoText Entry Manually

When you've turned off AutoComplete, you can insert an AutoText entry by typing the first four letters of its name (or enough letters to distinguish it from any other AutoText entry) and then pressing F3 to insert the entry.

Inserting an AutoText Entry from the Insert Menu

You can also insert an AutoText entry from the Insert menu:

1. Display the appropriate AutoText submenu.
   - To display the AutoText submenu of AutoText entries associated with the current style, choose Insert ➤ AutoText.
   - To display the AutoText submenu of all AutoText categories, pull down the Insert menu and hold down Shift as you select AutoText.

2. Choose the entry you want either from the AutoText submenu or from a category from the AutoText submenu, as shown in Figure 10.4.

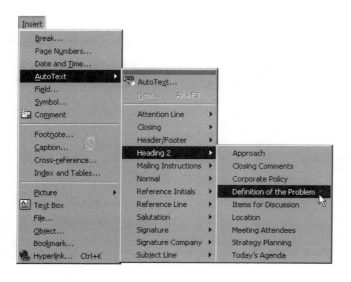

FIGURE 10.4:
You can insert Auto Text entries from the Insert ➤ AutoText submenu.

Changing an AutoText Entry

You can't edit an AutoText entry on the AutoText tab of the AutoCorrect dialog box. Instead, to change an AutoText entry, simply insert it in text (as described in the previous section), then make edits to it by using regular Word editing techniques. Once you have the material for the entry to your satisfaction, select it, choose Insert ➤ AutoText ➤ New to display the Create AutoText dialog box, enter the name of the existing AutoText entry in the Please Name Your AutoText Entry text box, click the OK button, and confirm that you want to replace the entry.

Deleting an AutoText Entry

To delete an AutoText entry:

1. Click the AutoText button or choose Insert ➤ AutoText ➤ AutoText to display the AutoText tab of the AutoCorrect dialog box.

2. Select the entry in the list box.

3. Click the Delete button to delete the entry.

4. Either delete more AutoText entries while you're at it, or click the Close button to close the AutoCorrect dialog box.

Automatic Bullets and Numbering

In this section, we'll look at the options Word offers for adding automatic bullets and numbering to your documents. First we'll look at straightforward bullets and numbering; then we'll look at how to modify the bullets and numbers to produce special effects. In the next chapter, we'll look at heading numbering, which can almost magically speed up the creation of long documents that consist of numbered subitems.

The bullets and numbering that Word applies automatically are paragraph formatting rather than actual characters on the page. In other words, once you've added a bullet to a list, you can't just select the bullet and delete it as you might delete a character—you have to remove it from the paragraph's formatting. We'll look at this process later in the section *Removing Bullets and Numbering*.

Adding Bullets and Numbering

You can add straightforward bullets and numbering to existing text by using the buttons on the Formatting toolbar.

To add bullets, first select the paragraphs you want to add bullets to, and then click the Bullets button on the Formatting toolbar. Word will add the bullets and apply a hanging indent to each of the paragraphs but leave them in their current style.

> **TIP**
>
> **To continue a numbered or bulleted list, press ↵ at the end of the list. To discontinue the list, press ↵ twice at the end of the list.**

To add numbers, select the paragraphs you want to number and then click the Numbering button on the Formatting toolbar.

For a variety of styles of bullets and numbering, select your victim paragraphs, and then either right-click in the selection and choose Bullets and Numbering from the context menu, or choose Format ➤ Bullets and Numbering to open the Bullets and Numbering dialog box (see Figure 10.5).

Choose the tab that corresponds to the type of list you want to create: Bulleted, Numbered, or Outline Numbered, and then click the style that suits you best. Click the OK button to apply the bullets or numbering and close the Bullets and Numbering dialog box.

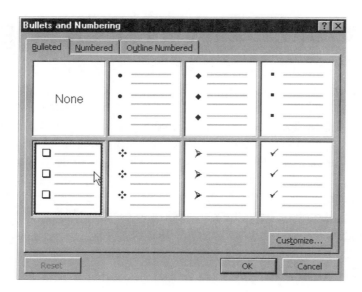

FIGURE 10.5:
The Bullets and Numbering dialog box gives you plenty of choices for bulleting and numbering your lists.

NOTE   **We'll look at outline numbering in detail in Chapter 11, which discusses outlines in Word.**

Removing Bullets and Numbering

To remove bullets or numbering from selected paragraphs, either click the Bullets button or the Numbering button, or choose Format ➤ Bullets and Numbering to display the Bullets and Numbering dialog box, select the None option, and click the OK button.

Modifying the Bullets and Numbering Styles

If you find the choices offered in the Bullets and Numbering dialog box inadequate for your needs, you can create your own bullets or numbers to adorn your text.

To create your own styles of bullets and numbering:

1. Select the paragraphs you want to add bullets or numbers (or both) to.
2. Right-click and select Bullets and Numbering from the context menu, or choose Format ➤ Bullets and Numbering, to display the Bullets and Numbering dialog box.

3. Select the appropriate tab and the format that suits you best, and then click the Customize button. Word will display the Customize Bulleted List dialog box, the Customize Numbered List dialog box, or the Customize Outline Numbered List dialog box as appropriate. Figure 10.6 shows the Customize Bulleted List dialog box, and the steps that follow discuss the options available in this dialog box; the Customize Numbered List dialog box and Customize Outline Numbered List dialog box look a little different, but the options work in similar ways.

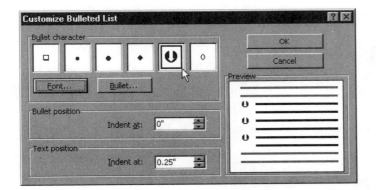

FIGURE 10.6:
In the Customize Bulleted List dialog box, you can choose almost any bullet character that your computer can produce.

4. In the Bullet Character group box, choose from one of the six bullets displayed; or click the Bullet button to open the Symbol dialog box, choose a character, and then click OK to return to the Customize Bulleted List dialog box. Then click the Font button to display the Font dialog box, and choose a suitable font, font size, and other formatting for the bullet; click the OK button to close the Font dialog box and return to the Customize Bulleted List dialog box.

5. In the Bullet Position group box, use the Indent At measurement to specify any indent the bullet should receive.

6. In the Text Position group box, use the Indent At measurement to specify the indent of the text. Usually, you will want this to be more than the indent for the bullet.

7. Click the OK button to apply the formatting to your list.

Captioning

Word's captioning features offer relief for those needing to ensure that the figures, graphics, tables, slides, video clips, equations, and so on throughout their long documents are numbered consistently and sequentially. You can forget about laboriously renumbering all subsequent figures when you delete one at the beginning of a chapter—Word will handle it for you in seconds.

You can add automatic numbering to captions of your own devising, or you can designate boilerplate captions that Word will add automatically to every table or equation or video clip or whatever you insert in your document.

Inserting a Caption

To insert a caption:

1. Select the item that you want to caption. For example, select a picture or a table.

2. Choose Insert ➤ Caption. Word will display the Caption dialog box (see Figure 10.7).

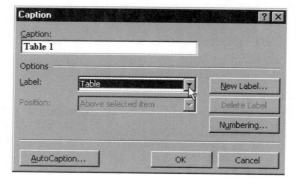

FIGURE 10.7:
The Caption dialog box

3. From the Label drop-down list, choose Figure, Equation, or Table. Word will display it in the Caption text box.

• To add a new label to the list (and to the Caption text box), click the New Label button. In the New Label dialog box that Word displays, enter the text for the new label in the Label box and click the OK button. Word will insert the new label in the Caption box with its regular numbering.

TIP

To delete a caption you've created, select the caption in the Label drop-down list and click the Delete Label button. You can tell which captions are Word's and which are yours because Word won't let you delete any of its captions. (The Delete Label button will be dimmed.)

4. Adjust the numbering of the caption if necessary: Click the Numbering button to display the Caption Numbering dialog box (see Figure 10.8). Click the OK button when you've finished.

    • From the Format drop-down list, choose the numbering format you want: 1, 2, 3; a, b, c; A, B, C; i, ii, iii; or I, II, III.

    • To include the chapter number with the illustration (for example, to produce "Figure 10.8" and so on), select the Include Chapter Number check box. Specify the style at the beginning of each chapter from the Chapter Starts with Style drop-down list and then choose a separator character from the Use Separator drop-down list. As you can see from this book, periods are the classiest separator characters, but Word also offers hyphens, colons, and em- and en-dashes.

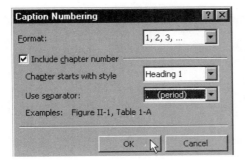

FIGURE 10.8:
Specify different numbering for your caption in the Caption Numbering dialog box.

5. In the Position drop-down list, choose whether you want the caption to appear above or below the selected item.

6. Click the OK button in the Caption dialog box to apply the caption numbering and return to your document. Add your specific caption to the generic caption that Word has inserted, as I've done throughout this book.

Using AutoCaption for Truly Automatic Captions

You can also choose to add automatic captions to recurring elements in a Word document. For example, if you're adding a number of tables to a document, you could have Word automatically add captions to each table as you insert it to prevent you from accidentally missing a table or using a wrong or inconsistent caption.

To add automatic captions to an element:

1. Choose Insert ➤ Caption to display the Caption dialog box.
2. Click the AutoCaption button to display the AutoCaption dialog box (see Figure 10.9).

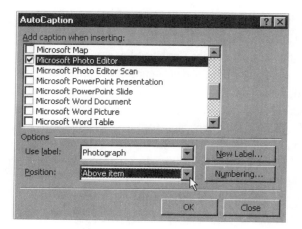

FIGURE 10.9:
In the AutoCaption dialog box, choose the element or elements to which you want to add automatic captions, and then customize the captions and numbering.

3. In the Add Caption When Inserting list box, select the check box for the element you want to have captioned automatically. If you want several elements to have the same caption, select each one.
4. In the Options area, specify what the label should be and whether Word should position it above or below the element.
   - The Use Label drop-down list offers standard choices: Equation, Figure, or Table. If you chose Microsoft Equation or Microsoft Word Table in the Add Caption When Inserting box, Word will offer you Equation and Table, respectively. Otherwise, it will offer you Figure as a generic title.
   - To change the label, click the New Label button and insert the text of the new label in the New Label dialog box.
   - To specify the numbering for the element, click the Numbering button and make your choices in the Caption Numbering dialog box. (For details, see the section, *Inserting a Caption* earlier in this chapter.) Click the OK button when you've finished.

- Use the Position drop-down list to specify the position of the caption: Above Item or Below Item.
5. To add a different AutoCaption to another item, repeat steps 3 and 4 ad lib.
6. Click the OK button to close the AutoCaption dialog box and return to your document.

Updating Captions

Word renumbers captions whenever you insert a new caption. If you move a caption to a different position in the document or delete a caption, you will need to tell Word to update the captions. To do so, select the whole document (choose Edit ➤ Select All or Ctrl+click in the selection bar) and press the F9 key.

> **TIP**
>
> If you want to update only one caption (or a number of captions one-by-one) without updating other fields in the document, select that caption and press F9.

Using Bookmarks

Word's electronic bookmarks provide a way of assigning names to parts of your documents so you can access them swiftly. A bookmark can mark a single point in the text, one or more characters, a table, a graphic—pretty much any item in a document.

Adding a Bookmark

To add a bookmark:
1. Position the insertion point where you want to insert the bookmark. If you want the bookmark to mark a particular section of text, a graphic, a text box, a table, or another element, select that item.
2. Choose Insert ➤ Bookmark to display the Bookmark dialog box (see Figure 10.10).
3. Enter the name for the bookmark in the Bookmark Name text box.
   - Bookmark names can be up to forty characters long and can contain letters, numbers, and underscores, but not spaces or symbols. The names must start with a letter; after that, you can mix letters, numbers, and underscores to your heart's desire.
   - To reuse an existing bookmark name, select it in the Bookmark Name list box.

4. Click the Add button to add the bookmark and close the Bookmark dialog box.

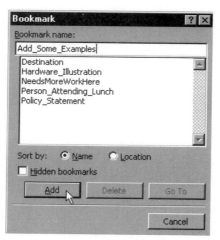

FIGURE 10.10:
In the Bookmark dialog box, enter the name for the bookmark and click the Add button.

Going to a Bookmark

Once you've added bookmarks to a document, you can quickly move to them by using either the Bookmark dialog box or the Go To dialog box.

To move to a bookmark using the Bookmark dialog box:

1. Choose Insert ➤ Bookmark to display the Bookmark dialog box.
2. In the Bookmark Name list box, select the bookmark you want to move to.
   - To sort the bookmarks alphabetically by Name, select the Name option button in the Sort By area; to sort them by their location in the document (for example, from start to finish), select the Location option button.
   - To display hidden bookmarks, such as those that Word uses to mark cross–references, select the Hidden Bookmarks check box.
3. Click the Go To button to move to the bookmark and then click the Close button (into which the Cancel button will have changed) to close the Bookmark dialog box.

To move to a bookmark by using the Go To dialog box:

1. Double-click in open space in the page/section or current-position areas of the status bar, press F5, or choose Edit ➤ Go To to display the Go To tab of the Find and Replace dialog box (see Figure 10.11).
2. Choose Bookmark in the Go To What list box.
3. Select the bookmark from the Enter Bookmark Name drop-down list and then click the Go To button.
4. Click the Close button to close the Go To dialog box.

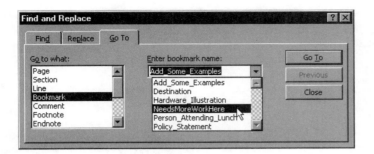

FIGURE 10.11:
Choose the bookmark to move to on the Go To tab of the Find and Replace dialog box and then click the Go To button.

Viewing Bookmarks

Word doesn't normally display bookmarks, which makes it easier to read your documents. But when you do need to see where your bookmarks are, you can display them by choosing Tools ➤ Options to display the Options dialog box and selecting the Bookmarks check box in the Show area on the View tab; then click OK.

Empty bookmarks appear as a heavy I-beam, disconcertingly similar to a mouse pointer on steroids, while bookmarks that contain text or another item enclose it within square brackets. This illustration shows both types of bookmarks.

> The [Vice President of Communications] will meet you at I for lunch.

Deleting a Bookmark

To delete a bookmark:

1. Choose Insert ➤ Bookmark to display the Bookmark dialog box.
2. In the Bookmark Name list box, select the bookmark you want to delete.
3. Click the Delete button to delete the bookmark. The bookmark's contents will not be affected.
4. Repeat steps 2 and 3 as necessary and then click the Close button to close the Bookmark dialog box.

> **TIP**
>
> You can also delete a bookmark by selecting it and pressing the Delete key. Using this method will delete the bookmark's contents as well.

Chapter

11

OUTLINES

- **Using outlines in Word**
- **Creating an outline**
- **Working in the outline**
- **Creating outline numbered lists**

Outline view is one of Word's most useful features if you're writing anything longer than a couple of pages. Using Outline view and Word's heading styles, you can collapse a document to an outline showing any number of heading levels from one to seven. For example, you can collapse a document to show three levels of headings, hiding any subheadings and body text between the headings. You can then zero in on a crucial heading and expand the text underneath it so that you can make a strategic addition or two, and then collapse that text again to move quickly to another heading. You can also move blocks of text around in your document quickly, or promote or demote a whole series of headings in one move.

Outline numbered lists offer capabilities similar to those offered in Outline view. We'll look at how to create and use outline numbered lists at the end of this chapter.

Unfortunately, Outline view is also one of Word's least used capabilities, particularly among the people who'd benefit most from using it. Outline view seems complex, but you can easily learn to use it within fifteen minutes. This chapter is short, and the clock is running…

How Outlines Work

Outlines work by using Word's nine heading styles, Heading 1 through Heading 9. These styles are predefined, so you can't delete them, no matter how hard you try, though you can format them however you like. (These styles are also used for tables of contents, which are closely related to outlines. We'll look at tables of contents in Chapter 12.)

To recap Chapter 2 quickly, Word offers paragraph styles for formatting paragraphs and character styles for formatting characters. By using paragraph styles, you can quickly apply consistent formatting to all the instances of any element in a document. For example, by setting Heading 1 to be 24-point Gill Sans Ultra with 18 points of space above it and 12 points below it (and also using indentation, borders, shading, and other formatting, to your liking) and then applying the Heading 1 style to each heading, you can make sure they all look the same on the page. (For more details, see the section titled *Style Formatting* in Chapter 2.)

TIP	Even if you're creating a short document, Outline view can save you time. As discussed in the section titled *Creating a New Style* in Chapter 2, most Heading styles are typically followed by a different paragraph style, on the assumption that you won't want to type several headings in a row—for example, you might want a Heading 1 paragraph to be followed by Body Text, or by some special graphical element that would offset the heading and draw the reader's attention. In Outline view, however, pressing Enter creates another paragraph with the same paragraph style, so you can quickly crank out a full chapter's worth of Heading 1 paragraphs, Heading 2 paragraphs, or whatever.

Creating an Outline

Creating an outline in Word could hardly be simpler. You can start with either the blank slate of a new document and build an outline from scratch, or you can start with an existing document.

Creating a New Outline

To create an outline in a new document:

1. Start a new document by choosing File ➤ New and choosing the template you want in the New dialog box, as discussed in the section titled *Creating a New Document* in Chapter 1.
2. Choose View ➤ Outline to switch to Outline view. Word will display the Outlining toolbar (see Figure 11.1).
3. Make sure that the paragraph style in the Style drop-down list on the Formatting toolbar is set to Heading 1 style. (Word will usually start the new document with a paragraph in Heading 1 style, depending on which template you chose in step 1. Styles are discussed in the section titled *Style Formatting* in Chapter 2.)
4. Enter the first-level headings, pressing Enter after each one. Word will start each new paragraph in Heading 1 style no matter what the Style for Following Paragraph for the Heading 1 style is set to.
5. To enter a second-level heading, press Tab to switch to Heading 2 style. Type the text for the heading and press Enter; Word will start a new paragraph also based on the Heading 2 style.
    *   To enter third-level headings, fourth-level headings, and so on, press Tab to move down through the Heading styles.
    *   To move back up through the heading styles, press Shift+Tab.
6. Save the document as usual.

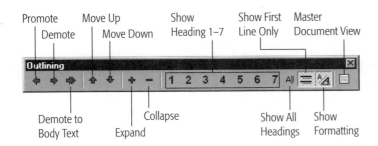

FIGURE 11.1:
The Outlining toolbar provides quick access to the main features of Outline view.

Outlining an Existing Document

To outline an existing document:

1. Open the document.
2. If the document isn't already formatted with styles, apply Heading styles to the headings by using the Formatting toolbar or the Format ➤ Style command (described in the section titled *Applying Styles* in Chapter 2).
3. Switch the document to Outline view as described in the next section, *Viewing an Outline*.

Viewing an Outline

To switch a document to Outline view, choose View ➤ Outline or click the Outline View button on the horizontal scroll bar (if you have it displayed). Word will shuffle your document into Outline view and display the Outlining toolbar.

When you choose Outline view, Word displays the Outlining toolbar and an outline symbol to the left of the first line in each paragraph, as shown in Figure 11.2. A fat plus sign appearing next to a heading indicates that the heading has subheadings or text (or both) underneath it; a fat minus sign means that the heading has nothing between it and the next heading. A small empty square indicates a paragraph of non-heading text.

> **TIP**
>
> If you've defined Word's Heading styles with large font sizes, you won't be able to see many headings onscreen at once in Outline view with formatting displayed. Either zoom the view to a smaller percentage—perhaps 75% or 50%—to display more headings onscreen, or click the Show Formatting button to toggle off the formatting.

To collapse or expand the outline to different levels, use the Expand and Collapse buttons and the seven numbered buttons on the Outlining toolbar. The Expand button reveals the subtext for the selected heading—for example, if you position the insertion point in a Heading 2 paragraph and click the Expand button, Word will display any Heading 3 paragraphs beneath the Heading 2 paragraph. If there are no Heading 3 paragraphs, Word will display paragraphs with the next Heading level style (Heading 4, then Heading 5, then Heading 6, and so on); if there are no headings at all between the selected Heading paragraph and the end of the document, Word will display body text. The Collapse button reverses the process, collapsing the outline one available level at a time.

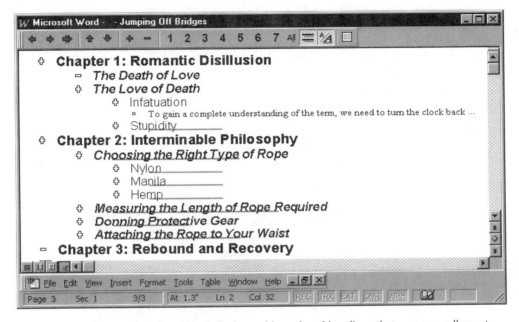

FIGURE 11.2: In Outline view, Word displays a hierarchy of headings that you can collapse to different levels.

The seven Show Heading *n* buttons on the Outlining toolbar expand or collapse the whole outline to that level of heading, while the All button toggles the display of all heading levels and body text.

You can also collapse (or expand) all the headings under a heading by double-clicking the fat plus sign next to it.

The Show First Line Only button on the Outlining toolbar toggles the display between only the first line of non-heading paragraphs and all lines of non-heading paragraphs. This option can be a great help in getting an overview of a large part of your document.

Promoting and Demoting Items

So much for expanding and collapsing your outline so that you can see the appropriate parts of it. Now let's look at how to deal with the resulting outline itself.

Two of the most useful buttons on the Outlining toolbar are the Promote and Demote buttons, which you can use to reorganize the headings in a document quickly. Click these once to promote or demote the current heading or selected headings one level of heading at a time.

When you select a heading using its outline symbol (the fat plus sign or fat minus sign that appears to the left of a paragraph, as described in the previous section), you select all of its subheadings as well (whether or not they're displayed). When you promote or demote a heading with its subheadings selected, you promote or demote the subheadings as well. For example, if I demote the Chapter 2 heading shown here from Heading 1 to Heading 2, the Heading 2 paragraphs will be demoted to Heading 3, the Heading 3 paragraphs to Heading 4, and so on.

Heading 1	✛ **Chapter 2: Interminable Philosophy**
Heading 2	✛ *Choosing the Right Type of Rope*
Heading 3	✛ Nylon
Heading 3	✛ Manila
Heading 3	✛ Hemp
Heading 2	✛ *Measuring the Length of Rope Required*
Heading 2	✛ *Donning Protective Gear*
Heading 2	✛ *Attaching the Rope to Your Waist*

To promote (or demote) a heading without promoting (or demoting) all of its subheadings, first expand the outline to display the subheadings. Then click in the heading and click the Promote (or Demote) button until the heading has reached the level you want it to be.

> **TIP**
>
> **To select a heading without selecting its subheadings, click in the selection bar next to the heading. To select several headings, click and drag in the selection bar.**

 To demote a heading to text, click the Demote to Body Text button. Word will apply Normal style to it.

> **TIP**
>
> You can also demote the paragraph you're working in by pressing Tab and promote it by pressing Shift+Tab. To type a real tab in Outline view (without promoting or demoting anything), press Ctrl+Tab.

Moving Items Up and Down the Outline

Outline view makes reordering the items in an outline speedy and simple. To move a heading up and down the outline, simply expand or collapse the outline so that the heading is displayed, and then click the symbol next to the heading and drag it up or down the outline. You'll see a line move up or down the screen with the mouse-pointer arrow indicating where the paragraph will end up when you let go of it.

> ⊕ _Measuring the Length of Rope Required_
> ‡⊕ _Donning Protective Gear_
> ⊕ _Attaching the Rope to Your Waist_

Alternatively, select the heading (and any subheadings you want to move with it) and click the Move Up or Move Down button to move it up or down the outline one displayed paragraph at a time.

Using Heading Numbering

Heading numbering can be a great asset in Outline view. Instead of renumbering your chapters as you drag them about the outline, you can let Word take care of the numbering automatically.

To apply heading numbering to a document:

1. Right-click in a heading and choose Bullets and Numbering from the context menu, or choose Format ➤ Bullets and Numbering to display the Bullets and Numbering dialog box.
2. If the Outline Numbered tab is not displayed, click it to bring it to the front of the dialog box (see Figure 11.3).

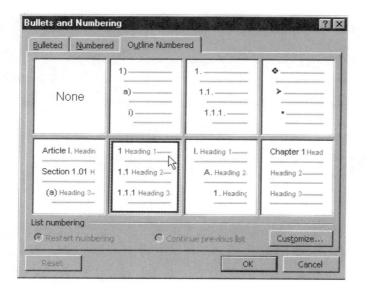

FIGURE 11.3:
Choose heading numbering on the Outline Numbered tab of the Bullets and Numbering dialog box.

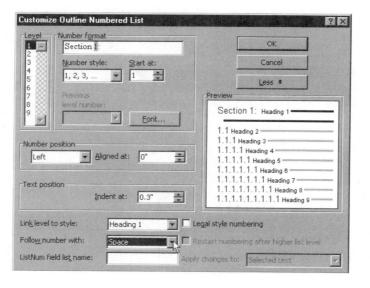

FIGURE 11.4:
In the Customize Outline Numbered List dialog box, choose how you want the heading numbering to appear.

3. Choose one of the numbering styles that includes the word "Heading," then click the Customize button to display the Customize Outline Numbered List dialog box (see Figure 11.4). If you see a Customize Outline Numbered List dialog box that is smaller than this one, click the More button to display the bottom section.

4. In the Level list box, choose the heading level on which to work.

5. In the Number Format box, choose how you want the numbering for the heading to appear. For example, you could enter a word in front of the number to produce numbering like **Part 1**, or you could enter a colon or other separator character after the number. The Preview box will show the effects of the change.

6. In the Number Style drop-down list, choose the style of numbering: 1, 2, 3; I, II, III; A, B, C; and so on.

7. In the Start At box, adjust the starting number (or letter) if necessary.

8. In the Previous Level number drop-down list, choose the number for the previous level if you want to produce a multipart number (e.g., **3.2.4**). This works only for levels below Level 1.

9. To change the font formatting of the numbering, click the Font button to display the Font dialog box. Choose font formatting as usual, then click OK to apply the formatting and close the Font dialog box.

10. In the Number Position group box, change the alignment and positioning of the number as necessary.

11. In the Text Position box, adjust the indent of the text as necessary.

12. In the Link Level to Style drop-down list, make sure that the level is associated with the appropriate paragraph style.

13. In the Follow Number With drop-down list, choose whether to follow the number with a tab, a space, or nothing.

14. Repeat steps 4 through 13 as necessary for other heading levels.

15. In the Apply Changes To drop-down list, make sure that Whole List is selected.

16. Click the OK button to apply the outline numbering to the document.

Formatting in Outline View

As we saw in the section titled *Viewing an Outline* earlier in the chapter, you can click the Show Formatting button on the Outlining toolbar to stop Word from display-ing character formatting in Outline view. This feature can help you get more headings onscreen in a readable format.

You can apply character formatting and style formatting as usual in Outline view, but you can't apply paragraph formatting. Bear in mind when applying style formatting to headings that you may not see the effect of the changes you're making. Consider split-ting the window (by double-clicking or dragging the Split bar at the top of the vertical scroll bar) and switching one of the resulting panes to Normal view or Page Layout view (see Figure 11.5)—or simply switch to another view altogether when you need to apply formatting.

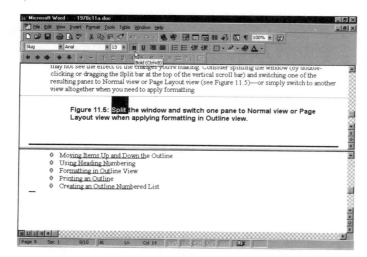

FIGURE 11.5:
Split the window and switch one pane to Normal view or Page Layout view when applying formatting in Outline view.

Printing an Outline

When you print from Outline view, Word prints only the information displayed onscreen—for example, to print only the first three levels of headings, click the Show Heading 3 button and choose File ➤ Print.

Creating an Outline Numbered List

You can also create an outline numbered list using styles other than the Heading styles. For example, you might want to create an outline numbered list as part of a document without disturbing the headings.

To create an outline numbered list:

1. Right-click and choose Bullets and Numbering from the context menu, or choose Format ➤ Bullets and Numbering to display the Bullets and Numbering dialog box.

2. If the Outline Numbered tab is not displayed, click it to bring it to the front of the dialog box.

3. Choose a style with appropriate numbering, then click the OK button.

TIP You can customize the style by selecting it on the Outline Numbered tab and then clicking the Customize button to display the Customize Outline Numbered List dialog box. Customize the style as described in steps 4 through 13 of the previous section, but leave the Link Level to Style drop-down list set to (no style).

4. Enter the text for the list:

- Press Enter to create another paragraph at the same numbering level as the previous one.

- To demote the current paragraph by one level, click the Increase Indent button or press Tab with the insertion point at the beginning of the paragraph.
- To promote the current paragraph by one level, click the Decrease Indent button or press Shift+Tab with the insertion point at the beginning of the paragraph.

To remove outline numbering from a list, click the Numbering button.

Chapter 12

TABLES OF CONTENTS AND INDEXES

FEATURING

- **Creating tables of contents**
- **Creating tables of authorities**
- **Creating tables of figures**
- **Creating indexes**

Tables of contents and indexes are another area in which word processing programs beat human intervention hands-down. Once you've formatted your document's headings with Word's Heading styles, you can not only outline your documents (as we saw in the previous chapter) but also generate tables of contents in seconds. Tables of figures require hardly any effort; and though tables of authorities and indexes require a little more effort, once you've put the Word codes in place, you can recompile your table of authorities (or index) in moments.

Table of Contents

Word uses paragraph styles to create tables of contents, so make sure you've applied styles to your document before starting. Typically, Word will use the Heading 1 through Heading 9 styles to create the table of contents (assigning the styles TOC 1 through TOC 9 to the resulting entries), but you can also use other styles for the table of contents if you've arranged your document that way. (You can also use table of contents fields, which are much slower to use; we'll look at fields in Chapter 14.)

Creating a Table of Contents from Heading Styles

To create a table of contents:

1. Position the insertion point where you want the table of contents to appear in your document.

2. Choose Insert ➤ Index and Tables to display the Index and Tables dialog box (see Figure 12.1).

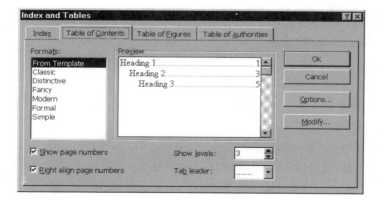

FIGURE 12.1:
Choose options for your table of contents on the Table of Contents tab of the Index and Tables dialog box.

3. If the Table of Contents tab isn't at the front of the dialog box, click it to bring it there.

4. Pick a format for the table of contents from the Formats box. (Watch the Preview box to see what looks best—often From Template is a good choice if you're working with a template that has table of contents styles defined.)

5. In the Show Levels box, choose the number of heading levels you want to include (from one to nine).

6. Choose options for page numbers in the bottom left corner of the dialog box—whether to include page numbers and (if you do) whether to right-align them or have each appear directly after the heading title it refers to.

7. If you chose to include page numbers, check the Tab Leader setting (it may be set to [None], Periods, Hyphens, or Underscores); and, if need be, choose a better tab leader character than the one Word suggests.
8. Click the OK button to insert the table of contents.

NOTE Word inserts the table of contents as a field, which can be disconcerting: depending on the options you have set in Word, when you click in the table of contents you may highlight all of it unexpectedly.

Creating a Table of Contents from Different Styles

If you want to create a table of contents from styles other than Heading 1 through Heading 9, click the Options button on the Table of Contents tab in the Index and Tables dialog box. Word will display the Table of Contents Options dialog box (see Figure 12.2).

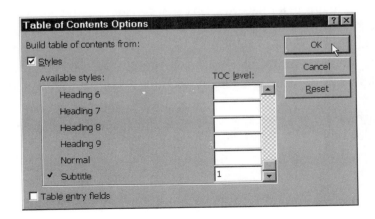

FIGURE 12.2:
In the Table of Contents Options dialog box, choose the styles you want to include in your table of contents by entering the level you want to assign to each heading in the corresponding TOC Level box.

Scroll through the list of styles to the ones you want. Type the TOC entry level you want to assign it in the box next to the heading level style. Remove the level assignments from boxes next to the Heading styles that you don't want to use.

> **TIP** You can create a table of contents that omits certain heading styles and assigns higher priority than usual to the other styles. For example, by deleting the **2** Word typically puts next to Heading 2 and the **3** next to Heading 3, and by entering **2** next to Heading 3 and **3** next to Heading 9, you can create a table of contents in which the order of importance is Heading 1, Heading 3, and then Heading 9; the other Heading levels will not appear. You can also create a table of contents that doesn't use any of the heading styles, should your documents be laid out in such a way as to make this necessary (e.g., without headings or with headings used for elements that you don't want in the table of contents).

Click the OK button to close the Table of Contents Options dialog box and return to the Index and Tables dialog box, where the Preview box will reflect your changes. Click the OK button to insert the table of contents.

Changing the TOC Styles

If the TOC styles in the current document's template are too fancy or plain for your liking, you can change them easily from the Index and Tables dialog box. However, this works only for the From Template format—you can't change Word's own precious TOC formats, such as Classic or Distinctive.

Click the Modify button to display a stripped-down edition of the Style dialog box we met in Chapter 2. Choose the TOC style to change in the Styles list box and then click the Modify button. Modify the style as described in the section titled *Modifying a Style* in Chapter 2.

When you've finished changing the styles, click the Apply button to return to the Index and Tables dialog box.

Updating Your Table of Contents

To update a table of contents, right-click in it and choose Update Field from the context menu. Word will display the Update Table of Contents dialog box; choose Update Page Numbers Only if you haven't added any headings to the table of contents or if you've applied formatting to it that you don't want to lose; otherwise, choose Update Entire Table to update the headings and the page numbers.

> **TIP**
>
> You can also update a table of contents by choosing Insert ➤ Index and Tables again. Word will ask if you want to overwrite the current table of contents; click the OK button if you do. This way you can also modify the table of contents if you want to.

Table of Figures

Word's tables of figures are specialized tables of contents produced from the automatic captions we discussed in Chapter 10.

To insert a table of figures:

1. Place the insertion point where you want the table of figures to appear in your document.
2. Choose Insert ➤ Index and Tables to display the Index and Tables dialog box. Click the Table of Figures tab to bring it to the front (see Figure 12.3).
3. In the Caption Label box, choose the type of caption you want for the table of figures.
4. In the Formats box, choose a format for the table of figures. You'll notice that this list is different from the list for the tables of contents, but you can still choose From Template if you have custom styles defined.
5. Choose options for page numbers and tab leaders as appropriate.

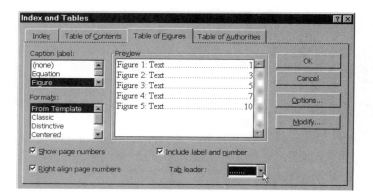

FIGURE 12.3:
Choose options for the table of figures on the Table of Figures tab of the Index and Tables dialog box.

6. Clear the Include Label and Number check box if you don't want **Figure 44.1** or something similar appearing in the list of figures. Watch the Preview box for the effect this will produce.

7. If you want to build a table of figures from table entry fields rather than captions, or as well as captions, click the Options button and make your choices in the Table of Figures Options dialog box. You can also choose to produce the table of figures from a style other than Caption (for example, you could use Heading 8, or any other style that you had chosen to use to identify your figures). Click the OK button after you've made your choices.

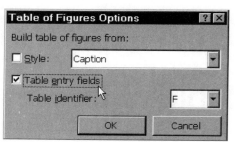

8. Click the OK button to close the Index and Tables dialog box and have Word insert the table of figures in your document.

Figure 1: *Monet at work in Robespierre's boudoir* (Fred Shakespeare) 7
Figure 2: *Miller visiting the Atomic Energy Research Bureau* (Andy Zloty) 12
Figure 3: *Everything Reminds Me of Croydon* (Rikki Nadir) 24

TIP You can quickly modify the Table of Figures style by clicking the Modify button on the Table of Figures tab of the Index and Tables dialog box.

Table of Authorities

Word can also produce tables of authorities for any case, statute, or treatise you happen to be working on. (Tables of authorities are specialized tables citing the sources referenced in legal or scholarly works. You probably won't want to use them unless you're producing legal documents, theses, or the like.)

Before you can create the table of authorities, you need to mark the citations to be included.

To mark citations for a table of authorities:

1. Select the first citation (a long citation—one with all the details) and press Alt+Shift+I to display the Mark Citation dialog box (see Figure 12.4) with the citation displayed in the Selected Text and Short Citation boxes.

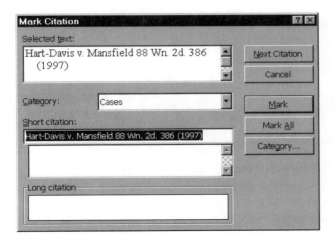

FIGURE 12.4:
Coordinate your citations in the Mark Citation dialog box.

2. Use shortcut keys (such as Ctrl+B for boldface; see the section *Character Formatting Using Keyboard Shortcuts* in Chapter 2 for the other shortcuts) to format the citation in the Selected Text box. Alternatively, right-click, choose Font from the Context menu, and choose Formatting in the Font dialog box.

3. Edit the Short Citation box to match the other citations of this authority in the document.

4. Choose a category from the Category drop-down list: Cases, Statutes, Other Authorities, Rules, Treatises, Regulations, Constitutional Provisions, or a category that you've defined by using the Category button.

5. Click either the Mark button to mark each citation for this authority in turn or the Mark All button to mark them all at once. Word will perform the marking and will add the citation to the list in the Short Citation list box, with its full text appearing in the Long Citation box.

6. Click the Next Citation button to have Word look for the next citation; when it finds it, repeat the marking process.

7. Click the Close button when you've finished marking all the citations.

Compared to marking the citations, creating the table of authorities is easy.

To create the table of authorities:

1. Place the insertion point where you want the table of authorities to appear within the document.

2. Choose Insert ➤ Index and Tables to display the Index and Tables dialog box, then click the Table of Authorities tab to bring it to the front (see Figure 12.5).

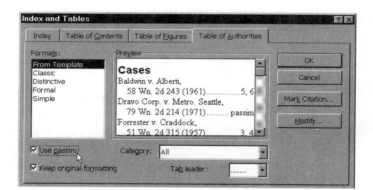

FIGURE 12.5:
Choose options for your table of authorities on the Table of Authorities tab in the Index and Tables dialog box.

3. Choose a format for the table of authorities from the Formats list box.

4. In the Category drop-down list, choose whether to include all authorities, or only those for Cases or Statutes, and so on.

5. Make sure the Use Passim check box has been selected if you want authorities with five or more references to be marked with passim (throughout the document) rather than with page references.

6. Click the OK button to have Word compile the table of authorities.

Cases
Butcher v. Hitchcock 88 Wn. 2d. 388 (1997)...24, 36, 40, 46
Drax Industries v. Bond UK, 87 Wn., 2d 315 (1994)..passim
Hart-Davis v. Mansfield, 87 Wn., 2d 386 (1994)...32, 33

> **TIP**
>
> **To update a table of authorities, right-click in it and choose Update Field. To modify the styles in a table of authorities, click the Modify button on the Table of Authorities tab in the Index and Tables dialog box.**

Index

If you've ever used a good index or been frustrated by an inadequate one, you know that good indexes simply *must* be harder to put together than tables of contents. And indeed they are—though Word gives you as much help as it can in automating the procedure. You don't even have to wait until the end of your project before starting to put the codes for the index entries in. You can add them as you go along, which helps make sure you don't forget to index vital elements in the mad rush to complete a project. Generally speaking, though, waiting until the end of the project lets you benefit most from Word's indexing features.

Creating an index in Word consists of marking index entries throughout your document and then telling Word to create the index. Once the index has been created, you can rearrange your document at will and easily update the index to make sure it includes the latest page numbers.

Marking Index Entries

To mark index entries:

1. Select a word or phrase you want to make into an index entry.
2. Press Alt+Shift+X to open the Mark Index Entry dialog box (see Figure 12.6) with the selected word or phrase in it. (You can also choose Insert ➤ Index and Tables and click the Mark Entry on the Index tab of the Index and Tables dialog box.)
3. Click the Mark button to mark this particular instance of the selected word or phrase as an index entry, or click the Mark All button to mark every instance of the selected word or phrase.
   - To create a subentry, verify the selected entry in the Main Entry box and enter the subentry in the Subentry box.

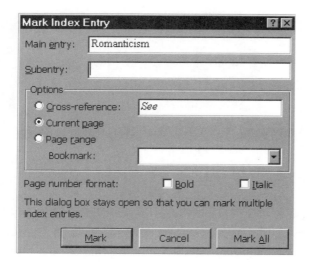

FIGURE 12.6:
Set up your index entry in the Mark Index Entry dialog box.

- To create a cross-reference, click the Cross-reference option button in the Options box and enter the name of the entry to see after the word **See** (which you could change to **See also** if you wanted to).
- To enter ranges of pages (e.g., 10–12), which are a little trickier, mark the range with a bookmark before inserting the index entry. (See the section titled *Using Bookmarks* in Chapter 10 for a discussion of the whys and wherefores of bookmarks.) Once you've placed the bookmark, choose the Page Range option button in the Options group box and select the name of the bookmark from the Bookmark drop-down list.

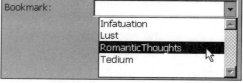

4. The Mark Index Entry dialog box stays open until you close it so you can add cross-references or subentries to your original entry. (Once you've marked an entry, the Cancel button changes to a Close button.)
5. Repeat steps 1 through 4 for the remaining entries in your document.

Inserting the Index

To create and insert the index:

1. Place the insertion point at the end of your document (or wherever you want the index to appear).

2. Choose Insert ➤ Index and Tables to display the Index and Tables dialog box. Click the Index tab to bring it to the front of the dialog box (see Figure 12.7).

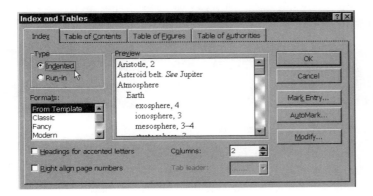

FIGURE 12.7:
Choose index options on the Index tab of the Index and Tables dialog box.

3. Choose the type of index in the Type box: Indented usually is easier to read, but Run-in can save you a lot of space if your index is long.

> **TIP**
>
> There's a quicker way to mark index entries, but it requires a good deal of preparation. You create a *concordance file* consisting of a two-column table (Table ➤ Insert Table, as discussed in the section titled *Inserting a Table* in Chapter 7) that contains, in the left-hand column, all the words you want indexed (one per cell), and in the right-hand column, the entries for those words. For example, in the left-hand column you might enter **John Smith** as the name for Word to find, and in the right-hand column **Smith, John** for the entry. When you've created the concordance file, save it and close it. Then, with the document to be indexed open, click the AutoMark button on the Index tab of the Index and Tables dialog box and choose the concordance file in the Open Index AutoMark File dialog box. The moment you click the Open button, Word marks all the entries for you as fast as it can.

4. Choose a style for the index from the Formats list box. Watch the Preview box to get a rough idea of how it will look.

5. Choose the number of columns in which to lay out the index in the Columns box. A two-column index is normal, but three columns sometimes work well on 8 ½ "x11" paper (or when you're desperate for space).

6. Click the OK button to insert the index. Word will repaginate your document and build the index.

NOTE   To update an index, right-click anywhere in it and choose Update Field from the context menu.

Chapter 13

MASTER DOCUMENTS

- **Creating a master document from scratch**
- **Creating a master document from an existing document**
- **Creating subdocuments within the master document**
- **Working with the master document and subdocuments**

Word's master documents and subdocuments can make large projects easier to handle. A *master document* is essentially a regular document made up of a number of *subdocuments*, which in turn are regular Word documents linked to the master document. Once you've created a master document and subdocuments, different people can work in the subdocuments, and when they're done, you can switch to the master document to see how the whole project is shaping up.

You can decide to use master documents and subdocuments at almost any stage of a project—you can create a master document at the beginning of a long work, or you can convert an existing document to a master document once you realize that it will be too big or unwieldy in a single file.

> **TIP**
> For the sake of simplicity, use master documents and subdocuments only when you really need to. For many projects, you'll find it easier to have everything in a single document, without the complications that subdocuments can cause. (If your computer has the 16MB of RAM needed to run Word under Windows 95 or Windows NT at a respectable speed, it should be able to handle Word documents several hundred pages long without perceptible problems.) For other projects—particularly for long documents that contain many graphics files (which make for large Word files) and for documents in which you need to have different people review different sections simultaneously—master documents and subdocuments can be a great boon.

Creating a Master Document

The first step is to create a master document. You can create one either from scratch or from an existing document. There's essentially no difference between the processes—you can open an existing document and make sure it has the appropriate headings, or you can create a new document and type in the headings. Both get you to the same stage.

To create a master document from scratch or from an existing document:

1. Create or open your master document.
   - To create a master document from scratch, choose File ➤ New and select a template from the New dialog box as usual.
   - To create a master document from an existing document, open that document.
2. Choose View ➤ Master Document. Word will switch the document to Master Document view and will display the Outlining toolbar and the Master Document toolbar. By default, the Master Document toolbar will appear at the right-hand end of the Outlining toolbar, but you can click its handle and drag it to a better location if you prefer.

3. Adapt the existing outline or create a new outline for the document using the outlining techniques discussed in Chapter 11. You can use any number of heading levels, but use the same heading style for the heading that each subdocument will start with. For medium-sized projects, you'll usually find it easiest to use Heading 1 for the titles of the subdocuments.

4. Select the text that you want to turn into subdocuments, making sure that the first heading in the selected text is the level of heading at which you want Word to divide the selected text into subdocuments. For example, if you used Heading 1 style for the chapters, make sure that the first heading in the selected text is Heading 1 style.

    *   If you're creating a master document from scratch, you can enter text in the master document and then select it.

5. Click the Create Subdocument button on the Master Document toolbar. Word will turn the selected text into subdocuments, dividing it at each occurrence of the selected heading level it finds. (For example, if the first heading in the selected text is Heading 2, each Heading 2 section will become a separate subdocument.) The start of each subdocument will be indicated by a subdocument icon in the selection bar at the left side of the screen, as shown in Figure 13.1, and each subdocument will be separated from the others by section breaks.

    *   If you're creating a master document from scratch and want to enter text directly into the subdocuments, select the subdocument heading and then click the Create Subdocument button. You can then enter text into the subdocument as you wish.

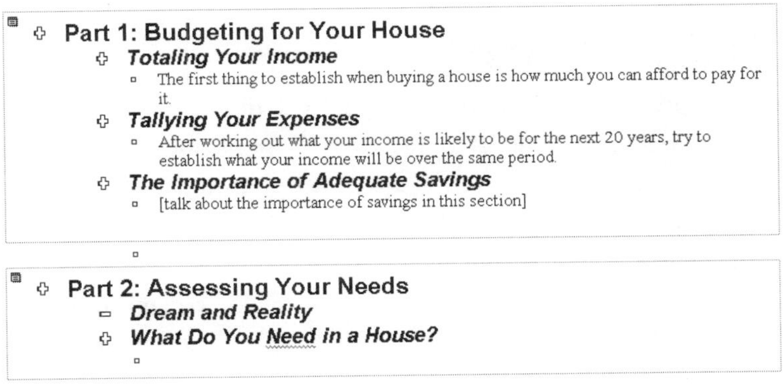

⊡ ⊹ **Part 1: Budgeting for Your House**
　⊹ *Totaling Your Income*
　　▫ The first thing to establish when buying a house is how much you can afford to pay for it.
　⊹ *Tallying Your Expenses*
　　▫ After working out what your income is likely to be for the next 20 years, try to establish what your income will be over the same period.
　⊹ *The Importance of Adequate Savings*
　　▫ [talk about the importance of savings in this section]

　　　▫

⊡ ⊹ **Part 2: Assessing Your Needs**
　▫ *Dream and Reality*
　⊹ *What Do You Need in a House?*
　　▫

FIGURE 13.1:
Word displays each subdocument in a different section with a subdocument icon to mark the beginning of a new subdocument.

---

6. Choose File ➤ Save to save the master document; if it's a new document, choose the folder and enter a document name as usual in the Save As dialog box and then click the Save button. Word will

save the master docu-ment in the regular way, and will automatically save all the subdocuments in the same folder, naming them by the headings with which they start. If any subdocument filename (including its path) will be more than 255 characters long, Word will truncate the filename at 255 characters.

> **TIP** Because Word automatically saves the subdocuments in the same folder as the master document, make sure you save the master document to an appropriate folder before creating the subdocuments.

Working with Master Documents and Subdocuments

Once you've created your master document and subdocuments, you can work either in the master document or in the subdocuments. Usually, you'll find it easier to work in the subdocuments when creating and formatting the text—especially if you want to have several of your co-workers work on different subdocuments at the same time. For arranging and managing the project, you'll need to work in the master document.

Working in the Master Document

When you open a master document, Word will display its contents in a collapsed form as a list of hyperlinks to the subdocuments included in the master document (see Figure 13.2). To work in the master document, click the Expand Subdocuments button to display the contents of the subdocuments.

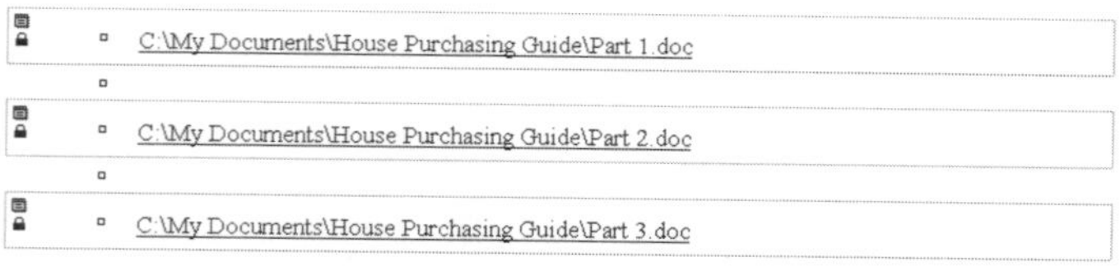

C:\My Documents\House Purchasing Guide\Part 1.doc

C:\My Documents\House Purchasing Guide\Part 2.doc

C:\My Documents\House Purchasing Guide\Part 3.doc

FIGURE 13.2:
Word opens a master document in a collapsed form. To work in it, click the Expand Subdocuments button.

Once you've expanded the subdocuments, you can work with the whole master document in Master Document view or Outline view for rearranging the document's outline, or in Normal view, Page Layout view, or Online Layout view for working with and formatting the full text of the document.

TIP   **To switch quickly between Master Document view and Outline view, click the Master Document View button at the right-hand end of the Outlining toolbar.**

Word separates the subdocuments in the master document into different sections with an extra section between each subdocument, so section breaks are already in place that you can use for setting up different headers (or footers) in the subdocuments.

Master documents give you several possibilities for printing:

- To get a complete view of your project, choose File ➤ Print Preview in your master document.
- To print the whole of your project, open the Master Document, click the Expand Subdocuments button to expand it, switch to Normal view (View ➤ Normal), and choose File ➤ Print.
- To print an outline of the master document, switch to Master Document view or Outline view and collapse or expand the outline to the level of detail you want. Then choose File ➤ Print.

Inserting a Subdocument in the Master Document

Once you've created your master document, you can easily insert existing documents as subdocuments. As we saw in *Creating a Master Document* earlier in this chapter, Word automatically saves subdocuments that you create from a master document in the same folder as the master document; but you can manually insert subdocuments from any available drive and folder into an existing master document. (To keep a project tightly coordinated, however, you may want to move documents to the same folder as the master document before inserting them as subdocuments.)

To insert an existing document as a subdocument:

1. Expand the master document to show all levels of text by clicking the All button on the Outlining toolbar.

2.   Position the insertion point between the two subdocuments in the master document where you want to add the existing document as a subdocument.

◇ **Part 1: Budgeting for Your House**
  ◇ *Totaling Your Income*
    ▫ The first thing to establish when buying a house is how much you can afford to pay for it.
  ◇ *Tallying Your Expenses*
    ▫ After working out what your income is likely to be for the next 20 years, try to establish what your income will be over the same period.
  ◇ *The Importance of Adequate Savings*
    ▫ [talk about the importance of savings in this section]

    ▫ |

◇ **Part 2: Assessing Your Needs**

---

3.   Click the Insert Subdocument button on the Master Document toolbar. Word will display an Insert Subdocument dialog box that looks suspiciously like the Open dialog box in disguise.

4.   Choose the document to insert and click the Open button. Word will insert it in the master document.

  • If the subdocument is based on a different template from the master document, it will inherit the master document's settings while the master document is open. (If you open the subdocument later without the master document open, it will appear in its original template.)

Removing a Subdocument from Its Master Document

To remove a subdocument from a master document, select the subdocument icon in the master document and click the Remove Subdocument button. Word will remove the link between the subdocument and the master document, but the subdocument text will remain in the master document and the subdocument file will remain in its previous location on disk. You can then delete the text or move it into another subdocument if necessary—or you can change it without worrying about changing the text in the subdocument at the same time.

Merging Subdocuments

You may occasionally need to combine two or more subdocuments into one subdocument—for example, if you realize that material planned as two sections really should be one section.

To merge subdocuments:

1. Open the master document and click the Expand Subdocuments button to view the subdocuments (rather than the list of hyperlinks).

2. If the subdocuments aren't next to each other, drag them so that they are. Click on the subdocument icon for the subdocument you want to move, then drag it to where you want it to appear.

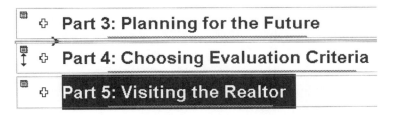

3. Select the first subdocument to merge by clicking its subdocument icon.

4. Select the second subdocument by holding down Shift and clicking its subdocument icon. Repeat this if you want to merge more than two subdocuments.

5. Click the Merge Subdocument button to merge the subdocuments. Word will remove the subdocument icon from the second and subsequent subdocuments, and when you save the master document, Word will save the merged subdocuments under the first subdocument's filename.

Splitting a Subdocument

If you realize that, for example, you need to divide one of your chapters into two chapters, you can split the subdocument in question. In Master Document view, enter another heading of the same level as those that start the other subdocuments at the point where you want to split the subdocument, and then select the heading and click the Split Subdocument button.

Renaming a Subdocument

If you need to rename a subdocument, you *must* do it from the master document in Master Document view so that Word can track the change. *Never* rename a subdocument with the Windows Explorer or another file management program; if you do, Word will lose track of the subdocument.

> **WARNING** As mentioned in *Creating a Master Document* earlier in this chapter, subdocuments that you insert into a Master document remain in their original folders; if you rename a subdocument without letting the Master document handle the process, the Master document will no longer know where the subdocument is.

In Master Document view, click the hyperlink for the subdocument to open the subdocument, choose File ➤ Save As to display the Save As dialog box, enter the new filename or folder for the subdocument, and click the Save button. If you create subdocuments from a master document, Word automatically saves them in the same folder. If you insert them from other folders, they remain in those folders. Once you've saved the subdocument, choose File ➤ Close to close the subdocument and return to the master document.

Working in Subdocuments

Working in subdocuments is quite straightforward, as they're regular Word documents connected to their master document. You can either open a subdocument in the regular way (via the Open dialog box) or from a master document (by clicking on its hyperlink if the subdocuments are collapsed, or by double-clicking its subdocument icon if the subdocuments are collapsed or expanded).

When you've finished working in a subdocument, save and close it as usual. If you accessed it from the master document, Word will return you to the master document.

> **WARNING** The main thing to remember when working with master documents and subdocuments is that only one person can make changes to any one subdocument at a time. Anyone who opens another copy of a subdocument won't be able to save changes to it. And if one person has a master document open, no one else will be able to save changes to it or any of its subdocuments.

Locking and Unlocking Master Documents and Subdocuments

As we saw in the previous section, one way to protect your master document and subdocuments against changes is to keep the master document open all the time. There is a more practical choice, though: you can *lock* them against changes. This can be particularly valuable when you're sharing documents on a network.

To lock a master document or subdocument:

1. Open the master document and click the Expand Subdocuments button to expand the subdocuments.

2. Click in the subdocument you want to lock. If you want to lock the master document, click anywhere in it (i.e., *not* in any of its subdocuments).

3. Click the Lock Document button on the Master Document toolbar to lock the subdocument or master document.

   - If the master document or subdocument contains unsaved changes, Word will prompt you to save them.
   - When you lock a master document, Word displays the words **(Read-Only)** in the title bar.
   - When you lock a subdocument, Word displays a padlock icon beneath the subdocument icon in Master Document view.

To unlock a locked master document or subdocument, click in it and then click the Lock Document button. Word will remove the **(Read Only)** or padlock icon from the master document or subdocument respectively.

WARNING Locking subdocuments works only while the master document is open—once the master document has been closed, you can open any of its supposedly locked subdocuments without encountering any security. To learn more about tighter security for your documents, turn to Chapter 18.

Chapter 14

FIELDS

- **Understanding and working with fields**
- **Inserting fields in your documents**
- **Updating fields**
- **Locking fields**
- **Formatting fields**

Fields (at least in the context of computers) have such a bad reputation that many people try to avoid them. In the previous chapters, we've skirted around the subject of fields but shirked discussing them explicitly. The automatic page numbers in headers and footers in Chapter 5, the mail-merge instructions in Chapter 9, the automatic numbering and captioning in Chapter 10, the tables of contents and indexes in Chapter 12, and the master documents and subdocuments in Chapter 13—those were all fields. Now the time has come to look at what fields really are and what they do.

Fields can be as confusing as they are powerful in Word, which is why we've avoided them so far in this book. In this section, we'll look briefly at what fields are, what they let you do, and how to use them to maximum effect with minimum effort. If you're feeling brave, we'll point you in the direction of the gruesome details, but we won't dirty our fair hands with the worst of them.

What Is a Field?

A field is a special code that tells Word to insert particular information in a document. For example, as we saw in Chapter 5, you can use fields to insert information such as page numbers and dates in your documents and have this information updated automatically.

Word lets you view either the field *codes* (the instructions that tell Word what information to put in your document) or the *results* of the field codes (the information the codes produce). Usually, you'll want to see the results, but when you're laying out a document that contains many fields, you may find it easier to display the codes.

Fields get their information from a variety of sources, such as the following:

- Date and time information comes from your computer's clock. (If it's wrong, the fields will be wrong too.)
- User information comes from the information stored on the User Information tab of the Options dialog box.
- File information comes from the Properties dialog box—some of it you can fill in when you save the document (Keywords, Comments, and so on), and some of it is generated automatically (details on who last saved the file and when, and so on).

What Are Fields For?

As we've seen, fields are good for inserting information in your documents and for automatically keeping that information up–to–date. For example, in Chapter 12 we looked at how you can use index entry fields to mark the entries for your index, rearrange your document, and then have Word generate the index instantly from the index entry fields.

You can also use fields to perform calculations, as we saw with the {=SUM(ABOVE)} field in Chapter 7, or to insert page numbers in your documents, as we saw in Chapter 5.

Inserting Fields

So far, the field codes we've looked at in this book are ones that come with special ways to insert them—the Page Numbers, Date, and Time buttons on the Header and Footer toolbar, for instance, or the Insert Merge Field button on the Mail Merge toolbar, or the index entry fields. But you can also insert most any field code from the Field dialog box.

To insert a field code manually at the insertion point:

1. Choose Insert ➤ Field to display the Field dialog box (see Figure 14.1).

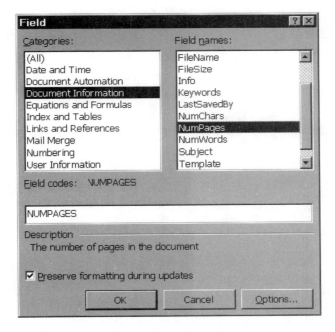

FIGURE 14.1:
Choose the field you want to insert in the Field dialog box.

2. Choose the category of field in the Categories list. (The first choice, All, shows the fields in alphabetical order and is helpful if you know the name of the field but not which category Word lumps it into. Otherwise, choose a category, and Word will display all the fields for that category in the Field Names list box.)

3. Choose the field name you want from the Field Names list box.

4. To set options for the field, click the Options button to display the Field Options dialog box (see Figure 14.2). Choose formatting, formats, or

switches for the field—the contents of the Field Options dialog box will vary depending on the field you've chosen—and click the Add to Field button to add them to the field. Use the Undo Add button to correct any mistakes. When the field in the Field Codes box looks right, click the OK button to return to the Field dialog box.

5. Click OK to close the Field dialog box and insert the field (and any formatting or switches) in the document.

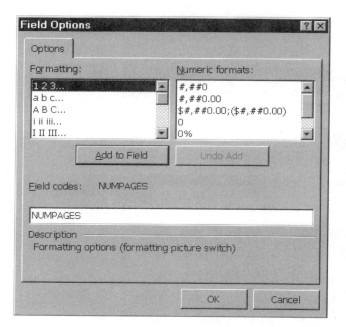

FIGURE 14.2:
Choose formatting or formats for the field in the Field Options dialog box.

WARNING You *can* type field codes straight into your document, provided you press Ctrl+F9 to insert the {} field-delimiter characters rather than trying to type them in from the keyboard—but it's a great waste of time and effort. Using the Insert ➤ Field command is almost always faster and simpler.

Viewing Field Codes

By default, Word displays the *results* of field codes rather than the codes themselves, so if you insert a date code in your document, you'll see something like **July 16, 1997** rather than **{ TIME \@"M/d/yy" }** or a similar code.

To display a field code rather than the field result, right-click in any field and choose Toggle Field Codes from the context menu. (To display the field result again, repeat the maneuver.) Alternatively, click in the field and press Shift+F9.

To toggle between field codes and field results for all fields in a document, either press Alt+F9 or choose Tools ➤ Options to display the Options dialog box and bring the View tab to the front. Select the Field Codes check box in the Show area to display field codes; clear it to display field results. Click the OK button to close the Options dialog box.

You may find it helpful to display field codes when arranging documents (e.g., forms, which we'll look at in Chapter 16) that contain many of them. You may find it even more helpful to split the window and view field codes in one half and field results in the other half—choose Window ➤ Split or double-click the split bar located at the top of the vertical scroll bar. Display the field codes in one pane by placing the selection point in the pane, displaying the Options dialog box (Tools ➤ Options), and selecting the Field Codes check box in the Show area of the View tab, or by using the Alt+F9 shortcut. Do not use the Shift+F9 shortcut because it will toggle the field display in both panes.

> **NOTE**
>
> To display index entry (XE), table of authorities (TA), table of contents (TC), and referenced document (RD) codes, you'll need to display hidden text rather than field codes. Choose Tools ➤ Options to display the Options dialog box, click the View tab, then select the Hidden Text check box or the All check box in the Nonprinting Characters area. Click the OK button to close the Options dialog box.

Displaying Field Shading

To make things easier when working with documents that include fields, you can turn field shading on and off. Turning it on can not only help you see where all your fields are (again, with the exception of the XE, TA, TC, and RD fields), but also prevent you from deleting fields while under the impression they're just text. At other times, though, field shading can be distracting, and you may want to turn it off so you can treat the field results as regular text.

C:\My Documents\Manufacturing Options in Malaysia.doc (Guy Hart-Davis)   Page **5** of **14**

To turn field shading on and off, display the Options dialog box by choosing Tools ➤ Options. On the View tab, choose the appropriate option from the Field Shading drop-down list: Never, Always, or When Selected (the latter displays field shading when the insertion point is anywhere in the field, not just when the whole field is selected). Click the OK button to close the Options dialog box and implement your choice.

NOTE | **Field shading is just a visual aid for working onscreen—it does not print under any circumstances.**

Updating Fields

For your fields to be most useful, you'll need to update them so the information is current. You can manually update fields either one at a time or all at once, or have Word update them all for you under certain circumstances.

TIP | **If you have fields that you don't want to update, you can lock them or unlink them. See *Locking Fields* later in this chapter for details.**

Updating Fields Manually

To update a single field manually, right-click in it and choose Update Field from the context menu. Alternatively, click anywhere in the field and press the F9 key.

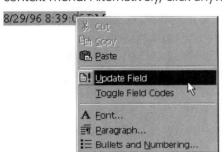

To update several fields at once manually, select the text that contains them, then either right-click and choose Update Field from the context menu or press the F9 key.

To update all the fields in a document at once, choose Edit ➤ Select All, then either right-click and choose Update Field from the context menu or press the F9 key.

Updating Fields Automatically When You Print

By updating fields whenever you print your documents, you can spare yourself the embarrassment of having your printouts contain out-of-date information.

To update fields when you print, display the Options dialog box by choosing Tools ➤ Options. On the Print tab, select the Update Fields box in the Printing Options area, then click the OK button to close the Options dialog box. Every time you print Word will update all the fields first.

NOTE A side effect of updating fields automatically when you print is that when you close the document, Word will ask if you want to save changes. This can be confusing if you know you've just opened the document and printed it without making any changes manually.

Updating Fields Automatically at Other Times

Word doesn't offer an option for automatically updating fields other than when you print. However, if you need to update all fields in your document automatically—for example, to see the latest sales figures and costs *right now* for the widgets your company has been manufacturing—a couple of possibilities are available:

- Record a macro named UpdateAllFields. Start the macro recorder and assign a key (this process is discussed in Chapter 15 in the section titled *Recording a Macro*). Then choose Edit ➤ Select All, press F9, and press ← (the left-arrow key, *not* the Backspace key) once. Stop the macro recorder, and your macro is ready to update all the fields in the current document at the touch of a button.

- If you want to update all fields either when you open a document or when you close it, copy the UpdateAllFields to an AutoOpen macro or AutoClose macro in the template. (See the section titled *Word's Five Automatic Macros* in Chapter 15 for details on these macros.)

Locking Fields

Updating fields is all very well, but sooner or later you'll find yourself with a field that needs to stay the same while all the other fields in the document get updated. In this case, you can either *lock* the field for the time being to prevent updates (so that you can unlock it later if need be) or *unlink* the field to prevent it from being updated from now until Armageddon.

To lock a field, click in it and press Ctrl+F11; to unlock it, click in the field and press Ctrl+Shift+F11.

> **TIP**
>
> A locked field looks just the same as an unlocked field—for example, you'll still see field shading when the insertion point is in it (if field shading is turned on). One way to tell if it's locked is to try to update it—Word will beep if the field is locked. Another way is to right-click on it and see if the context menu contains the Update Field item—if it doesn't, the field is locked.

To unlink a field, click in it and press Ctrl+Shift+F9. (If you do this by accident, you can choose Edit ➤ Undo to undo the action—but make sure you do so straightaway. If you don't catch the mistake in time to undo it, you'll have to recreate the link from scratch.) Once you've unlinked a field, it'll appear as regular text—no updating, no shading, nothing special.

Formatting Fields

Formatting fields could hardly be easier—simply format either the field code or the field result by selecting either the one or the other and using the regular formatting techniques described in Chapter 2. Generally speaking, formatting the field results will give you a better idea of how your document will look.

> **NOTE** You can also format fields by using special switches (such as * CardText * Caps); you'll find a horrendous number of them in the Word Help file (look under *Formatting Field Results*). If you get heavily into fields, you may want to investigate these switches. For all conventional documents, though, you can achieve the same effects by making careful choices in the Field Options dialog box or the Font dialog box and having Word do all the work for you.

Getting from Field to Field

The easiest way to move from one field to another is by pressing the F11 key to move to the next field (going from the beginning of your document towards the end) and by pressing Shift+F11 to move to the previous field. This option moves you to the next or previous field without discriminating about what kind of field it is.

If you need to move to a field of a particular type—for example, to move to each XE (index entry) field in turn—double-click in the page/section or selection point area of the status bar or choose Edit ➤ Go To to display the Go To tab of the Find and Replace dialog box (see Figure 14.3). Choose Field in the Go to What list box, and then choose the type of field from the Enter Field Name drop-down list. You can then click the Next button to go to the next instance of that particular type of field (skipping all other intervening fields) or click the Previous button to go to the previous instance of that field. You can enter a **+** or **–** value after the field name to skip ahead (or back) a specified number of fields of the same type. For example, to skip ahead five index entry fields, enter **XE+5** and click the Next button.

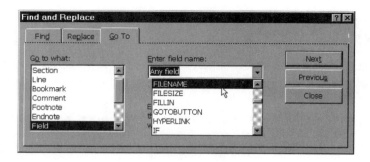

FIGURE 14.3:
Use the Go To tab of the Find and Replace dialog box to move quickly to a particular type of field.

Once you've used Go To to go to a field, Word sets the Object Browser to browse by field. You'll see that the Next Page and Previous Page buttons at the foot of the vertical scroll bar turn from black to blue, and if you move the mouse pointer over them, you'll see that the ScreenTips identify them as Next Field and Previous Field, respectively. You can then click these buttons to move to the next or previous field; you can also press Ctrl+PageDown or Ctrl+PageUp for the same effect.

To reset the Object Browser to browse by page, click the Select Browse Object button

and choose the Browse by Page icon from the pop-up panel, as shown here. (To switch back to Browse by Field after that, you can click the Select Browse Object button again and choose the Browse by Field icon—the square with **{a}** in it— from the pop-up panel.)

Printing Out Fields

Normally you won't want your field codes to print—but should you ever need to, you can print them by selecting the Field Codes check box in the Include with

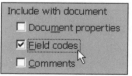

Document area on the Print tab of the Options dialog box (Tools ➤ Options). Remember to clear this check box the next time you print. If you don't, Word will merrily keep printing the field codes rather than the results.

Chapter 15

MACROS

FEATURING

FEATURING

- **Recording a macro**
- **Assigning a macro to a toolbar button, menu selection, or key combination**
- **Running a macro**
- **Editing a macro**

Macros is in many ways Word's most powerful feature—and its least used. This is unfortunate, because if you devote even a little while to learning about them, macros can save you a great deal of time and effort. In this chapter, we'll look briefly at what macros are and how you might use them; we'll also look at how you can quickly record macros using Word's macro recorder and then easily tweak those macros to make them more powerful.

What Are Macros?

A macro is a sequence of commands that you can repeat at will. For example, you might create a macro to automate basic formatting tasks on a type of document you receive regularly in an inappropriate format, such as documents for which you need to perform the complex replace operations we considered at the end of Chapter 6.

In Word, you can create macros either by turning on Word's macro recorder and performing the sequence of actions you want the macro to contain, or by opening the Visual Basic macro editor and typing in the commands yourself. You can also compromise by recording the basic sequence of actions, and then opening the macro and editing any inappropriate actions out of it so they're not repeated ad nauseam every time you run the macro. While editing the macro, you can add further actions one by one as needed and add control structures, such as message boxes, input boxes, and dialog boxes, to interact with the users of the macro.

Once you've created a macro, you can assign it to a menu item, a key combination, or a toolbar button and run it at any time. You can even create macros that run automatically when you start Word—for example, to customize your screen preferences or to present a menu of documents to work on.

Uses for Macros

There are any number of uses for macros, as you'll see if you begin to dabble in them. You might want to write a simple macro that saves you time by applying complex formatting to a word (bold, strikethrough, Abadi MT Condensed Light font, 14 points, magenta) without changing its style; or you can write a macro that draws information from three corporate databases every morning, adds in stock prices downloaded from the Dow Jones online service, formats all of this information attractively in your daily choice of five formats, and e-mails it to a distribution list of grateful recipients. As you can imagine, writing this second macro would be a much more complex process than writing the first one—and far more rewarding.

Recording a Macro

Recording a macro is by far the easiest way to create a macro. You simply switch on the macro recorder, assign a method for running the macro (a toolbar button, a menu item, or a key combination), perform the actions you want in the macro, and then switch the macro recorder off again. You can then run the macro at any time by choosing the toolbar button, menu item, or key combination you assigned it.

Starting the Macro Recorder

 To start the macro recorder, double-click the REC indicator on the status bar. Word will display the Record Macro dialog box (see Figure 15.1).

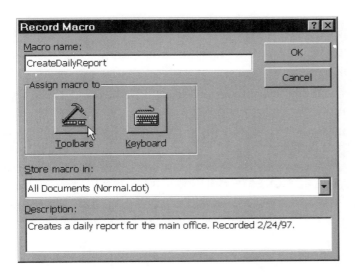

FIGURE 15.1:
In the Record Macro dialog box, enter a name for the macro you're about to record and give it an illuminating write-up in the Description box.

Naming the Macro

Enter a name for the new macro in the Macro Name text box:

- The macro name can be up to 80 characters long and can contain both letters and numbers, but it must start with a letter. It cannot contain spaces, punctuation, or special characters (such as **!** or *****), though underscores are allowed.

Enter a description for the macro in the Description box. This description is to help you (and anyone you share the macro with) identify the macro; it can be up to 255 characters long.

If you want to restrict the macro to just the current template, choose the template from the Store Macro In drop-down list. If you want the macro to be available no matter which template you're working in, make sure the default setting, *All Documents (Normal.dot)*, appears in the Store Macro In drop-down list box.

Assigning a Way to Run the Macro

Next, click the Toolbars button or the Keyboard button in the Assign Macro To group box.

- If you chose Toolbars, Word will display the Customize dialog box (see Figure 15.2) with the Commands tab displayed and Macros selected in the Categories list box. Click the macro name in the Commands list box and drag it to any convenient toolbar or menu bar. Word will add a button or menu item for the macro, giving it the macro's full and unappealing name, such as **NORMAL.NEWMACROS.CREATEDAILYREPORT**. You can now rename the button or menu item by right-clicking it and entering a more attractive and more descriptive name in the Name box. For a menu item, put an ampersand (**&**) before the character that you want to use as an access key for the item. Click the Close button to close the Customize dialog box.

- If you chose Keyboard, Word will display the Customize Keyboard dialog box (see Figure 15.3). Place the insertion point in the Press New Shortcut Key box and then press the key combination you want. A key combination can be any one of the following: Alt plus a regular key not used as a menu access key or a function key, Ctrl plus a regular key or a function key, Shift plus a function key, Ctrl+Alt, Ctrl+Shift, Alt+Shift, or even Ctrl+Alt+Shift (for special occasions) plus a regular key or function key. Look at the Current Keys list box to make sure the key combination you choose isn't already in use (if it is, press Backspace and press another combination), and then click the Assign button. Click the Close button to close the Customize Keyboard dialog box.

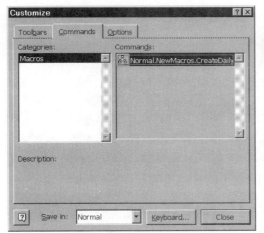

FIGURE 15.2:
Choose a way to run the macro in the Customize dialog box.

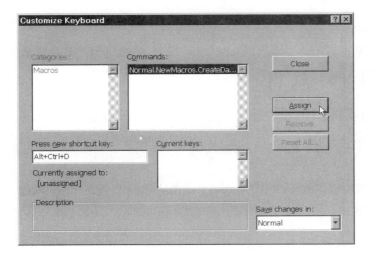

FIGURE 15.3:
Set a shortcut key for the macro in the Customize Keyboard dialog box.

Word will display the Stop Recording toolbar and will add a cassette-tape icon to the mouse pointer to remind you that you're recording. In case you miss these hints, the REC indicator in the status bar will be black.

Recording the Macro

Now record the sequence of actions you want to immortalize. You can use the mouse to select items from menus and toolbars, and to make choices in dialog boxes, but not to select items onscreen—to select items onscreen, you must use the keyboard.

> **TIP**
>
> **When you make choices in a dialog box—for example, the Paragraph dialog box—Word records the current settings for all the options on that tab of the dialog box when you click OK. So when you make a change to, say, the left indentation of a paragraph, Word will record all the other settings on the Indents and Spacing tab as well (Alignment, Before and After spacing, and so forth). You can, however, edit these out later if you don't want them.**

To perform any actions you don't want recorded, you can pause the macro recorder at any time by clicking the Pause Recording button on the Stop Recording toolbar. Click the Pause Recording button again to resume recording.

To stop recording, click the Stop Recording button on the Stop Recording toolbar.

Word has now recorded your macro and assigned it to the control you chose.

Running a Macro

To run a macro, click the toolbar button or choose the menu item or press the key combination you assigned to it.

If you chose not to assign a button, menu item, or key combination (perhaps because you have too many macros, as I do), you can run a macro by choosing Tools ➤ Macro ➤ Macros to display the Macros dialog box, selecting the macro from the Macro Name list, and clicking the Run button.

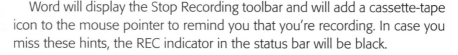

TIP

To stop a macro you've started running, press Ctrl+Break (Break is usually written on the front face of the Pause key). Visual Basic will display an angry dialog box telling you that "Code execution has been interrupted." Click the End button to dismiss this dialog box.

Editing a Macro

If you make a mistake while recording a macro, you can, of course, always choose to re-record it; but often a better option is to edit out the mistakes. If you're prepared to spend a few minutes looking at the Visual Basic for Applications programming language (VBA for short), you can usually figure out which is the offending line and simply remove it. You can also add further commands at this stage, as we'll see in a minute.

To edit a macro:

1. Choose Tools ➤ Macro ➤ Macros to display the Macros dialog box.

2. Select the macro you want to edit and click the Edit button to display the macro ready for editing in the Visual Basic Editor (see Figure 15.4).

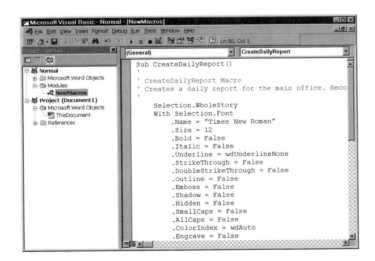

FIGURE 15.4:
The Visual Basic Editor

> **TIP**
>
> You can also choose Tools ➤ Macro ➤ Visual Basic Editor to run the Visual Basic Editor, then select the module you want to work with. In the Project window in the top left corner of the Visual Basic Editor, expand the object for the current template (in this case, Normal). Then expand the Modules object and double-click the module that contains the macro. By default, Word puts macros into a module named NewMacros. Word will display the contents of the module in the window on the right side of the Visual Basic Editor. In the right-hand window, scroll to the macro you want to edit.

3. Make such changes as necessary in the macro by adding, deleting, and editing actions.

4. Choose File ➤ Save *templatename* to save the template and the changes you've made to it.

5. Choose File ➤ Close and Return to Microsoft Word to close the Visual Basic Editor and return to Word.

Getting Help on Visual Basic

The Visual Basic Editor offers comprehensive help on the Visual Basic for Applications programming language. To view it, choose Help ➤ Microsoft Visual Basic Help or Help ➤ Contents and Index. Most of the statements and functions have examples, which can be particularly helpful when creating and troubleshooting your macros.

> **NOTE**
>
> If your computer doesn't offer you any help on VBA, whoever installed Word (or Office) on your computer might not have installed the relevant files (perhaps to save space). If that's the case, you'll need to dig out your CD of Word (or Office) and run the Setup program again. See the Appendix for details on running this program.

Testing Your Macro

If you're having problems with your macro, the quickest way to find out what's going wrong is to open the macro in the Visual Basic Editor and run it by clicking the Run Sub/User Form button on the Standard toolbar. If the macro encounters an error and crashes, Visual Basic for Applications will display an error box onscreen and will select the offending statement in the macro editing window.

> **TIP** Always test your macros on documents (or copies) that you don't care about.

For subtler problems—say the macro is selecting almost, but not quite, the text you want, and you can't make out which command is superfluous (or plain wrong)—you may want to arrange the Visual Basic Editor and Word windows so that you can see them both (for example, by right-clicking in open space on the Windows Taskbar and choosing Tile Windows Horizontally from the context menu). Position the insertion point appropriately in the Word window, then click on the Visual Basic Editor window to activate it. Position the insertion point in the macro you want to run, and press F8 to step through the macro command by command (see Figure 15.5). The Visual Basic Editor will highlight each command as it's executed, and you can watch the effect in the Word window so that you can catch errors.

Two Vital Visual Basic Programming Statements

If you're going to learn any Visual Basic for Applications statements at all, the two most useful ones (in my estimation) are Goto and If... Then... Else... EndIf. With knowledge of these two statements and a decent dose of ingenuity, you can make even simple macros jump through enough hoops to be quite useful. They're also surprisingly easy, so don't give up just yet.

Goto

The Goto statement is amazingly straightforward:

Goto *Label*

where *Label* is a word (any word other than a VBA command) followed by a colon on a line by itself in the macro; note that the Goto statement does not include the colon.

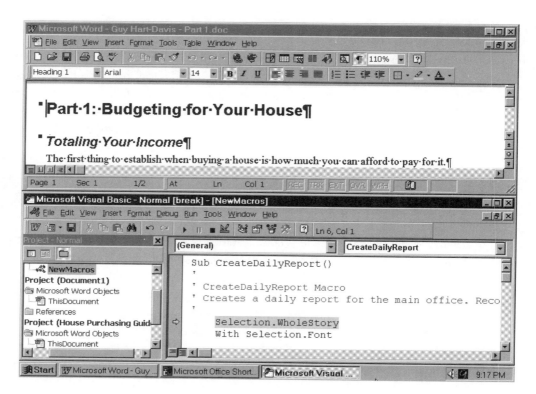

FIGURE 15.5: To catch something that the macro is doing wrong, arrange the Word and Visual Basic Editor windows so that you can see both, then step through the macro by pressing the F8 key.

For example, you could use the label below together with a **Goto ChangePrinter** statement:

```
ChangePrinter:
```

The quintessential Goto statement is **Goto Bye**, where you have a label named **Bye:** at the end of the macro. You might include a Goto Bye statement for times when somebody chooses Cancel or No in a message box or dialog box. Word will jump straight to the Bye line from the Goto Bye line, ignoring any other statements in-between. You can also use Goto to loop back to an earlier part of the macro.

When using Goto to loop back to an earlier part of a macro, be careful not to create an infinite loop that the macro will endlessly pursue. This usually means including an If statement (see the next section) so that the loop is only repeated if the specified condition is met (or not met).

If... Then... Else... EndIf

The If statement is the easiest conditional command to use. Its format is

If *Condition* **Then** *Instruction* **Else** *Instruction* **EndIf**

For example, the statement below checks the user's response to the message box; if the user chooses the Yes button, Word executes the CreateDailyReport macro; if the user chooses the No button, Word goes to the Bye label (and terminates the macro without changing anything).

```
Response = MsgBox("Do you want to create a daily
report?" "vbYesNo, "Create Daily Report")
If Response = 1 Then
     CreateDailyReport
Else
     Goto Bye
EndIf
```

You can also include an ElseIf condition that will run if the If condition is not met. For details, consult Visual Basic's Help file.

Adding Message Boxes and Input Boxes

Once you've got your macro performing the actions you intend for it to perform, you may find yourself needing to make it more accessible to the user. Here we'll look at two quick ways to do that—giving the user simple choices with message boxes, and soliciting input from the user with input boxes.

Controlling the Macro with Message Boxes

In your daily work, you've probably seen Word do two things with message boxes—give you information about what's going on without letting you choose what to do about it, and give you information and then let you make a choice about what to do. You can do the same with message boxes in your macros.

VBA offers the following types of message boxes:

Value	Constant	Buttons
0	vbOKOnly	OK
1	vbOKCancel	OK, Cancel
2	vbAbortRetryIgnore	Abort, Retry, Ignore
3	vbYesNoCancel	Yes, No, Cancel
Value	**Constant**	**Buttons**
4	vbYesNo	Yes, No
5	vbRetryCancel	Retry, Cancel

You can refer to these message box types by using either the value or the constant. For example, you can specify either **1** or **vbOKCancel** to produce a message box with OK and Cancel buttons.

You can also add icons to the message box by including the value argument.

Value	Constant	Displays
16	vbCritical	Stop icon
32	vbQuestion	Question icon
48	vbExclamation	Exclamation point icon
64	vbInformation	Information icon

Again, you can refer to these icons by using either the value or the constant: Either **48** or **vbExclamation** will produce an exclamation icon.

Use a plus sign to link the value or constant for the message box with the value or constant for the icon. For example, to produce a message box containing Yes and No buttons together with a question icon, you could use **vbYesNo + vbQuestion** (or **4 + 32**, **vbYesNo + 32**, or **4 + vbQuestion**).

To simply display information for the user in a message box, use the OK box (the default selection) with the following format:

MsgBox *Message$* [, *Type*][, *Title$*]

NOTE In Visual Basic for Applications syntax, the boldface represents words that don't change; italic represents variables (for example, here *Message$* is a variable string); the *$* indicates a string, usually text typed between double quotation marks; and the [] indicates that an argument is optional.

For example, this statement displays the Daily Report macro message box shown below:

```
MsgBox "The macro has created the daily report for
you.", vbOKOnly + vbInformation, "Create Daily Report"
```

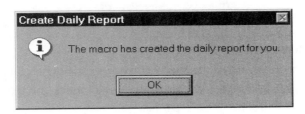

More useful to you and the users of your macro is a message box that lets them make a choice that the macro then acts upon. For this, use a message box such as Type 1 or Type 4:

```
Response = MsgBox("Do you want to create a daily
report?", vbYesNo + vbQuestion, "Create Daily Report")
If Response = vbYes Then
    Goto CreateDailyReport
Else
    Goto Bye
EndIf
```

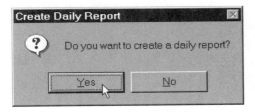

Here, if the user chooses the Yes button, Word goes to the CreateDailyReport label and continues running the macro from there; if not, it terminates the macro by going to the Bye label at the end. The condition checks the Response generated by the choice the user made in the message box to see if it's a vbYes (clicking the Yes button). Here's the full list of buttons; again, you can refer to them by either the constant or the value.

Value	Constant	Button Selected
1	vbOK	OK
2	vbCancel	Cancel
3	vbAbort	Abort
4	vbRetry	Retry
5	vbIgnore	Ignore
6	vbYes	Yes
7	vbNo	No

Getting Input from the User

The InputBox statement lets you quickly get one piece of information from the user by displaying a small dialog box onscreen into which the user types a response and then chooses OK. The syntax is simple:

*Variable$* = **InputBox$**(*Prompt$*[,*Title$*][, *Default$*])

For example, if you want to offer different users a choice of different types of daily reports based on who they are, you can check to see who they are by using an input box, and then take action based on the name:

```
FName$ = InputBox$("Please enter your first name:",
"Create Daily Report") If FName$ = "Taylor" Then...
```

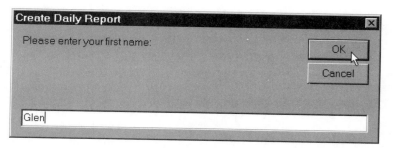

In this example, we're using a *string* (denoted by the dollar sign, *$*) to retrieve text entered by the user rather than a value entered by the user. To retrieve a value, omit the dollar signs from the relevant parts of the statement (the first item and the InputBox definition):

Value = **InputBox**(*Prompt$*[,*Title$*][, *Default*])

Deleting a Macro

To delete a macro that you no longer need, display the Macros dialog box by choosing Tools ➤ Macro ➤ Macros. Choose the macro in the Macro Name list box and click the Delete button. Choose Yes in the warning message box. Click Close in the Macros dialog box.

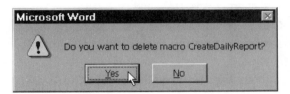

TIP Instead of deleting macros that you might potentially reuse, consider storing them in another template. (Create the template as usual by choosing File ➤ New and clicking the Template option button in the Create New group box in the New dialog box; then click OK.)

Word's Five Automatic Macros

Word provides names for five automatic macros that can be most helpful in customizing your Word environment. When you create a macro using one of these five names (or rename an existing macro with one of these names), the macro takes on the automatic characteristics listed below:

AutoExec   Runs whenever you start Word. You can use an AutoExec macro to set screen preferences, to open the last couple of files you worked on, or to open, say, a log file that you need to update every morning at work.

AutoNew   Runs whenever you open a new file based on the template containing an AutoNew macro (you can have more than one AutoNew macro, but only one in any given template). Adding an AutoNew macro to a template is a great way to create forms (which we'll look at in the next chapter) by automatically pulling the latest information from a database into the new document.

AutoOpen   Runs whenever you reopen a file based on the template containing the AutoOpen macro. Again, AutoOpen is template-specific, so if you want to switch to a particular printer for a document based on a certain template, this would be an easy way to do that.

AutoClose   Runs whenever you close a file based on the template containing the AutoClose macro. You might want to pair AutoClose with AutoOpen to undo any environmental changes you make—for example, to switch back to the regular printer from the special one.

AutoExit   Runs whenever you close Word. This might be a great way to back up special files automatically every day—or to launch another application by using the Shell command.

> **TIP**
>
> **You can either record an automatic macro using one of the above names or rename an existing macro (we'll look at renaming macros in just a moment). Either way, pay attention to which template you put your AutoNew, AutoOpen, and AutoClose macros in.**

Organizing Your Macro Modules

If you use macros often, sooner or later you'll need to rename macro modules or move them or copy them from one template to another.

To do so, open the Organizer dialog box by choosing Tools ➤ Macro ➤ Macros and clicking the Organizer button in the Macros dialog box. Word will display the Macro

Project Items tab of the Organizer dialog box (see Figure 15.6), displaying the macro modules in Normal (the global template) in one panel and the macro modules in the current document in the other panel.

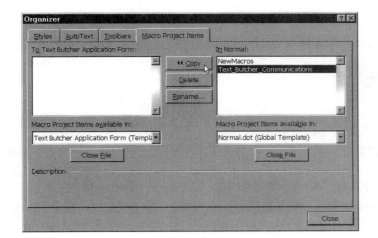

FIGURE 15.6:
The Organizer box lets you rename macros quickly, and copy and move them from one template to another.

To work with the template for the current document, select it from the Macro Project Items Available In drop-down list in the panel listing the current document. Otherwise, open the templates you want: Click the Close File button on either side of the dialog box to close the file currently open; then click the Open File button (into which the Close File button will have metamorphosed) and choose the correct template from the Open dialog box that Word then displays.

Once you've renamed, copied, or moved macros as described below, click the Close button to close the Organizer dialog box. Word will invite you to save any changes to affected templates that are not open; click the Yes button.

Deleting a Macro Module

To delete one or more macro modules from a template, choose the module or modules from either panel of the Organizer dialog box, and click the Delete button. Choose Yes in the confirmation message box.

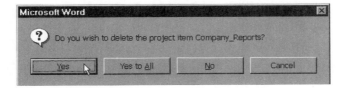

> **TIP** Any copies of the macro module in other templates are unaffected.

Renaming a Macro Module

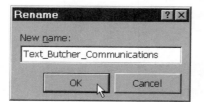

To rename a macro module, select it (from either the left-hand panel or the right-hand panel of the Organizer dialog box) and click the Rename button. Enter the new name for the module in the Rename dialog box and click the OK button. Again, instances of the module in other templates will be unaffected.

Copying and Moving Macro Modules between Templates

To copy one or more macro modules from one template to another, open the templates in question in the Organizer dialog box. Select the module or modules to copy in either panel of the dialog box (the arrows on the Copy button will change direction to point to the other panel). Then click the Copy button.

If the recipient template contains a module of the same name as one you're copying, Word will display a warning message box telling you that the project item cannot be copied.

> **TIP** To move a macro from one template to another, copy it as described here, and then delete the macro from the source template.

Chapter 16

FORMS

FEATURING

- **Creating a form**
- **Automating a form**
- **Filling in a form**
- **Distributing information from a form**

Word's powerful features for creating business forms streamline the handling of repetitive information at work. Of course, you can use the features discussed earlier in this book to create forms that can be printed out and filled in by hand; but in this chapter, we'll look at online forms for gathering, storing, and distributing information.

The usual procedure is to start a form as a new template, lay out the text and form fields, format the whole thing, and protect the form so the user can change only the form fields, not the text you've entered. Then the user can start a new copy of the form based on the template you've created, fill in the relevant fields, and save it as a document, leaving the template unaffected and ready for more customers.

Creating a Form

First, start a new template for the form by choosing File ➤ New and clicking the Template option button in the Create New group box in the New dialog box. If Word offers a template suitable as a starting point for your new form, select that template; otherwise, choose the Blank Document on the General tab. Click the OK button to start the form.

Before you do anything else, save the form (as a template) in whichever of the folders in the Templates folder best suits your purpose. Then choose File ➤ Properties to display the Properties dialog box and add a lucid description of the template in the Comments box on the Summary tab.

Next, display the Forms toolbar by right-clicking either the menu bar or any displayed toolbar and choosing Forms from the context menu. The Forms toolbar (see Figure 16.1) contains nine buttons for working with forms.

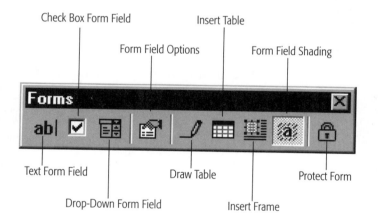

FIGURE 16.1:
The Forms toolbar provides quick access to form fields.

Now enter the skeleton of your form as you would any regular Word document: Type in text, insert graphics, create tables, and format the document. Figure 16.2 shows the beginning of an employment application form.

You can use tables, offset by the creative use of borders and shading (discussed in Chapter 2), to lay out many types of forms effectively. Draw tables by clicking the Draw Table button on the Forms toolbar and drawing as described in Chapter 7; insert tables as needed by clicking the Insert Table button or by using the Draw Table button and its associated features.

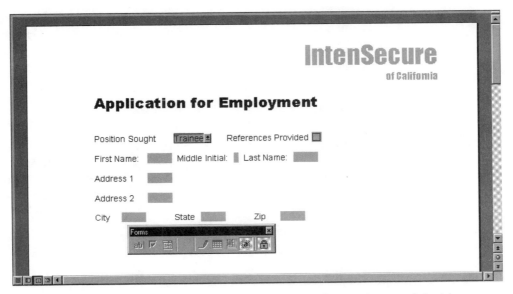

FIGURE 16.2: Putting together an online form with drop-down lists, text boxes, and check boxes

Adding Form Fields

Once you've got the basic text and layout of your form in place, it's time to add form fields to it. Word provides check boxes (which can be checked or not checked), text boxes (in which the user can enter text of a type you choose), and drop-down lists (from which the user can choose one predefined option from a list).

Check Boxes

To insert a default-sized check box in the form at the insertion point, click the Check Box Form Field button on the Forms toolbar. Double-click the check box to open the Check Box Form Field Options dialog box (see Figure 16.3), and then choose the options you want:

- In the Check Box Size group box, choose Exactly and specify a point size for the check box if you don't like Word's automatic point size.
- If you want the check box to be selected by default, select Checked in the Default Value group box.
- If you want to run a macro either when the user enters the check box or when they leave it, choose a macro name from the Entry or Exit drop-down list in the Run Macro On group box.

- In the Field Settings group box, enter an identifying name for the check box in the Bookmark text box, and then make sure the Check Box Enabled check box has been selected. (You may occasionally want to disable a check box so that the user can't access it at all.)

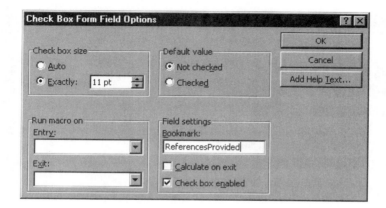

FIGURE 16.3:
Set options for the check box in the Check Box Form Field Options dialog box.

Click the OK button when you've finished making your selections. Word will apply your choices to the check box you inserted.

Text Boxes

To add a text box to the form at the insertion point, click the Text Form Field button on the Forms toolbar. Double-click the text form field that Word inserts to open the Text Form Field Options dialog box (see Figure 16.4), and then choose the options you want:

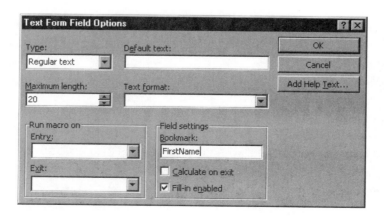

FIGURE 16.4:
Set options for the text form field in the Text Form Field Options dialog box.

- In the Type drop-down list, choose the type of text form field you want: Regular Text, Number, Date, Current Date, Current Time, or Calculation.

> **NOTE** When you choose a type other than Regular Text, the Default Text and Text Format boxes change names accordingly—for example, their names change to Default Date and Date Format if you choose Date.

- In the Default Text box, enter any default or sample answer you want the form to display. (If you choose Current Date or Current Time, this box isn't available.)
- In the Maximum Length box, limit the text box entry to a specified number of characters if you'd like. (For example, if you were adding text boxes for a phone number, you might use three boxes of three, three, and four characters, respectively. For a middle initial field, you'd probably set a one-character limit.)
- From the Text Format drop-down list, choose how you want the entry to look. The choices for text are Uppercase, Lowercase, First Capital (i.e., sentence case), and Title Case; for numbers, dates, times, and calculations, you get a more exciting range of choices.
- If you want to run a macro either when the user moves to the text form field or when they leave it, choose a macro name from the Entry or Exit drop-down list in the Run Macro On group box.
- In the Field Settings group box, enter an identifying name for the text form field in the Bookmark text box, and then make sure the Fill-in Enabled check box has been selected. (If you choose Current Date, Current Time, or Calculation, this check box will be unavailable because Word will supply the information itself.)

Click the OK button when you've finished making your selections. Word will apply your choices to the text form field.

Drop-Down Form Fields

 To add a drop-down form field to the form, position the insertion point at the appropriate place and click the Drop-Down Form Field button on the

Forms toolbar. Then double-click the drop-down form field to display the Drop-Down Form Field Options dialog box (see Figure 16.5) and choose options for the field:

- Create the drop-down list by entering each item in the Drop-Down Item box and clicking the Add button to add it to the Items in Drop-Down List box. Repeat as often as needed, up to a maximum of 25 items. Use the Move buttons to move the selected item in the Items in Drop-Down List box up and down the list. Use the Remove button to remove a selected entry from the list.

NOTE   **You can enter up to 25 items in the drop-down list.**

- If you want to run a macro either when the user moves to the drop-down form field or when they leave it, choose a macro name from the Entry or Exit drop-down list in the Run Macro On group box.
- In the Field Settings group box, enter an identifying name for the drop-down form field in the Bookmark text box, and then make sure the Drop-Down Enabled check box is selected.

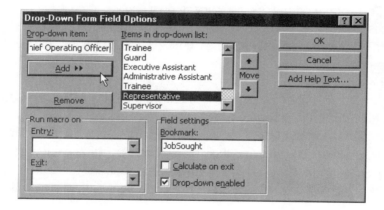

FIGURE 16.5:
Set options for the drop-down form field in the Drop-Down Form Field Options dialog box.

Click the OK button when you've finished making your selections. Word will apply your choices to the drop-down form field.

Adjusting Form Fields

Once you've inserted your form fields, you can drag-and-drop them (or cut and paste them) to move them to the most suitable place in your form.

You can format text form fields and drop-down lists by selecting them and applying formatting as described in Chapter 2. (Some formatting, such as point size and underline, works for check boxes as well—if for some strange reason you want to underline a check box.) You'll find this much easier to do if you keep form-field shading switched on (if it's off, click the Form Field Shading button on the Forms toolbar).

If you need to rename a form field, open its Form Field Options dialog box by either double-clicking the form field or right-clicking and choosing Properties from the context menu. Enter the new name in the Bookmark text box, click the OK button, and the change is made.

Running Macros from Form Fields

As mentioned in the previous sections, you can set one macro to execute when the user enters a form field (using the mouse, the Tab key, or the ↵ key) and another macro to execute when the user leaves that field. You can use this feature to automate your forms to a high degree. For example, you can make sure the user fills in a particular field by automatically moving the insertion point to that field when the user creates the copy of the form from the template and running a macro when the user exits the field to make sure that the user has entered something in the field, and that something is suitable in format, length, and so on. If the user has failed on either count, you can make Word display a message box and then move the insertion point right back to that field time and time again until they get it right.

Less fascist, but equally helpful, might be a macro that runs on exit from a field that skips the user to a relevant section of the form when they make a particular choice, so they don't have to tab their way through an entire subsection of fields that are meaningless to them.

> **TIP**
>
> Remember that you can also add AutoNew, AutoOpen, and AutoClose macros (as discussed in Chapter 15) to form templates that automate your forms even further.

Adding ActiveX Controls

In addition to the straightforward form fields discussed in the previous section, Word 97 provides ActiveX controls that you can use in forms and dialog boxes. ActiveX controls include items such as toggle buttons (for toggling an option on and off), option buttons (for picking one choice out of two or more mutually exclusive choices), and spin buttons (for adjusting a number box), and can store VBA code inside themselves.

Using ActiveX controls effectively is a topic beyond the scope of this book, but if you find yourself needing to create forms with more capabilities than the regular form fields can offer, you would do well to spend time investigating the ActiveX controls.

To work with ActiveX controls, display the Control Toolbox toolbar (see Figure 16.6) by right-clicking the menu bar or any displayed toolbar and choosing Control Toolbox from the context menu of toolbars.

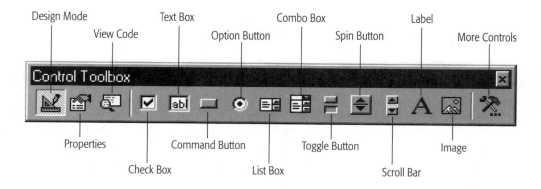

FIGURE 16.6: Use the buttons on the Control Toolbox toolbar to insert ActiveX controls.

Testing Your Form

You can quickly see how your form looks by protecting it with the Protect Form button on the Forms toolbar. This will allow you to see the drop-down form fields (and other form fields) in all their glory and to improve the layout of the form. You'll also be able to move through the text field by field by pressing Tab (and Shift+Tab to go backwards) or by clicking in fields with the mouse.

Adding Help Text to a Form Field

If your form has even vestigial ambiguity, you'll probably want to add help text to its form fields. To do so, display the Form Field Options dialog box by double-clicking the field you want to add help text to (or by right-clicking in it and choosing Properties from the pop-up menu) and click the Add Help Text button. Word will display the Form Field Help Text dialog box (see Figure 16.7).

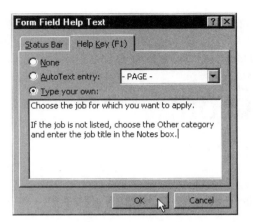

FIGURE 16.7:
In the Form Field Help Text dialog box, add help text on either the Status Bar tab or the Help Key (F1) tab—or both.

On the Status Bar tab of the Form Field Help Text dialog box, add any help text that you want to appear in the status bar when the user moves to the field in question. If you have a predefined AutoText entry suitable for help, select the AutoText Entry option button and specify the entry in the drop-down list; otherwise, click in the Type Your Own box (thereby selecting the Type Your Own option button) and enter the text. Status Bar help text can have a maximum of 138 characters; remember that some of these may not be visible if the user is running Windows at a low resolution (such as 640x480) because the later characters will run off the right edge of the screen.

On the Help Key (F1) tab, add further help text as appropriate. Help Key help text can have up to 255 characters, and you can space the text over half-a-dozen lines, adding indents if need be. Here's an example of the Help box that the user will see when they press the F1 key:

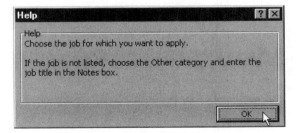

When you've finished adding help text in the Form Field Help Text dialog box, click the OK button to return to the Form Field Options dialog box. Choose OK to apply your changes to the form field and return to the form.

Protecting the Form

Once you've finished laying out the form, you need to protect it so that users will be able to use but not alter the form fields you've so carefully included. You can protect the form either with or without a password: If you protect it with a password, anyone will be able to fill in the form fields, but they'll need to enter the password to change the form itself; if you protect it without requiring a password, anyone can unprotect (and then alter) the form without any effort at all.

- To protect the form without a password, click the Protect Form button on the Forms toolbar.
- To protect the form with a password (heavily recommended), choose Tools ➤ Protect Document. Word will display the Protect Document dialog box (see Figure 16.8). Choose the Forms option button in the Protect Document For area, enter a password (of up to 15 characters) in the Password text box, and click the OK button.

FIGURE 16.8:
To protect your form against unauthorized changes, display the Protect Document dialog box, choose Forms in the Protect Document For area, and enter a password in the Password box.

- Word will ask you to confirm the password (to eliminate the chance of a typo). Enter the password again in the Confirm Password dialog box and click the OK button.

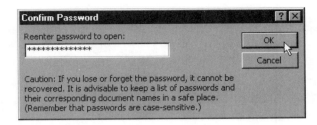

Now that the form is protected, users can access only the form fields, and they can move from one field to the other by pressing Tab (or Shift+Tab to move backwards). They can then fill in the form quickly.

TIP   For more information on locking and protecting documents, see the *Locking and Protecting Documents* section in Chapter 18.

Filling in the Form

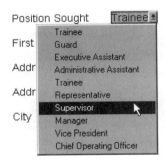

To fill in a form based on a template, simply open a document based on that template and move from form field to form field, entering text in the text boxes, selecting and clearing check boxes, and making choices from drop-down lists.

Any macros set to run when the user enters a form field will run when you move to that field (by using Tab or Shift+Tab, PageUp or PageDown, or by clicking in the field); any macros set to run when the user exits a form field will run when you leave the field.

When you've finished filling in the form, save it.

> **TIP**
> A thoroughly automated form will offer to save itself: Consider offering this option to save the form as soon as the user starts filling the form in (either with an AutoNew macro or with a macro set to run on exit from, say, a Last Name text box, by which time the user should have filled in enough information for the form to start being useful); and to close it and save changes when the user completes the last required item.

Printing Forms

When you have filled in the form, you can print it in full by choosing File ➤ Print or by clicking the Print button on the Standard toolbar. But if you want to print the data entered in the form without printing the standard text of the form, first choose Tools ➤ Options to display the Options dialog box, click the Print tab, and select the Print Data Only for Forms check box in the Options for Current Document Only area. Then choose File ➤ Print, and Word will print just the data entered into the form.

> **TIP**
> This is a great way of filling in often-used preprinted forms on special paper: Scan the form into your computer, and recreate it in Word with form fields. You can then fill in the form online and print only the data out onto the preprinted form sheets.

Saving Only the Data from a Form

Word also lets you save the data from a form without saving the form itself, which can help you more swiftly enter form data in a database. To save the data without the form, display the Options dialog box by choosing Tools ➤ Options, click the Save tab, and select the Save Data Only for Forms check box in the Save Options area. Then click the OK button to close the Options dialog box, and save the form as normal.

TIP If you automate your form using macros, the saving macro could automatically choose to save only data for forms.

Retrieving Information from a Form

Having users fill in forms online so you can then print them out and get information from the hard copy is all well and good, but it's hardly true to Babbage's vision when he started punching cards for the Difference Engine. If you're going to create a form online and have your victim fill it out online so you can then store it online, go the whole hog and use the information online too.

In this section, we'll outline the steps for creating a macro that accesses the filled-in employment application and inserts relevant pieces of information from it into a letter inviting the applicant in for an interview (or turning them down). This letter can either be a form or an unprotected document containing bookmarks.

This is where naming your form fields carefully pays off. In your template for the letter to the applicant, set up form fields (or bookmarks) for the information you want to pull from the application: the various name and address fields, the position sought, and so on.

The VBA command to use for retrieving the result of a form field is:

```
ActiveDocument.FormFields("BookmarkName").Result
```

The VBA command for setting the result of a form field is:

```
ActiveDocument.FormFields("BookmarkName").Result =
"ResultToSet"
```

Armed with just these two commands, you can quickly retrieve information from one form and transfer it into another document. For example, your macro might retrieve part of the information from the open application form like this:

```
FirstName$ =
ActiveDocument.FormFields("FirstName").Result
```

```
MiddleInitial$ =
ActiveDocument.FormFields("MiddleInitial").Result
LastName$ =
ActiveDocument.FormFields("LastName").Result
JobSought$ =
ActiveDocument.FormFields("Job").Result
ReferencesProvided =
ActiveDocument.FormFields("References").Result
```

Having retrieved that information (and the rest), it would then open a new document based on the Letter-to-the-Applicant template and fill in the relevant fields (FirstName, MiddleInitial, LastName) in the letter:

```
ActiveDocument.FormFields("FirstName").Result =
FirstName$
ActiveDocument.FormFields("MiddleInitial").Result =
MiddleInitial$
ActiveDocument.FormFields("LastName").Result =
LastName$
ActiveDocument.FormFields("JobSought").Result =
JobSought$
If ReferencesProvided = 1 Then
    ActiveDocument.FormFields("ReferencesProvided")
.Result = "We will check your references within the
next week."
Else
ActiveDocument.FormFields("ReferencesProvided")
.Result =  Please provide the names of two
references as soon as possible."
EndIf
```

WARNING This macro will not work if you just type these lines of code in. You have to create the form and letter first.

Once you've transferred all the relevant information from the application form to the letter, it'll be ready for a quick scan by the human eye to make sure everything's okay. Oh, and while that's going on, why not have Word transfer the name and address information to an envelope and print that automatically? Time's a wasting…

Chapter 17

CUSTOMIZING WORD

- **Customizing toolbars, menus, and keyboard shortcuts**
- **Creating your own toolbars and menus**
- **Setting environment options**
- **Creating a special-purpose template**

One of Word's most appealing features—aside from its ability to help you produce all kinds of good-looking documents swiftly and easily—is that you can customize the user interface to the *n*th degree. By "user interface" I mean the screen, the menus, the toolbars, the keyboard shortcuts, and so on.

We saw in Chapter 15 how you can assign macros to toolbars, menu items, and keyboard shortcuts so you can run the macros quickly. In this section, we'll look at how you can create your own toolbars and menus and how you can strip down—or even remove completely—the menus that Word provides. We'll also look at the environment options that Word provides—such as the Edit and File Locations options—and see how you can optimize Word for your work. Finally, we'll discuss creating a template in Word that constrains users to performing only some actions on special documents.

Customizing Toolbars and the Menu Bar

As we saw in Chapter 1, not only can you display any number of Word's toolbars onscreen at one time, but you can also float them (and the menu bar) in the middle of the screen and reshape them at will. In this section, we'll look at how you can create new toolbars, modify your own toolbars or Word's existing ones, and delete your own toolbars.

Creating a New Toolbar

To create a new toolbar:

1. Right-click on the menu bar or on any displayed toolbar to display the context menu of toolbars, then choose Customize to display the Customize dialog box.

2. On the Toolbars tab, click the New button to display the New Toolbar dialog box.

3. Enter a name for the new toolbar in the Toolbar Name text box.

4. If you want to make the toolbar available only to the current template, choose the template's name in the Make Toolbar Available To drop-down list. Otherwise, make sure Normal is selected in the Make Toolbar Available To drop-down list.

5. Click the OK button to create the toolbar. Word will display the new toolbar (with space for just one button, and most of its name truncated) somewhere within easy commuting distance of the Customize dialog box (see Figure 17.1)

6. Click the Commands tab to display it, then add the buttons you want to the new toolbar:

   • From the Categories list, select the type of command you're looking for. The Categories list includes all the regular menus (from File through Help), together with Web, Drawing,

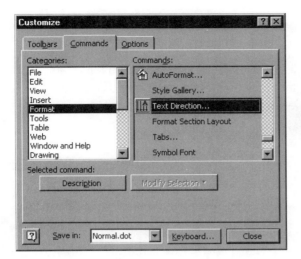

FIGURE 17.1:
Drag buttons from the Customize dialog box to the new toolbar.

AutoShapes, Borders, Mail Merge, Forms, Control Toolbox, All Commands, Macros, Fonts, AutoText, Styles, Built-in Menus, and New Menu.

- When you choose the category, the available items for it appear in the Commands list box. Click the item you want and drag it to the toolbar. To see a description of the selected item (for example, to make sure you've gotten hold of the command you thought you had and not one of its close relatives), click the Description button first to display a description of the command.

- If the item you dragged to the toolbar has a button associated with it, Word will add that button to the toolbar. (You'll see any button associated with an item beside the listing of the item in the Commands list box.) If the item doesn't have a button associated with it, Word will create a text button containing a description of the button you dragged. For example, if you drag the Heading 1 style to the toolbar, Word will create a button named *Heading 1 Style*. You can now rename the button by right-clicking it and entering another name in the Name box, or you can choose an image from the button by right-clicking and choosing Change Button Image from the context menu.

- To rearrange the buttons on the new toolbar, drag and drop each button while the Customize dialog box is open. To remove a button from the toolbar, drag it off and drop it somewhere in the document or in the Customize dialog box.   .

7. Click the Close button in the Customize dialog box when you've finished creating your toolbar.

Modifying a Toolbar

To modify a toolbar:

1. Display the toolbar onscreen by right-clicking the menu bar or any displayed toolbar, then selecting that toolbar in the context menu of toolbars. Alternatively, choose View ➤ Toolbars and select the toolbar from the Toolbars submenu.

2. Add, move, copy, or remove buttons as appropriate:

   - To remove a button from the toolbar, hold down Alt and drag the button off the toolbar and into an open space in a document. Drop the button there, and it'll disappear.

> **WARNING**
>
> If you remove a custom button (one that you've created) from a toolbar this way, Word will delete the details of the button, so that you'll have to re-create it if you want to use it again. If you want to store your custom buttons safely, create a toolbar as described in the previous section, *Creating a New Toolbar*, and use it for safely storing buttons for future use.

   - To move a button from one toolbar to another, hold down Alt and drag the button from one toolbar to the other. You can also rearrange the buttons on a toolbar by holding down Alt and dragging the buttons.
   - To copy a button from one toolbar to another, hold down Ctrl and Alt, then drag the button from one toolbar to the other.
   - To add buttons to a toolbar, choose Tools ➤ Customize and add the buttons to the toolbar as described in the previous section. Close the Customize dialog box when you've finished.

Deleting a Toolbar

To delete a toolbar you've created, right-click in the menu bar or any displayed toolbar and choose Customize from the context menu to display the Customize dialog box. On the Toolbars tab, select the toolbar you want to delete, and then click the Delete button. Word will display a message box asking if you want to delete the toolbar; choose OK. Click the Close button to exit the Customize dialog box.

NOTE **Word won't let you delete any of its toolbars—you can only delete ones you've created.**

Renaming a Toolbar

To rename a toolbar you've created, right-click in either the menu bar or any displayed toolbar and choose Customize from the context menu to display the Customize dialog box. Highlight the toolbar to re-name in the Toolbars list box on the Toolbars tab. Click the Rename button to display the Rename Toolbar dialog box and specify the new name for the toolbar in the Toolbar Name text box, as shown here. Click the OK button to rename the toolbar, and then click the Close button to close the Customize dialog box.

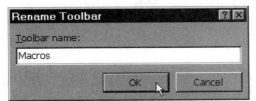

Copying a Toolbar from One Template to Another

To copy a toolbar you've created from one template to another, open the Organizer dialog box by choosing Tools ➤ Templates and Add-Ins and clicking the Organizer button in the Templates and Add-Ins dialog box. Click the Toolbars tab to bring it to the front of the Organizer dialog box (see Figure 17.2), displaying the toolbars in Normal (the global template) in one panel and the toolbars in the current document in the other panel.

To work with the template for the current document, select it from the Toolbars Available In drop-down list in the panel listing the current document. Otherwise, open the templates you want: Click the Close File button on either side of the dialog box to close the currently open file; then click the Open File button (into which the Close File button will have metamorphosed) and choose the correct template from the Open dialog box that Word then displays.

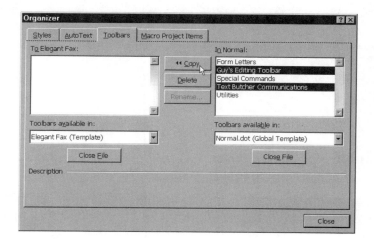

FIGURE 17.2:
The Organizer box lets you copy toolbars from one template to another quickly.

Copy the toolbar by selecting it from the left-hand or right-hand box and clicking the Copy button. When you click the Close button to exit the Organizer dialog box, Word will invite you to save any changes to affected templates; choose Yes.

Customizing Menus

You can customize menus by adding items to them, as we saw when creating macros in Chapter 15. You can also remove from menus any items that you don't use—or that you don't want other people to use. As if that weren't enough, you can remove entire menus and add menus of your own.

Adding Items to Menus

By strategically adding items to menus, you can have all the commands, styles, macros, and fonts that you need right at hand.

To add an item to a menu:

1. Right-click the menu bar or any displayed toolbar and choose Customize from the context menu, or choose Tools ➤ Customize, to open the Customize dialog box.

2. Click the Commands tab to bring it to the front (see Figure 17.3).

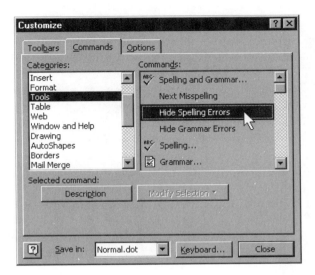

FIGURE 17.3:
Adding items to menus on the Commands tab of the Customize dialog box

> **NOTE** To make changes in a template other than Normal (the global template), open a document based on that template before starting these steps, and choose the template in the Save In drop-down list in the Customize dialog box.

3. In the Categories list box, select the category of item to add.

4. In the Commands list box, click the command and drag it to the name of the menu to which you want to add it. Keep holding the mouse button down as Word displays the menu, then drag the command down the menu (and across to any submenu if necessary) to where you want it to appear. Word will indicate with a black bar where the command will land, as shown on the next page. Drop it when it's in the right place. Alternatively, click the menu to display it before selecting and dragging the command to it.

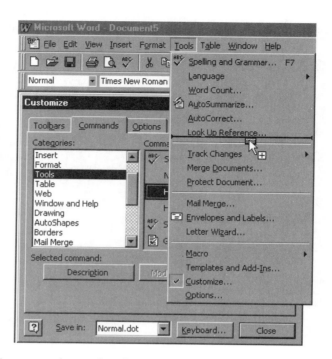

5. If the item you dragged to the menu has a button associated with it, Word will add that button to the menu along with the name of the command. (You'll see any button associated with an item beside the listing of the item in the Commands list box.) You can now rename the menu item by right-clicking it and entering another name in the Name box, or you can choose an image by right-clicking and choosing Change Button Image from the context menu (to add an existing button) or Edit Button Image (to create a new button in the Button Editor).

TIP   You can add an *access key* (also known as a "hot key" or—bizarrely—a "mnemonic") for the item by putting an ampersand (&) before the access key letter; for the best results, make sure the letter you choose isn't already an access key for another item on the menu.

6. Add more items to any of the menus, or click the Close button to close the Customize dialog box.

Modifying Menus and Removing Items

To remove one item quickly from a menu, press Ctrl+Alt+– (that's the hyphen key, but think of it as the minus key). The mouse pointer will change to a short, thick horizontal line. With this mouse pointer showing, pull down a menu and click the item you want to remove.

> **TIP**
>
> **If you decide not to remove an item, press Esc to restore the mouse pointer to normal.**

To remove a number of items from a menu, display the Customize dialog box by right-clicking and choosing Customize from the context menu or by choosing Tools ➤ Customize. Then:

- Reposition a menu item by clicking it and dragging it to a different position on that menu, on a different menu, or on a toolbar, as shown here.
- Remove a menu item by dragging it and dropping it in blank space in the document (or anywhere in the Customize dialog box). Word will display an X next to the mouse pointer as you drag the item to indicate that it will be removed.

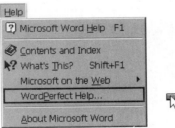

Restoring Word's Menus to their Defaults

You can restore any of Word's predefined menus in any given template to its default state—and at once wipe out any and all changes you've made to it—by opening the Customize dialog box, right-clicking the name of the menu you want to restore, and then choosing Reset from the context menu.

Customizing the Menu Bar

You can customize Word's menu bar by adding menus, removing menus, and renaming menus. To do so, first display the Customize dialog box by right-clicking either the menu bar or any displayed toolbar and choosing Customize from the context menu or by choosing Tools ➤ Customize. Then click the Commands tab to display it and verify the setting in the Save Changes In drop-down list to make sure you're working in the right template.

Adding Menus

To add a menu to the menu bar or to a toolbar:

1. Display the Commands tab of the Customize dialog box.
2. In the Categories list box, select New Menu.
3. Drag the New Menu item from the Commands list box and drop it where you want it to appear either on the menu bar or on a toolbar (see Figure 17.4). Word will name the new menu *New Menu*, which you'll probably want to change.

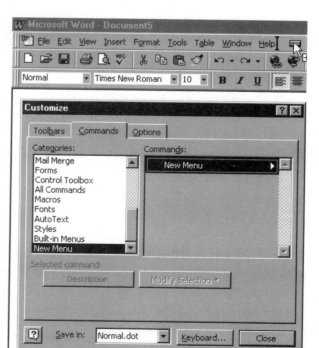

FIGURE 17.4:
To add a new menu, drag the New Menu item to the menu bar or to a toolbar.

4. Right-click the menu name to display the context menu, then drag through the Name box to select its contents. Enter a suitable name for the new menu. Put an ampersand before the letter you want to use as an access key. Make sure this access key letter isn't already assigned to another menu.

5. Repeat steps 3 and 4 if you need to add another menu. Otherwise, you can now add items to the menu as described in the section titled *Adding Items to Menus* earlier in the chapter.

6. When you're finished, click the Close button to close the Customize dialog box.

Removing Menus

You can remove a menu from the menu bar or from a toolbar in either of two ways:

- If you have the Customize dialog box open, click on the menu name, drag it off the menu bar or toolbar, and drop it either in open space in the Word window or in the Customize dialog box.
- If you do not have the Customize dialog box open, hold down the Alt key, click on the menu name, drag it off the menu bar or toolbar, and drop it in open space in the Word window.

Renaming Menus

To rename a menu, first display the Customize dialog box. Then right-click the menu name to display the context menu, edit the menu's name in the Name text box (putting an ampersand before the letter you want to use as an access key), and press Enter. You can then perform further customization or click the Close button to close the Customize dialog box.

Customizing Keyboard Shortcuts

Even if you're not a die-hard WordStar user who's finally upgraded to Word, you can speed and simplify your work by customizing the keyboard to suit your needs. While Word comes with an impressive array of preprogrammed keyboard shortcuts, you're likely to find other items that you need to have at hand instead. (If you *are* a former WordStar user, you can remap most of the keyboard...)

Assigning a Keyboard Shortcut

To set a keyboard shortcut:

1. Choose Tools ➤ Customize to display the Customize dialog box.

2. Click the Keyboard button to display the Customize Keyboard dialog box (see Figure 17.5).

3. Specify the template to change in the Save Changes In drop-down list if necessary. (Leave Normal selected if you want the changes to apply to all templates that don't have this keyboard combination set to another command.)

4. In the Categories list, select the category of item for the new keyboard shortcut.

5. Choose the item to add in the Commands list box. (If you chose Macros, Fonts, AutoText, Styles, or Common Symbols in the Categories list, the list box will change its name to suit your choice—Macros, Fonts, and so on.)

6. Click in the Press New Shortcut Key box and press the key combination you want; Word will display the combination you choose in the Press New Shortcut Key box. A key combination can be any of the following:

   - Alt plus a regular key not used for a menu access key
   - Alt plus a function key
   - Ctrl plus a regular key or function key
   - Ctrl+Alt plus a regular key or function key
   - Shift plus a function key

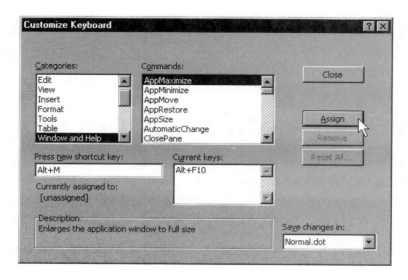

FIGURE 17.5:
Setting keyboard shortcuts in the Customize Keyboard dialog box

- Ctrl+Shift plus a regular key or function key
- Alt+Shift plus a regular key or function key
- Ctrl+Alt+Shift plus a regular key or function key

Because this last option involves severe contortions of the hands, it's not a great idea for frequent use.

> **NOTE** You can set up shortcut keys that have two steps—for example, Ctrl+Alt+F, 1 and Ctrl+Alt+F, 2—by pressing the second key (in this case, the 1 or the 2, though you can use any key) after pressing the key combination. These tend to be more trouble than they're worth unless you're assigning hundreds of extra shortcut keys.

7. Check the Currently Assigned To area under the Press New Shortcut Key box to see if that key combination is already assigned. (If it is and you don't want to overwrite it, press Backspace to clear the Press New Shortcut Key box, and then choose another combination.)
8. Click the Assign button to assign the shortcut.
9. Either assign more keyboard shortcuts or click the Close button to close the Customize Keyboard dialog box.
10. Click the Close button to close the Customize dialog box.

Removing a Keyboard Shortcut

Usually you remove a keyboard shortcut by assigning that shortcut to another item—for example, if you assign Ctrl+P to a Photograph style you've created, Word will overwrite Ctrl+P as the shortcut for the Print command. But sometimes you may need to remove a shortcut without assigning it to another item—for example, if you want to prevent the user from performing certain actions.

To remove a keyboard shortcut:

1. Choose Tools ➤ Customize to display the Customize dialog box.
2. Click the Keyboard button to display the Customize Keyboard dialog box (see Figure 17.5).
3. Specify the template you want to change in the Save Changes In drop-down list if necessary. (Leave Normal selected if you want the changes to apply to all templates that don't have this keyboard combination set to another command.)

4. In the Categories list, select the category of the item that currently has the keyboard shortcut you want to remove.
5. Choose the item in the Commands list box. (If you choose Macros, Fonts, AutoText, Styles, or Common Symbols in the Categories list, the name of the list box will change to match your choice—Macros, Fonts, and so on.)
6. In the Current Keys list box, select the key combination to remove (depending on the command, there may be several).
7. Click the Remove button.
8. Either remove more keyboard shortcuts or click the Close button to close the Customize Keyboard dialog box.
9. Click the Close button to close the Customize dialog box.

Resetting All Keyboard Shortcuts

You can quickly reset all keyboard shortcuts for the template specified in the Save Changes In drop-down list by clicking the Reset All button in the Customize Keyboard dialog box. Word will display a confirmation message box to make sure you want to take this drastic step.

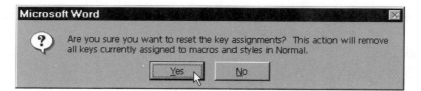

Choose Yes to reset the keyboard shortcuts, click the Close button to exit the Customize Keyboard dialog box, and then click the next Close button to close the Customize dialog box.

Choosing Environment Options

As we've seen in earlier chapters, Word offers any number of options for editing, printing, spelling and grammar, and the like, all stored on the ten tabs of the Options dialog box (Tools ➤ Options). In this section, we'll look at the different categories of options and discuss those not touched on in other sections of this book. We won't grind through all the details for every single option, but I'll try to indicate the most useful options for conventional uses of Word.

> **TIP**
>
> **For more detail on the options not discussed in depth in this section, consult Word's Help files by clicking the Help button (the ? button) in the Options dialog box and selecting an element in the dialog box or by choosing Help ➤ Microsoft Word Help.**

View Options

The options on the View tab (see Figure 17.6) let you specify which tools and elements you see onscreen.

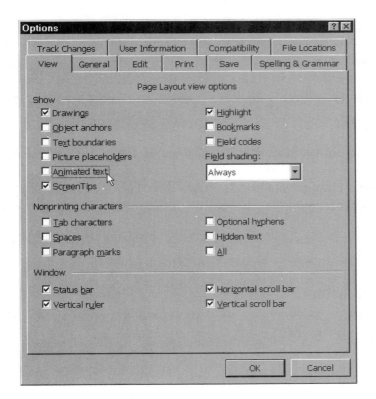

FIGURE 17.6:
Use the options on the View tab of the Options dialog box to set up your screen.

NOTE Word's different views offer some different view options—for example, Page Layout view does not offer the Wrap to Window and Draft Font options, but it does offer Text Boundaries (dotted lines around page elements), Drawings (for displaying drawing objects created in Word), and Object Anchors (the anchor symbols that indicate an item is attached to a particular paragraph). Online Layout view offers an Enlarge Fonts Less Than option instead of Style Area Width.

Show Options

Select the Picture Placeholders check box to have Word display empty boxes instead of graphics. This will let you scroll through your documents faster, particularly when using a slower computer.

Select the Wrap to Window check box to have Word adjust the line length to fit the window and make the text more readable.

Select the Field Codes check box to have field codes rather than results displayed in-text. Select the Bookmarks check box to have bookmark markers appear in-text.

Window Options

Choose whether to have the status bar, horizontal scroll bar, and vertical scroll bar displayed.

In the Style Area width box, enter a measurement other than "0" if you want to display the style area, a pane on the left side of the Word window which displays the style for each paragraph.

In Online Layout view, choose the smallest font size you want to have displayed by setting the font size in the Enlarge Fonts Less Than box.

Non–printing Characters

Choose which characters and items you want to see onscreen: tabs, spaces, paragraph marks, optional hyphens, hidden text, or all of the above.

General Options

The options on the General tab of the Options dialog box (see Figure 17.7) offer a mishmash of choices:

- Background Repagination repaginates your documents in the background as you work. On long documents, this may slow down your computer.

> **NOTE** **Background Repagination isn't available in Page Layout view, which is always up-to-date with its pagination.**

- Help for WordPerfect Users performs equivalent Word commands when you press a WordPerfect key combination. For example, if you type Home Home ↑ with Help for WordPerfect Users on, Word will move to the beginning of the document; if you type Home Home ↑ without Help for WordPerfect Users on, Word will move to the beginning of the line, beep, and then move up one line. When this option is on, **WPH** appears on the status bar.

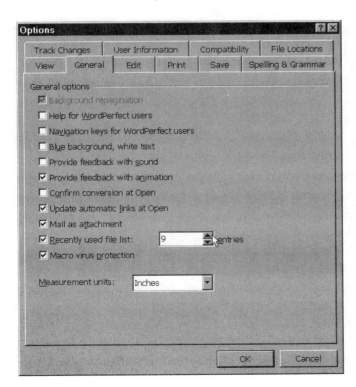

FIGURE 17.7:
The General tab of the Options dialog box

- Navigation Keys for WordPerfect Users makes the PageUp, PageDown, Home, End, and Esc keys behave in Word as they do in WordPerfect. When this option is on, **WPN** appears on the status bar. (If both Help for WordPerfect Users and Navigation Keys for WordPerfect Users are on, **WP** appears on the status bar.)

- Blue Background, White Text displays white text on a blue background, which can be visually restful. If you also choose View ➤ Full Screen, you can pretend you're using WordPerfect 5.1 for DOS.

- Provide Feedback with Sound controls whether Word plays sounds when something goes wrong or when Word completes an action (such as saving a file). If an irregular stream of cutesy sounds annoys you, clear this check box.

- Provide Feedback with Animation animates the mouse cursor when Word is performing an action, and animates Word actions such as closing dialog boxes. This check box is another candidate for clearing.

- Confirm Conversion at Open displays a Convert File dialog box when you open a file in a format other than Word. Select this check box if Word is misconverting your files and you want to try a different conversion.

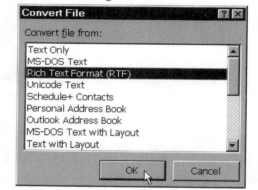

- Update Automatic Links at Open updates any links set for automatic updating in a document when you open that document. (See Chapter 19 for information on linking.)

- Mail as Attachment lets you e-mail a document as an attachment rather than inserting the contents directly into the e-mail message (see Chapter 18).

- Recently Used File List controls the number of latest-used files that appear at the foot of the File menu. Increase or decrease the number in the Entries box to list more or fewer files (from one to nine); clear the check box to have none appear (for example, for security reasons).

- Macro Virus Protection scans documents you open and warns you if they might contain a macro virus. Keep this check box checked, but be prepared for false alarms.

- Measurement Units controls the units in which the rulers, Paragraph dialog box, and so on, display measurement: choose Inches, Centimeters, Points, or Picas.

Edit Options

Because the options on the Edit tab of the Options dialog box (see Figure 17.8) can make a great deal of difference in your daily maneuverings, these options bear further investigation.

Typing Replaces Selection causes Word to overwrite selected text when you start typing. If this disconcerts you, clear the check box and Word will move the insertion point to the beginning of a selection when you start typing.

Drag-and-Drop Text Editing controls whether you can use drag-and-drop. If you don't use drag-and-drop, turning this off may speed up Word a bit.

When Selecting, Automatically Select Entire Word lets you quickly select multiple words. (See *Selecting Text with the Mouse* in Chapter 1 for details.)

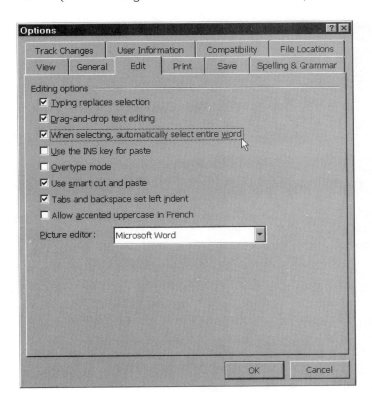

FIGURE 17.8:
Make sure the options on the Edit tab of the Options dialog box are set to suit your preferences.

Use the INS Key for Paste makes the Insert (or Ins, depending on your keyboard) key perform the Paste command. (On most computers, this has nothing to do with the Immigration and Naturalization Service.)

Overtype Mode turns on Overtype mode, discussed in *Insert and Overtype Modes* in Chapter 1.

Use Smart Cut and Paste adds and removes spaces as necessary when you cut, paste, and drag-and-drop text. You'll usually want to keep this check box selected.

Tabs and Backspace Set Left Indent lets you indent and outdent the left margin by pressing Tab and Backspace, respectively.

Allow Accented Uppercase in French does just that.

Print Options

The Print tab of the Options dialog box (see Figure 17.9) lets you select the default tray of paper for the printer and specify whether to print just the data when printing a form. There are also seven Printing Options and five Include with Document options.

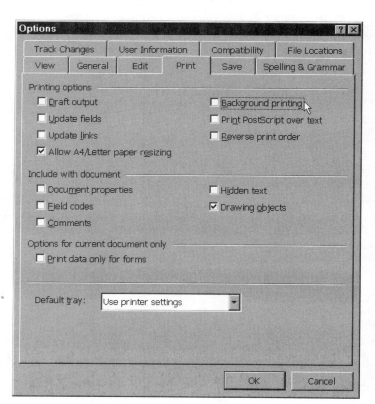

FIGURE 17.9:
Choose how to print your document and what to include with the document on the Print tab of the Options dialog box.

Printing Options

Draft Output lets you print a stripped-down version of your document on some printers. Your mileage may vary.

Update Fields updates all unlocked fields whenever you print.

Update Links updates all unlocked links whenever you print.

Allow A4/Letter Paper Resizing allows Word to resize documents formatted for A4 to print them on letter-size paper (which is proportioned a little differently), and vice versa. Word adjusts the printout, not the formatting of the document. If you work with documents from, say, a European firm, this capability can be a lifesaver.

Background Printing lets you keep working (albeit a bit more slowly) while Word is printing your documents.

Print PostScript over Text is primarily useful if you need to print a document created in Word for the Macintosh containing PostScript code for special printing effects.

Reverse Print Order prints documents from last page to first.

Include with Document

Choose whether to print document properties, field codes, comments, hidden text, and drawing objects (objects created in Word, including lines) when printing your document. Document properties and comments will each print on a separate page at the end of the document; field codes, hidden text, and drawing objects will print where they occur in the document.

WARNING Printing hidden text will alter the layout of your pages. Use Print Preview to check the effect that including hidden text will have before actually printing.

Save Options

The options on the Save tab of the Options dialog box (see Figure 17.10) can help keep your work safe when all around you people are losing their work (and blaming it on you).

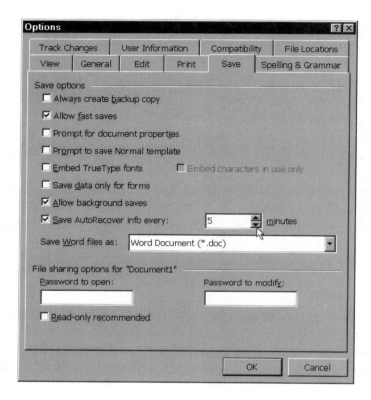

FIGURE 17.10:
Specify how to save your documents on the Save tab of the Options dialog box.

Save Options

Always Create Backup Copy creates a backup copy each time you save a document by renaming the previously saved version of that document to **Backup of *filename*** and giving it the extension .WBK. This is a valuable option—with two caveats: First, it will slow down your save operations a little, though usually not enough to worry about; and second, you need to understand that the backup is *not* the same as the currently saved version of the file—if you destroy the latest saved version, the backup will provide you with the previous version.

TIP

To make the backups of your documents virtually identical to the currently saved copies, always save twice in immediate succession. You could write a macro to do this.

Allow Fast Saves speeds up save operations by saving only the changes to a file, not actually saving the file itself. This option can create bizarre results—if you delete most of a large file (or most of a file containing graphics) and then fast-save it, the file size will still be large; and fast-saved documents will always be somewhat larger than regularly saved documents. Bear this in mind if disk space is at a premium or you're often transferring documents by modem.

> **TIP** You can't choose both Always Create Backup Copy and Allow Fast Saves at the same time—it's one or the other. Allow Fast Saves saves you only a little time unless you have a very slow computer or you're working with huge documents (or both).

Prompt for Document Properties displays the Properties dialog box automatically the first time you save a document. This is useful if you use the document properties information to identify your documents; if you don't, it rapidly proves tedious.

Prompt to Save Normal Template makes Word check with you before it saves changes to Normal.dot, the global template. Select this option if you spend time mucking about with Normal.dot and want to be able to escape any embarrassing changes you make by mistake. Otherwise, leave this check box selected to have Word save changes to Normal.dot automatically.

Embed TrueType Fonts lets you save the fonts used in a document with the document so that the fonts will appear in the document even on a computer that doesn't have those particular fonts installed.

> **WARNING** Using Embed TrueType Fonts can greatly increase the size of document files. Use it only if you're sharing files and need to ensure they look exactly the same on the other computers.

Save Data Only for Forms was discussed in Chapter 16.

Allow Background Saves notionally allows you to keep working while Word saves a file to disk. In my experience, it seems to help neither on fast computers nor slow ones.

Save AutoRecover Info Every *nn* Minutes causes Word to save an automatic backup of documents at a specified interval (from one minute to 120 minutes). You can use these AutoRecover files to recover documents if Word or your computer crashes.

When you exit Word successfully, it deletes any AutoRecover files made in that session. These backups are stored in the AutoRecover Files location specified on the File Locations tab of the Options dialog box (which we'll discuss in *File Locations Options* in a page or two). When you restart Word after a crash, it should open any AutoRecovered files that haven't been deleted and display them to you as **(Recovered)**. Check the files carefully and save them under new names if they're still viable.

File-Sharing Options

These options—for protecting your documents from intrusion, alteration, and damage—are discussed in Chapter 18.

Spelling & Grammar Options

The options on the Spelling & Grammar tab of the Options dialog box—for controlling Word's automatic spell-checking and grammar-checking, working with dictionaries, and so on—are discussed in Chapter 4.

Track Changes Options

Track Changes options let you specify the colors and marks to use with revision marks. See the *Tracking Changes* section in Chapter 18 for a full discussion of these options.

User Information Options

Make sure your name, initials, and mailing address are entered correctly on the User Information tab of the Options dialog box (see Figure 17.11). Among other things, Word uses the name for document properties information, the initials for comments, and the mailing address for envelopes.

Compatibility Options

The options on the Compatibility tab of the Options dialog box (see Figure 17.12) are for fine-tuning the way in which Word converts files created in other word processors or in other versions of Word. We won't go into these options in detail here. Briefly, the Font Substitution button allows you to specify which fonts to use when a document contains fonts that are not installed on your computer. The Recommended Options For drop-down list lets you pick the format in which a file was created, and the

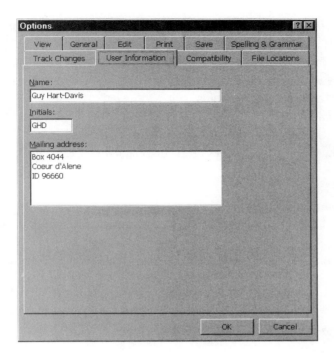

FIGURE 17.11:
Make sure your personal information is correct on the User Information tab of the Options dialog box.

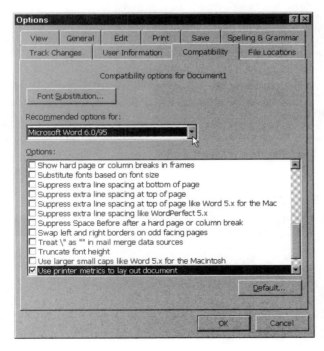

FIGURE 17.12:
The options on the Compatibility tab of the Options dialog box let you specify exactly how to convert documents created in different forms.

Options list box contains options for tweaking the conversion of that file format to Word.

The options on the File Locations tab of the Options dialog box (see Figure 17.13) let you specify where Word should locate documents, clip-art pictures, templates, AutoRecover files, and other files it maintains.

Documents is the category that can save you the most time: If you want Word to suggest saving documents somewhere other than where it's decided is most appropriate (probably the My Documents folder or the Personal folder), change Documents straight away.

To change a file location:

1. Choose the item to change in the File Types list box.
2. Click the Modify button to display the Modify Location dialog box (see Figure 17.14).
3. Choose the folder for the new location by using standard Windows techniques.
4. Click the OK button to close the Modify Location dialog box.

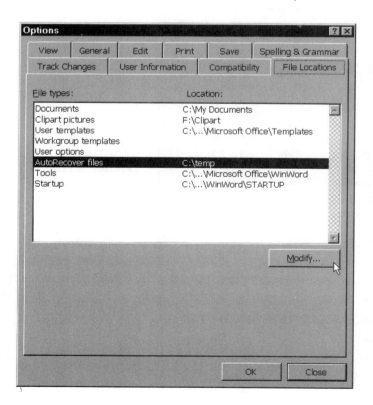

FIGURE 17.13:
Specify where Word should keep its various types of documents on the File Locations tab of the Options dialog box.

FIGURE 17.14:
In the Modify Location dialog box, choose the new location for the item.

Putting Customization to Use

This section discusses how you might design and implement a special-purpose template that focuses a user—or yourself—precisely on their tasks. You could use such a template to improve productivity by putting all the commands (Word's own commands along with custom items you've created) needed for a particular task right where you need them.

Your steps towards creating such a template would include the following:

1. Work out exactly what the user needs to be able to do and which Word commands and features they'll need in order to fulfill their mission.

2. Create a new template. Rather than destroying your Normal global template in the process, create a new template for this purpose. You could even use an AutoExec macro (described in Chapter 15) to start a new document based on your template whenever Word is run; this could help prevent a user from inadvertently starting their work in the wrong template.

3. Customize the menu bar and the toolbars to provide the most functionality with the least loss of screen real estate. You could remove from the menu bar all the menus that aren't necessary and replace them with more rewarding menus or buttons. For some purposes, you may be able to reduce all the actions to one menu or toolbar to make things simple for the user.

4. Write special-purpose macros for operations you know the user will need to perform for this type of document.

5. Customize keyboard shortcuts for the commands and macros needed most in this template so that the user can work without removing their hands from the keyboard if they want.

This procedure will take some time and effort, but it yields very worthwhile results.

Chapter 18

WORKGROUP FEATURES

FEATURING

- **Working with footnotes and endnotes**
- **Using comments**
- **Working with change marks**
- **Working with versions**
- **Locking and protecting documents**
- **Mailing documents around the office**

This is the Age of the Network, so Word provides a minor host of features to make workgroup computing faster and easier. You can use footnotes and end-notes either in the academic fashion or for conveying editorial comments while creating documents, while comments let you speak directly to others who are working on a document (literally so if you use sound comments). Change marks help track who made which change to a document (and when); and when change marks aren't enough, you can lock your documents to protect them from your co-workers. Word's built-in mail features make it easier to propagate your documents among those who need them.

Footnotes and Endnotes

Footnotes are notes placed at the foot of the page that refers to them. Endnotes are notes placed at the end of a document, as with magazine articles that cite references. Like heading numbering, footnotes and endnotes bring out some of the best features for automating documents.

Word automates the numbering of footnotes and endnotes (maintaining separate numbering for each), adjusts pages so that footnotes fit, and can even manage *Continued...* notices for footnotes that need to run to the next page. If your document has sections, you can choose to place the endnotes for any given section either at the end of the section or at the end of the document.

Inserting a Footnote or Endnote

To insert a footnote or endnote:

1. Choose Insert ➤ Footnote. Word will display the Footnote and Endnote dialog box (see Figure 18.1).

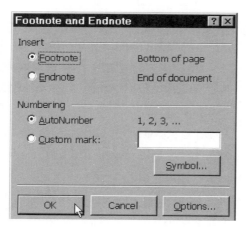

FIGURE 18.1:
To insert a footnote, choose Insert ➤ Footnote and select Footnote in the Footnote and Endnote dialog box.

2. To insert a footnote, choose Footnote in the Insert area; to insert an endnote, choose Endnote.

3. To choose footnote or endnote options, click the Options button. Word will display the Note Options dialog box (see Figure 18.2) with either the All Footnotes tab or the All Endnotes tab displayed, as appropriate. Choose options as follows:

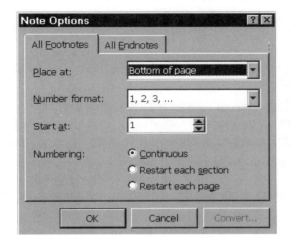

FIGURE 18.2:
Choose options for footnotes and endnotes in the Note Options dialog box.

- In the Place At drop-down list, choose whether to place footnotes at the bottom of the page or beneath the text on the page (i.e., higher than the bottom of the page if the text is short), and endnotes at the end of the document or the end of the section.
- In the Number Format drop-down list, choose an appropriate number format for your footnotes.
- In the Start At box, choose the number with which to start numbering the footnotes or endnotes.

TIP

When you're building a long work out of subdocuments, you may want to number footnotes or endnotes consecutively throughout the whole work. To do so, enter the appropriate number in the Start At box for the notes in each successive document.

- In the Numbering area, choose whether the note numbering should be continuous, if it should restart at each section, or if (for footnotes only) it should restart on each page.
- Click the OK button when you've chosen the note options.

4. If you want your footnote or endnote to be numbered with special symbols of your choosing, select Custom Mark in the Numbering box and click the Symbol button. In the Symbol dialog box, choose the symbol you want to use (use the Font drop-down list to see symbols from other character sets) and click OK. If you're using AutoNumber and it's showing an inappropriate format, go back to step 3 and change the numbering scheme in the Options dialog box.

5. Click OK to insert the footnote or endnote in your document.
   - If you're in Normal view, Word will display a Footnote pane or Endnote pane at the bottom of your screen.
   - If you're in Page Layout view, Word will move the insertion point to the bottom of the page (for footnotes) or the end of the section or document (for endnotes).

6. Type the text of the footnote or endnote after the reference mark that Word inserts.

7. Return to your document by choosing Close (from the Footnotes or Endnotes pane) or by clicking in the main document text or by pressing Shift+F5.

When you insert further footnotes or endnotes, Word will synchronize their numbering with the existing footnotes or endnotes.

Changing Footnote and Endnote Separators

By default, Word inserts a fine separator line across part of the page between the body text and footnotes and between the body text and endnotes:

---

are many things to consider now that we've put our faith in science and progress, and God

---

[1] *From Hydrogen to Helium: the Only One*, Theodoraki, Wittgenstein, *et al*, Broderbund, 1955, 188pp.

To change this line, choose View ➤ Footnotes in Normal view to display the Footnotes pane, then choose Footnote Separator from the drop-down list. The line then appears as a paragraph that you can select and delete (or edit). You can also add pictures using Insert ➤ Picture, or you can change to Page Layout view and add drawings by using the Drawing toolbar. Click the Close button to close the Footnotes pane when you're satisfied with the result.

Adding Continued Notices to Footnotes

To add *Continued...* notices to footnotes, choose View ➤ Footnotes in Normal view and choose Footnote Continuation Notice from the drop-down list on the Footnotes pane. Enter the text for the footnote continuation notice and format it using normal formatting techniques. Click the Close button to close the Footnotes pane and return to your document; Word will then display your *Continued...* message whenever a footnote runs over to the next page.

---

through stupidity and ignorance, and yet the one thing to be sure of is that we cannot doubt the courage of the Albigensians[2], who persisted in their Manichean beliefs despite

---

[1] *From Hydrogen to Helium: the Only One*, Theodoraki, Wittgenstein, *et al*, Broderbund, 1955, 188pp.
[2] For a comprehensive discussion of the Albigensian heresy and its development from Cathar roots (and its divergence from standard Catharistic doctrine over the centuries), see Peter del Torres' excellent book,
Continued on the next page

TIP You can also edit the separator between footnotes and *Continued...* notices by choosing Footnote Continuation Separator from the drop-down list on the Footnotes pane—for example, you might want to use a line as a separator.

Moving and Copying Footnotes and Endnotes

You can quickly move a footnote or endnote by selecting its reference mark within the text and using Cut and Paste or drag-and-drop to move the reference mark to a different location. If need be, Word will renumber that footnote or endnote and all affected footnotes or endnotes.

To copy a footnote or endnote, select its reference mark within the text and use Copy and Paste (or Ctrl+drag-and-drop) to copy it to another location. Again, Word will renumber the copied footnote or endnote and all affected footnotes or endnotes accordingly.

Deleting a Footnote or Endnote

To delete a footnote or endnote, simply select its reference mark within the text and press Delete (or right-click and choose Cut from the context menu). Word will renumber all subsequent footnotes or endnotes accordingly.

Viewing Footnotes or Endnotes

To view a footnote or endnote in a document, move the mouse pointer over the reference mark for that footnote or endnote. Word will display the text of the footnote or endnote in a pop-up box, as shown here; it will not display any graphical elements in the footnote.

From Hydrogen to Helium: the Only One, Theodoraki, Wittgenstein, et al, Broderbund, 1955, 188pp.

Theodoraki's excellent book

To work with footnotes or endnotes in Normal view, choose View ➤ Footnotes. Word will display the Footnotes pane by default. To switch to endnotes, select All Endnotes from the drop-down list.

When you choose View ➤ Footnotes in Page Layout view in a document that has both footnotes and endnotes, Word will display the View Footnotes dialog box so you can select which ones you want to view.

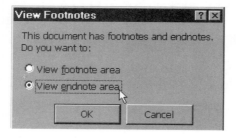

Choose View Footnote Area or View Endnote Area and click the OK button. Word will display the area you chose.

Converting Footnotes to Endnotes (and Vice Versa)

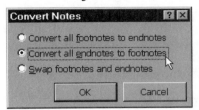

You can convert footnotes to endnotes (or vice versa) by choosing Insert ➤ Footnote to display the Footnote and Endnote dialog box, clicking the Options button to display the Note Options dialog box, and clicking the Convert button. In the Convert Notes dialog box (shown below), choose Convert All Footnotes to Endnotes, Convert All Endnotes to Footnotes, or Swap Footnotes and Endnotes; then click the OK button.

Word will perform the conversion you specified. If you convert footnotes to endnotes, or endnotes to footnotes, Word will renumber the resulting notes so they're in sync with the existing notes.

Click the OK button in the Note Options dialog box, then click the Close button in the Footnote and Endnote dialog box.

Comments

Similar to footnotes and endnotes are Word's comments, which can be most useful for making notes to yourself and your colleagues when creating a complex document. Word automatically marks each comment with the identity of the current user (as drawn from the User Information tab of the Options dialog box), so you can easily track who made which suggestions. When you move the mouse pointer over text that has a comment attached to it, Word highlights the word and—if you keep the mouse pointer there for a second—displays the text of the comment.

> **TIP**
>
> You can lock documents so that users who don't know the password can add comments but cannot change the text of the document itself. We'll look at locking and protecting documents later in this chapter.

Word's tools for working with comments are grouped on the Reviewing toolbar (see Figure 18.3), which you can display at any time by right-clicking the menu bar or any displayed toolbar and choosing Reviewing from the context menu of toolbars.

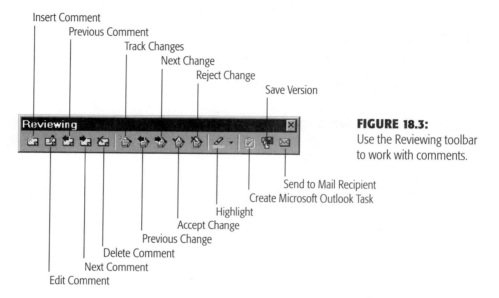

FIGURE 18.3:
Use the Reviewing toolbar to work with comments.

Inserting a Comment

To insert a comment at the insertion point:

1. Click the Insert Comment button on the Reviewing toolbar or choose Insert ➤ Comment. The current user's initials and a comment number will be inserted as hidden text in the document; Word will temporarily display this hidden text and will highlight the current word and the initials and comment number. Word will also open the Comments pane, again inserting the user's initials and a comment number.

2. Type the comment in the Comment pane.

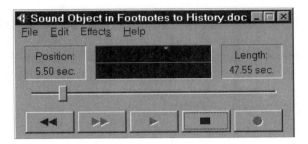 • To insert an audio comment, click the Insert Sound Object button on the Comments pane. Word will display your currently configured sound recorder. Record the comment (by clicking the Record button of the sound recorder) and close the sound recorder; Word will display a loudspeaker icon for the comment in the Comments pane.

3. Click the Close button to close the pane and return to the body text of your document. Word will faintly highlight the word to which the comment is attached.

Viewing Comments

You can review the comments in a document in several ways:

- To view a comment on-the-fly, move the mouse pointer over a faintly highlighted word. Word will intensify the highlighting and will display a screen tip with the text of the comment, as shown here. (For an audio comment, you'll see only the name of the commentator.) To edit the comment, right-click and choose Edit Comment from the context menu; Word will open the Comments pane. To delete the comment, right-click and choose Delete Comment from the context menu.

- Alternatively, click the Next Comment or Previous Comment button to move to the next comment or previous comment. Keep the mouse pointer over the Next Comment or Previous Comment button and Word will display the full highlight and the screen tip for the comment. Click the Edit Comment button to edit the comment in the Comments pane, or the Delete Comment button to delete the comment.

- Once you start reviewing comments, Word will set the Object Browser to browse by comments and will replace the Next Page and Previous Page buttons below the vertical scroll bar with Next Comment and Previous Comment buttons. Click these buttons to move from comment to comment in the document. To reset the Object Browser to browse by page, click the Select Browse Object button (the button between the Next and Previous buttons) and choose Browse by Page from the pop-up panel, as shown here. (You can also manually set the Object Browser to browse by comments by clicking the Select Browse Object button and choosing Browse by Comment from the pop-up panel.)

- To view comments in the comments pane, click the Edit Comment button or choose View ➤ Comments. Word will display the Comments pane at the bottom of the screen. Scroll through the comments using the scroll bar, or click a comment in the Comments pane to move the highlight in the main document window to the comment mark.

> **TIP** If you have hidden text displayed in your document, you can double-click in a comment marker to display the Comments pane.

To play a sound comment, double-click its icon in the Comments pane, or right-click the icon and choose Play from the Wave Sound Object submenu of the context menu.

By default, you'll see all the comments in the document displayed in the Comments pane in the order in which they appear in the text. To see only the comments entered by one author, choose the author's name from the Comments From drop-down list.

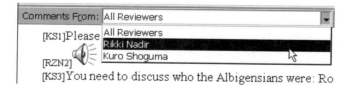

Reviewing Comments

To review comments, display them by choosing View ➤ Comments. You can then edit and delete comments, move them by dragging the comment marks about the document, and copy and paste (or drag and drop) comment text into the main document.

You can also either print just the comments from a document (by choosing File ➤ Print and choosing Comments in the Print What drop-down list in the Print dialog box) or print the comments along with the document (by choosing Tools ➤ Options to display the Options dialog box and selecting the Comments check box in the Include with Document area on the Print tab).

Editing and Deleting Comments

You can edit the comments in the comments pane using regular editing methods, but you can't delete an entire comment.

To delete a comment, display hidden text if it isn't already displayed, select its reference number in the text (*not* in the Comments pane) and press Delete. Alternatively, right-click in the reference number within the text and choose Cut from the context menu.

Track Changes

Word's Track Changes feature—known as *revision marking* in previous versions of Word—lets you track both the edits (additions and deletions) a team of users makes in a document and which user made which edits. You can then review the edits one by one and either accept or reject them with due consideration, or you can go ahead and blithely accept (or reject) all the edits in one fell swoop.

By default, Word marks additions with a single underline and deletions with a strikethough, but you can customize these settings to make them easier to distinguish from your regular text. Each user gets (by default) a different color of change mark, so you can quickly identify which user made which marks visually; again, this is customizable.

WARNING Track Changes tracks only where text is either added to or deleted from a document, and where attributes such as bold or italic are applied to or removed from the text—it doesn't track changes in style for whole paragraphs or changes in capitalization using Format ➤ Change Case.

You can turn Track Changes on and off at will. You can also turn the display of change marks on screen on and off while change marking is on. This can be helpful for seeing the text that remains during heavy editing.

TIP You can protect a document so that other users have to use change marks when they make changes to it. We'll look at protecting documents later in this chapter.

Turning Track Changes On and Off

To turn Track Changes on and off, either click the Track Changes button on the Reviewing toolbar or double-click the TRK indicator on the status bar. Alternatively, right-click the TRK indicator on the status bar and choose Highlight Changes, or choose Tools ➤ Track Changes ➤ Highlight Changes, and select the Track Changes While Editing check box in the Highlight Changes dialog box.

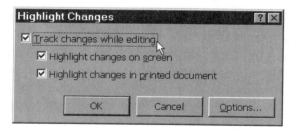

Choosing Track Changes Options

To choose different options for Track Changes:

1. Choose Tools ➤ Options to display the Options dialog box, then click the Track Changes tab (see Figure 18.4).

- You can also move quickly to the Track Changes dialog box (which contains the Track Changes tab from the Options dialog box) either by clicking the Options button in the Highlight Changes dialog box or by right-clicking the TRK indicator on the status bar and choosing Options from the context menu.

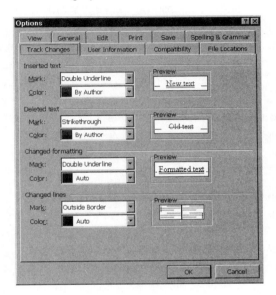

FIGURE 18.4:
Choose options for change marks on the Track Changes tab of the Options dialog box or in the Track Changes dialog box. Use the Preview boxes to see the effect your changes will have.

2. In the Inserted Text area, choose a means of marking new text and a color for that text: From the Mark drop-down list, choose None, Bold, Italic, Underline, or Double Underline, and from the Color drop-down list, choose By Author, Auto (which matches the default font color), or one of the sixteen text colors Word offers.
    - By Author assigns different colors to the first eight authors who use change marks on a document (for the ninth and subsequent authors, Word recycles the colors, starting from the top). Word identifies authors by the contents of the Name box on the User Information tab of the Options dialog box, so if you change your Name setting (from, say, **Joseph Takagi** to **Joseph Y. Takagi**), Word will mark subsequent changes in a different color.

TIP

By Author is the most convenient setting for tracking changes made by different authors, but you may sometimes want changes by two or more authors to appear in the same color—for example, if they are members of the same team or fulfilling the same role. In that case, choose an appropriate color manually.

3. In the Deleted Text area, choose how to mark deleted text (with Strikethrough or Hidden formatting or a caret [^] or pound sign [#]) and a color for that text (again, By Author, Auto, or a color of your choice).

4. In the Changed Formatting area, choose a means of marking text whose formatting has changed and a color for the marking. Word will then mark changes such as the application or removal of bold and italic.

5. In the Changed Lines area, choose a position for the vertical bars Word puts in the margin next to lines containing changes (None, Left Border, Right Border, Outside Border) and a color for them (Auto or your choice of color).

6. Click the OK button to close the Options dialog box or Track Changes dialog box. (If you opened the Track Changes dialog box by clicking the Options button in the Highlight Changes dialog, Word will return you to the Highlight Changes dialog box.)

Displaying Change Marks

Once you've turned Track Changes on, you can turn the display of change marks onscreen on and off by selecting and clearing the Highlight Changes on Screen check box in the Highlight Changes dialog box. Turning off the display of change marks onscreen can make heavily edited documents much easier to read and can make minor errors, such as extra spaces or missing spaces resulting from cutting and pasting, easier to find. It can, however, make it hard to tell that you're still using change marks for the edits you're making.

You can also turn the display of change marks in your printed documents on and off from the Highlight Changes dialog box: Simply select or clear the Highlight Changes in Printed Document check box. This way, you can print out drafts without showing all the editing going on in the background.

Reviewing Changes

Once you've had someone else—or half the office—go through your prized document and make their edits, you can quickly review the changes. If you've chosen to have change marks color-coded by user, you'll easily be able to see the different changes.

To review individual changes, move the mouse pointer over a changed word. Word will display a screen tip showing who made the change and the nature of the change they made: Inserted for added text, Deleted for deleted text, and Property Change for a change to an attribute such as boldface or italic.

> **Rikki Nadir, 11/28/96 1:59 PM:**
> Deleted

| painfully ~~overwhelming~~ <u>amounts of</u> evidence to

To accept or reject a change, click in it and click the Accept Change button or Reject Change button on the Reviewing toolbar. Alternatively, right-click in the change and choose Accept Change or Reject Change from the context menu.

To review a number of changes and either accept or reject them:

1. Right-click the TRK indicator in the status bar and choose Accept or Reject Changes from the context menu to display the Accept or Reject Changes dialog box.

2. If necessary, adjust the setting in the View group box:
   - Changes with Highlighting shows the changes in the document marked with change marks.
   - Changes without Highlighting shows the document without change marks (i.e., as if all the changes had been accepted).
   - Original displays the document without the changes (i.e., as if all the changes had been rejected).

3. Click the ← Find button or the Find → button to find either the previous or the next change in the document. Word will indicate the type of change (Deleted, Inserted, Property Change) in the Changes box (see Figure 18.5).

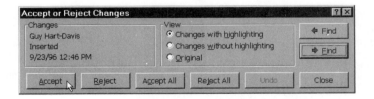

FIGURE 18.5:
Use the Accept or Reject Changes dialog box to review multiple changes.

4. Click the Accept button to accept the change or the Reject button to reject it.
5. Use the Find buttons to review the rest of the changes.
6. Click the Close button to close the Accept or Reject Changes dialog box.

TIP To accept or reject all changes in the document quickly, right-click the TRK indicator, choose Accept or Reject Changes, and click the Accept All button or the Reject All button in the Accept or Reject Changes dialog box. Word will display a confirmation message box; choose Yes. Then click the Close button to exit the Accept or Reject Changes dialog box.

Merging Revisions

You can also route multiple copies of your document around the office and have a number of people review it at the same time. When you get back several copies of the document with different people's revisions, you can merge the changes into your original document so that you can deal with them all at once.

To merge revisions:

1. Open the document containing the changes.
   - If you have several documents containing changes, open them all and activate one of them by clicking in it.
2. Choose Tools ➤ Track Changes ➤ Compare Documents to display the Select File to Compare with Current Document dialog box (see Figure 18.6).

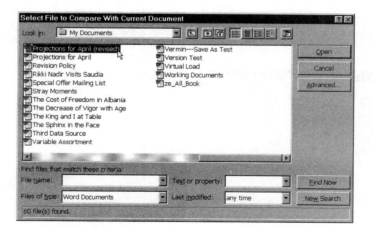

FIGURE 18.6:
Select the original document in the Select File to Compare with Current Document dialog box and click the Open button.

3. Select the original document and choose Open. Word will open the original document and merge the changes from the active document into the original.

4.   To merge revisions from other open documents, save and close the original version and then repeat steps 2 and 3.

Versions

Word's versioning features let you save multiple versions of a document within the same file. Instead of containing only the information in the document from when it was last saved, the file contains snapshots from whenever a version was saved. For example, if several people review a document of yours, each can save a version of the document when they're finished. When the document returns to you, you can review each version of the document and revert to an earlier version than the last if you want—which can prove handy if one of your colleagues has made ill-advised changes that could otherwise have ruined the document.

Saving Multiple Versions of a File

To save a version of a file:

1.   Choose File ➤ Versions. Word will display the Versions dialog box (see Figure 18.7).

2.   Click the Save Now button. Word will display the Save Version dialog box (see Figure 18.8).

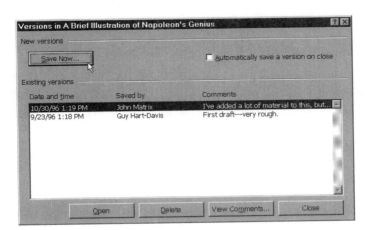

FIGURE 18.7:
To save a version, click the Save Now button in the Versions dialog box.

3.   Enter any comments about this version in the Comments on Version text box, then click the OK button.

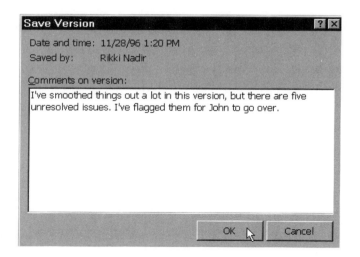

FIGURE 18.8:
Enter any comments on the version in the Save Version dialog box.

Saving Versions Automatically

If you need to keep a record of changes to the documents your company creates, you can try saving a version of the file automatically each time anyone closes it. This can help you track who has opened a file (even if they make no changes).

To have Word automatically save a version of the file whenever it is closed, choose File ➤ Versions and select the Automatically Save a Version on Close check box. Word will now automatically save a version of the file and will add the comment *Automatic version* to it.

Saving a Version as a Separate File

No matter how happy you are with Word's versioning features, when a document is complete and ready for delivery, you'll probably want to save a fresh copy of it so that it does not contain all the versions that have gone before. To do this, choose the version in the Existing Versions list box and click the Open button, then use File ➤ Save As to save the file under another name.

To delete a version, select it in the Existing Versions list box in the Versions dialog box and click the Delete button. (To delete multiple versions, use Shift+click or Ctrl+click to select them.)

Opening a Version

To open a version of the document, select it in the Existing Versions list box and click the Open button. Word will open it in a separate window. You can revert to this version of the document by closing all other versions of the document that you have open and using File ➤ Save As to save the document with the original name of the file (thus overwriting the other file that contains the versions).

Locking and Protecting Documents

By using Word's document locking and protection features, you can safely share your documents with fair protection against the documents being trashed.

Word offers four types of protection:

- You can save a document as *read-only recommended*. Whenever someone opens the file, Word displays a message box recommending that they open it as a read-only file, which means that they cannot save changes to the original. The user can choose to bypass this, however, so it isn't effective protection.
- You can password-protect a document so others can open it but can either only make changes using revisions marks or only insert comments unless they unprotect it by entering the correct password.
- You can password-protect a document so others can open it but cannot save changes to the original without entering the correct password.
- You can password-protect a document so nobody can open it without entering the correct password.

Saving Files as Read-Only Recommended

To save the open file as read-only recommended, choose File ➤ Save As and click the Options button in the Save As dialog box to display the Save dialog box, which you'll recognize as the torn-off Save tab from the Options dialog box. In the File Sharing Options area, select the Read-Only Recommended check box, then click the OK button. Word will return you to the Save As dialog box; choose Save.

Whenever anyone opens the document, Word will display a message box recommending that they open it as a read-only file.

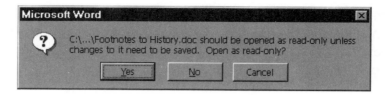

The user can choose Yes to open the document as a read-only file, No to open the document with full privileges, or Cancel to not open the document.

NOTE When you open a document as a read-only file, Word displays (Read-Only) after the document's title in the title bar.

To remove the read-only recommendation, open the document (not as read-only) and clear the Read-Only Recommended check box on the Save tab of the Options dialog box and save the file again.

Password-Protecting Files

As you can see, a read-only recommendation has no teeth—it's a suggestion that the user can instantly ignore. For files that you value more, you'll need to use password protection.

Word's passwords can be up to 15 characters long (letters, numbers, or keyboard symbols, even spaces) and are case sensitive—**02binSF** is different from **02BinSF**, and so on.

Protecting Documents for Tracked Changes and Comments

To protect the open document so that users can only make changes using change marks or only add comments:

1. Choose Tools ➤ Protect Document to display the Protect Document dialog box (see Figure 18.9).
2. In the Protect Document For area, choose whether to protect the document for tracked changes, comments, or forms.
3. Enter a password in the Password text box.

FIGURE 18.9:
In the Protect Document dialog box, choose whether to protect the document for tracked changes, comments, or forms, then enter a password.

4. Click the OK button. Word will display a Confirm Password dialog box, as shown here.

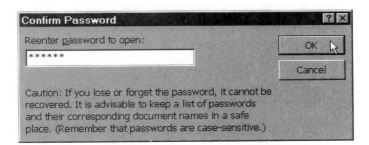

5. Enter the password again, then click the OK button. If you enter the same password, Word will close the Confirm Password dialog box and protect the document; if you get it wrong, Word will return you to the Protect Document dialog box for another try.

6. Save the document to set the protection.

When a user opens the protected document, Word will allow them only to make changes using change marks or only to insert comments (depending on which you chose).

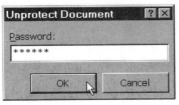

To remove the protection, choose Tools ➤Unprotect Document and enter the password in the Unprotect Document dialog box, as shown here.

If you get the password right, Word will unprotect the document; if you get it wrong, Word will display a message box to that effect.

Protecting Documents with Password to Modify

The next level of protection is *password to modify,* which means the user can only write changes to a file if they supply the correct password when opening the file. If they can't supply the password, they can open the file as read-only but cannot save changes under the document's original name.

To protect the file using password to modify:

1. Choose File ➤ Save As and click the Options button in the Save As dialog box to display the Save dialog box.
2. Enter a password in the Password to Modify text box.

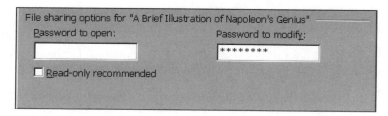

3. Click OK. Word will display the Confirm Password dialog box.
4. Enter the password again (to make sure you didn't misspell it the first time) and click OK. If you get the password right, Word will set the password and return you to the Save As dialog box.
5. Click the Save button to save the document. The password-to-modify protection will take effect when you close the document.

The next time the document is opened, the user will have to enter the password in the Password dialog box to open the file with write access.

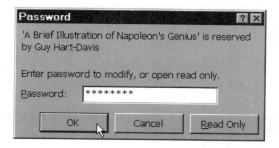

Alternatively, the user can choose the Read Only option to open the document as a read-only file.

TIP

To remove (or change) a password-to-modify, open the file (using the password), then choose Tools ➤ Options to display the Options dialog box. Click the Save tab to bring it to the front. Delete (or change) the password to modify and click the OK button. Save the file to store the change.

Preventing Others from Opening Word Documents

You can also prevent others from opening your Word documents unless they enter the correct password.

To password-protect a document:

1. Choose File ➤ Save As and click the Options button in the Save As dialog box to display the Save dialog box.
2. Enter a password in the Password to Open box.
3. Click the OK button. Word will display the Confirm Password dialog box.

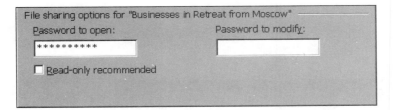

4. Enter the password again and click OK. If you get the password right, Word will set up the password and return you to the Save As dialog box.
5. Click the Save button to save the document. The password protection will take effect when you close the document.

The next time the document is opened, the user will have to enter the password in the Password dialog box to open the file at all.

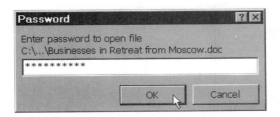

WARNING If you forget a password to open, you will never be able to reopen the document.

To remove a password from a document, open the document (by providing the password), choose Tools ➤ Options to display the Options dialog box, and click the Save tab. Delete the password to open and then save the file.

Sending Word Documents via E-Mail

With Word and the Microsoft Exchange features built into Windows 95 and Windows NT 4, you no longer need to have a Microsoft Mail network available to be able to send Word documents via e-mail.

To send a document via e-mail:

1. Start Word and open the document.
2. Choose File ➤ Send To ➤ Routing Recipient to display the Routing Slip dialog box (see Figure 18.10).

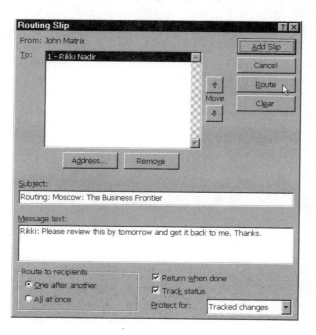

FIGURE 18.10:
Choose recipients for the open document, specify a subject, enter message text, and decide how to route the message in the Routing Slip dialog box.

3. Choose the recipients. Click the Address button to display the Address Book dialog box (see Figure 18.11).

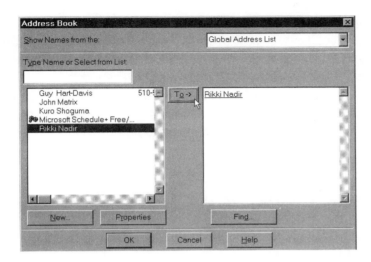

FIGURE 18.11:
Add recipients for the document in the Address Book dialog box.

4. Select the names of the recipients and click the To button to add them to the list.
  • You can Shift-click to select a range of recipients or Ctrl-click to select a group of recipients one by one.
  • If need be, choose another address book from the Show Names drop-down list.

5. Click the OK button when you've finished selecting your recipients. Word will return you to the Routing Slip dialog box.

6. Check the Subject line that Word has automatically entered from the Title of the file set in File ➤ Properties. Change this line if necessary.

7. Enter any message text in the Message Text box.

8. Choose how messages should be routed to recipients: One After Another, or All at Once.
  • If you choose One After Another, Word will send out only one copy of the document, and it will be passed on from one recipient to the next (we'll look at how the recipients pass the document on in a moment). Each will see their predecessor's comments, so you may want to arrange the To list carefully. (Highlight a name and use the Move buttons to move up or down the To list.)

9. Choose from among the options in the lower-right corner of the Routing Slip dialog box:

- Leave Return When Done selected if you want the document to come back to you after its routing experience.
- Check the Track Status box if you want to have an e-mail message sent to you each time one of the recipients in a One After Another routing sends the message on to the next recipient.
- Choose how to protect the document in the Protect For drop-down list: (none), Tracked Changes, Comments, or Forms.

10. To route the document now, click the Route button.

- To save your recipient list, subject, and message before routing the document so you can return to it to do more work, choose Add Slip. You can then choose File ➤ Send To ➤ Next Routing Recipient to send the document on its way. Word will display the Send dialog box, in which you can choose whether to send the document with or without the routing slip. Click the OK button when you've made your choice.

Receiving a Mailed Document

Here's what to do when you receive a mailed document:

1. Open the document in Word. If you're using Microsoft Outlook as your e-mail package, you can do so by simply double-clicking the document icon in the message, as shown in Figure 18.12.

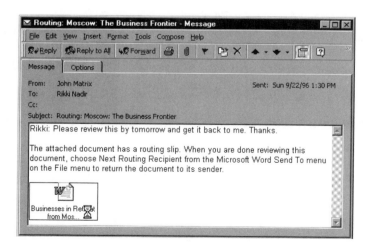

FIGURE 18.12:
Opening a mailed document from Outlook.

2. Review and revise the document as appropriate:
   - If the document is protected for tracked changes, the change marks will appear automatically whenever you alter the document.
   - If the document is protected for comments, you will only be able to insert comments.

3. When you're finished, choose File ➤ Send To ➤ Next Routing Recipient to send the document either on to the next recipient or back to the sender (depending on what the originator chose on the routing slip). Word will display the Send dialog box showing you where the document is headed and telling you that it contains a routing slip, as shown here. Click the OK button to send the document on its way.

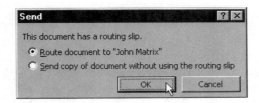

Chapter 19

OLE AND OFFICE BINDERS

- **Linking objects to your documents**
- **Embedding objects in your documents**
- **Creating Office binders**
- **Working with Office binders**

As we've seen so far in this book, Word's many features give you all types of text from regular text to complex tables. But sooner or later, you'll find yourself needing to include in your Word documents information created in other applications—part of a spreadsheet created in Excel, perhaps, or a couple of slides from a PowerPoint presentation. Beyond that, however, you may find you need to group several Word documents, together with that spreadsheet and presentation, to form a complex document.

In Chapter 1, we looked quickly at how you can insert pictures created in other applications into your documents. In this chapter, we'll look at how you can use Object Linking and Embedding (OLE) to enhance your Word documents. When that falls short of your needs, you can use Office binders, which we'll also examine in this chapter, to pull disparate elements together into a super-document.

Object Linking and Embedding

Object Linking and Embedding gives you two ways to include information from other applications in Word documents. By *linking* information from another application to a Word document, you can have the information automatically updated whenever you open or print the document (or, indeed, any time you choose to update the information manually). By *embedding* information from another application in a Word document, you can make that information part of the document, so you can change that information even when you don't have access to the original data source—for example, you can include data from an Excel spreadsheet in a Word document, transfer the document to your laptop, and then hit the road.

> **NOTE** *Object* is one of those great computer terms whose meaning people can never quite agree on. For the moment, think of an object as being a chunk of information (data) that knows which application it was created in—for example, a group of spreadsheet cells that knows it was created in Excel.

Linking

Linking connects information from another application to a Word document. The information appears in the Word document but stays connected to its source in the other application, so that if you change the information in the source, you can have Word automatically update the information in the document as well. For example, by linking the sales figures in an Excel spreadsheet to a Word document, you can make sure the Word document always has the latest sales figures in it.

> **TIP** Word includes linked information as a field. Fields are discussed in detail in Chapter 14.

To link information from another application to a Word document:
1. Start the source application for the object you want to link to a Word document.
2. Open the file containing the object.

3. Select the object to insert. For example, if you're inserting a group of cells from a spreadsheet, select those cells.

4. Choose Edit ➤ Copy (or click the copy button in that application) or press (Ctrl+C) to copy the object to the Clipboard.

5. Start Word if it isn't already running, or switch back to Word by clicking the Microsoft Word icon on the Taskbar or by pressing Alt+Tab until the Word icon has been selected in the task-switching list.

6. Position the insertion point where you want the linked item to appear.

7. Choose Edit ➤ Paste Special to display the Paste Special dialog box (see Figure 19.1).

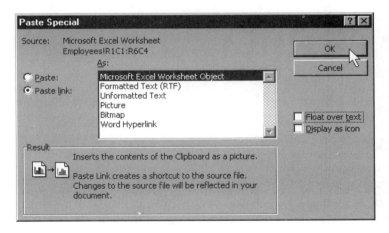

FIGURE 19.1:
To link information, select the Paste Link option in the Paste Special dialog box and choose the option from the As list box that describes the item as "Object"— here it's Microsoft Excel Worksheet Object.

8. Select the Paste Link option on the left side of the dialog box.

9. In the As list box, choose the option that describes the item you're linking as "Object." (Here it's Microsoft Excel Worksheet Object because Excel is the source application; with other source applications, you'll see different descriptions.)

10. To have the item float over the text, make sure the Float over Text check box is selected. To have the item appear in line, make sure the Float over Text check box is cleared.

11. To have the item display as an icon rather than at its full size, select the Display as Icon check box. To change the icon, click the Change Icon button and select a different icon in the Change Icon dialog box; then click OK. (The Change Icon button appears when you select the Display as Icon check box.)

12. Click the OK button to insert the object in your document (see Figure 19.2).

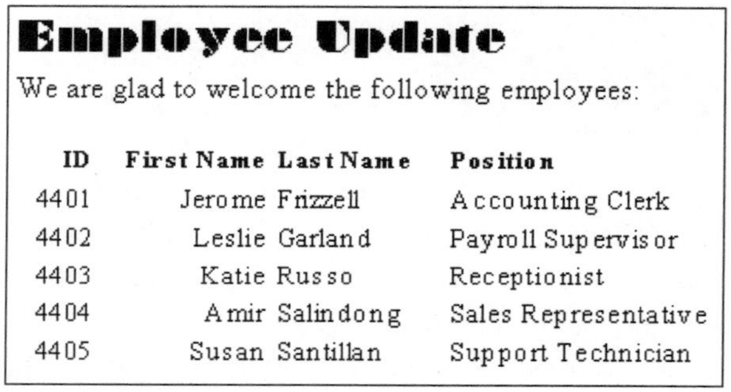

Employee Update

We are glad to welcome the following employees:

ID	First Name	Last Name	Position
4401	Jerome	Frizzell	Accounting Clerk
4402	Leslie	Garland	Payroll Supervisor
4403	Katie	Russo	Receptionist
4404	Amir	Salindong	Sales Representative
4405	Susan	Santillan	Support Technician

FIGURE 19.2:
The cells from the Excel spreadsheet inserted in the document.

You can now format the linked object, for example, by adding borders and shading (discussed in Chapter 2) or by placing it in a text box (discussed in Chapter 1).

TIP To open the source file for the linked object in the application that created it, double-click the linked object (or the icon for it) in your document.

Updating Links

You can update links either manually or automatically so that a link is updated every time you open the document that contains it or every time the source file is updated (when the document containing the link is open). You can also lock a link so that it cannot be updated.

To set updating for links:

1. Open the document containing the links in Word.

2. Choose Edit ➤ Links to display the Links dialog box (see Figure 19.3).

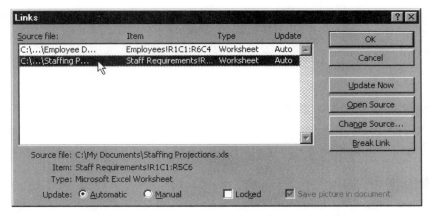

FIGURE 19.3: Choose how to update your links in the Links dialog box.

3. In the Source File list box, select the link or links on which to work. (Use Shift+click to select several adjacent links or Ctrl+click to select nonadjacent links.)

4. Choose how the link or links should be updated by selecting the Automatic option button or the Manual option button.
   - To update a link or links manually, click the Update Now button.
   - To lock the link or links, click the Locked check box. Word will then dim the Automatic option button and the Manual option button to indicate that the choices are not available. To unlock a link, select it in the list box and clear the Locked check box.

5. Click the OK button to close the Links dialog box.

Breaking Links

If you no longer need to be able to update a link, or if you're planning to share a document with someone who won't have the linked information available, you can break the link. Essentially, breaking the link turns the linked information into embedded information.

To break a link:

1. Choose Edit ➤ Links to display the Links dialog box.
2. Select the link or links in the list box.
3. Click the Break Link button. Word will display a message box to make sure that you want to break the link.
4. Click the Yes button to break the link.
5. Click OK to close the Links dialog box.

WARNING Once you've broken a link, you cannot restore it (except by reinserting the linked information, thus creating the link again).

Deleting Linked Objects

To delete a linked object, click it to select it, then press the Delete key or choose Edit ➤ Clear.

Embedding

To embed an object in a document, you follow a procedure similar to the one used for linking, but the result is completely different: Instead of creating a connection from the object in the document to its source file in the application that created it, Word saves all the information needed to edit the object in the Word document. Because the object is not connected to the file that it comes from, you cannot update the object in the Word document; but you can edit the object in the Word document to your heart's content without worrying about changing the source file.

TIP The advantage of embedding as compared to linking is that you can edit the embedded information in place, independent of the original data file. The disadvantage is that embedding objects in your documents makes the documents much larger than linking objects does because all the data contained in the object is stored in the Word document (instead of just the information pointing to the source file and source application).

Embedding an Existing Object

To embed an existing object in a document:

1. Start the source application for the object you want to embed in the Word document.
2. Open the file containing the object.

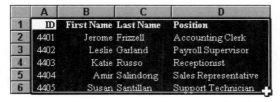

3. Select the object to embed. Again, we'll select the cells from our spreadsheet.

4. Choose Edit ➤ Copy (or click the Copy button in the application or choose Ctrl+C) to copy the object to the Clipboard.

5. Switch back to Word by clicking the Microsoft Word icon on the Taskbar or by pressing Alt+Tab until the Word icon is selected in the task-switching list.

6. Position the insertion point where you want to embed the object.

7. Choose Edit ➤ Paste Special to display the Paste Special dialog box (see Figure 19.4).

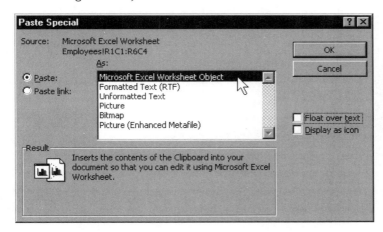

FIGURE 19.4:
To embed information, select the Paste option in the Paste Special dialog box and choose the option in the As list box that describes the item as "Object"—here it's Microsoft Excel Worksheet Object

8. Select the Paste option.

9. In the As list box, choose the option that describes the item you're embedding as "Object." (Here it's Microsoft Excel Worksheet Object because Excel is the source application; with other source applications, you'll see different descriptions.)

10. To have the item float over the text, make sure the Float over Text check box is selected. To have the item appear in line, make sure this check box is cleared.

11. To have the item display as an icon rather than at its full size, check the Display as Icon box. To change the icon, click the Change Icon button (which will materialize when you select the Display as Icon check box) and select a different icon in the Change Icon dialog box; click OK to return to the Object dialog box.

12. Click OK to insert the object in your document.

So far this all seems singularly similar to linking. But you'll notice the difference when you double-click the embedded object—it displays a border from its source application (here, the row and column headings for the spreadsheet), and the toolbars and menus change to those of the source application, so you can edit the object within Word as if you were working in the source application (see Figure 19.5).

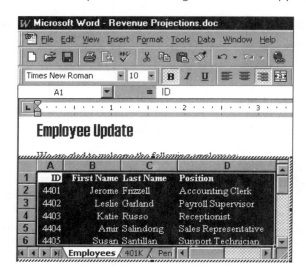

FIGURE 19.5:
Double-click an embedded object to edit it in place. Word will display the menus and toolbars from the source application.

> **TIP**　To edit a sound clip or video clip, right-click the object, choose the Object submenu (e.g. Media Clip Object), and then choose the Edit item. Double-click an embedded sound or video clip to run it.

Embedding a New Object

You can also create a new object and embed it at the same time. For example, you could insert a sound clip in your document as follows:

1. Choose Insert ➤ Object to display the Object dialog box (see Figure 19.6).

2. Click the Create New tab to bring it to the front of the dialog box (unless it's already there).

3. From the Object Type list, choose the type of object you want to insert. (Here I've chosen Wave Sound.)

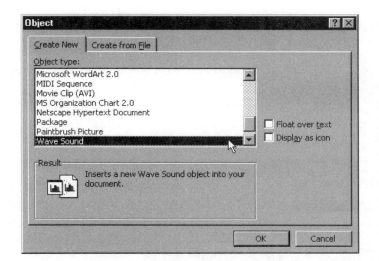

FIGURE 19.6:
On the Create New tab in the Object dialog box, choose the type of object to create, then click the OK button.

4. To have the item float over the text, make sure the Float over Text check box is selected. To have the item appear in line, make sure this check box is cleared.

5. Select the Display as Icon check box if you want the object to display as an icon in the document. To change the icon for the object, click the Change Icon button (which will appear when you select the Display as Icon check box)and select a different icon in the Change Icon dialog box; click the OK button to return to the Object dialog box.

6. Click OK. Word will start the application you chose.

7. Create the object as usual in that application.

8. Choose File ‰ Exit and Return to Document Name to close the application and return to the Word document. Word will insert the object, which you can then position and format as necessary.

Deleting an Embedded Object

To delete an embedded object, select it by clicking it, then press the Delete key or choose Edit ➤ Clear.

Office Binders

Office binders are a way of putting together projects that contain files created in Word, Excel, PowerPoint, and Project.

A binder contains *sections*, each of which can contain either a complete Office file (Word document, PowerPoint slide presentation, Excel spreadsheet, and so on) or part of a file.

Creating a Binder

To create a binder, choose Start ➤ Programs ➤ Microsoft Binder to open a Microsoft Office Binder window with a fresh binder (see Figure 19.7).

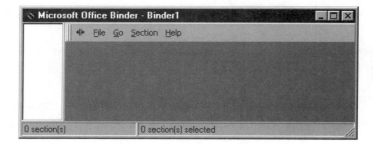

FIGURE 19.7:
The Microsoft Office Binder window

- To start a binder from a template that comes with Office (e.g., Report), from the Windows Desktop, choose Start ➤ New Office Document to display the New dialog box for Office documents, then click the Binders tab (see Figure 19.8). Select the template for the new binder and then click the OK button.

Adding Items to a Binder

The easiest way to add files to the binder is to open an Explorer window (or My Computer window) and drag the files from that window to the left pane of the binder window. When you drop the first file in the left pane, the Office Binder copies across the information to the binder and activates the application in which the file was created, displaying the application's menus and toolbars along with the information in the file (see Figure 19.9).

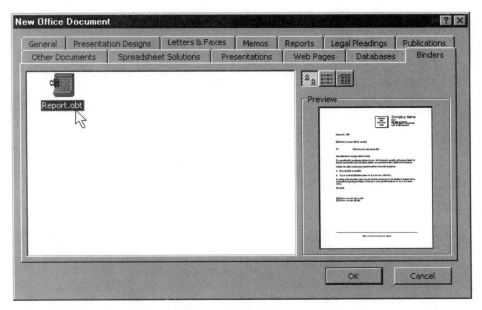

FIGURE 19.8:   To start a new binder based on a template, choose the template on the Binders tab of the New dialog box for Office documents.

You can also add files by choosing Section ➤ Add from File to display the Add from File dialog box (see Figure 19.10). Select the file, and click the OK button.

Adding Sections to a Binder

To bridge the transitions between the different files you place in the binder, you can add blank sections to the binder and then enter material in those sections.

To add a section to a binder, right-click anywhere in the left pane of the Office Binder window and choose Add from the context menu to display the Add Section dialog box.

In the Add Section dialog box (which you'll recognize as the New dialog box in disguise), choose the template for the type of section you want to add and click the OK button.

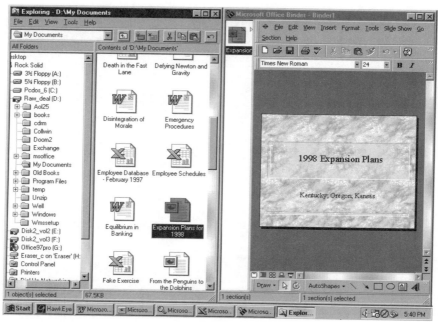

FIGURE 19.9: I've just dragged the file *Expansion Plans for 1998---Presentation.ppt* from the My Computer window to the Binder window. The Office Binder has displayed the first slide in the presentation, together with the PowerPoint menus and toolbars.

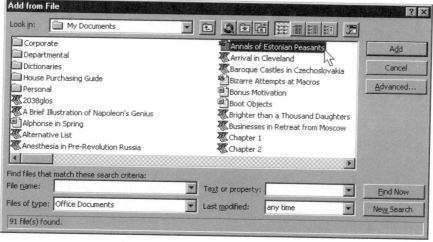

FIGURE 19.10: You can also add files to the binder by choosing them in the Add from File dialog box and clicking Add.

Once Office Binder has inserted the new section, you are to all extents and purposes working in an Excel chart or worksheet, a PowerPoint presentation, or a Word document. To give yourself a little more room to maneuver, you can hide the left pane of the Office Binder window by clicking the Show/Hide Left Pane button; click the button again to display the pane again.

> **TIP**
>
> **To save a section of a binder as a separate file, click that section in the left pane of the Office Binder window and drag it to another location, such as an Explorer (or My Computer) window or to the desktop. The section will be saved in its new location under the name you assigned it in the binder.**

Moving Items around in the Binder

To move an item up or down the binder, you can simply click and drag the icon for the item in the left pane of the Office Binder window. If you're rearranging more items, you may find it easier to choose Section ➤ Rearrange and work in the Rearrange Sections dialog box (see Figure 19.11). Highlight the section you want to move in the Reorder Sections box, then click the Move Up or Move Down button to move the section to its new location (each click moves it up or down one file). Repeat as needed for other sections, then click the OK button to close the Rearrange Sections dialog box.

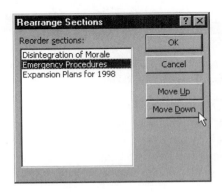

FIGURE 19.11:
In the Rearrange Sections dialog box, select the section you want to move in the Reorder Sections box, then click the Move Up or Move Down button to put it in its new place.

Removing Items from a Binder

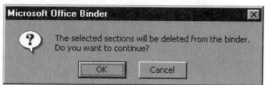

To remove an item from the binder, right-click it in the left pane of the Office Binder window and choose Delete from the context menu.

Word will display a confirmation message box to make sure you want to remove the item from the binder; click OK to remove it.

Editing in the Binder

You can create and edit your documents in the binder if necessary, but generally you'll do better to create a binder from already existing documents. If you then need to modify those documents, open them in their source applications and edit them there rather than editing them in the binder, then put the edited version back in the binder (where they will replace the previous version).

When working in a binder, you'll find that a few features of particular applications either don't work or are not available. For example, you cannot use Excel's AutoCalculate feature in a binder because the binder's status bar replaces Excel's status bar (which contains the AutoCalculate feature).

> **TIP**
> If you need to use toolbars, macros, or AutoText entries that are stored in the template to which a Word document in a binder is attached, drag the template to the binder as well.

Creating Consistent Headers and Footers

Here's how to create consistent headers and footers in all the sections of a binder:

1. Choose File ➤ Binder Page Setup to display the Binder Page Setup dialog box (see Figure 19.12).

2. In the Apply Binder Header/Footer To group box, choose whether to apply the header or footer to all supported sections or only to specified sections. If you choose the Only Sections Selected Below option button, select the check box next to each section in which you want to have the header or footer appear.

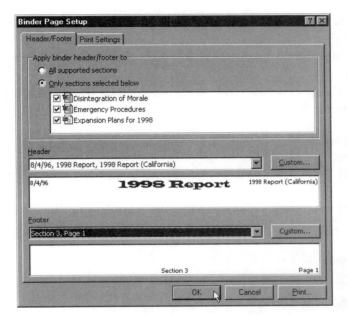

FIGURE 19.12:
You can create consistent headers and footers quickly and easily in the Binder Page Setup dialog box.

3. Next, either choose a ready-made header from the Header drop-down list, or click the Custom button to display the Custom Header dialog box (see Figure 19.13). You can enter text in the Left Section, Center Section, and Right Section boxes, and you can use the buttons to change the font and enter automatic information about the binder—the page number, the binder name, and so on. Click the OK button when you're finished.

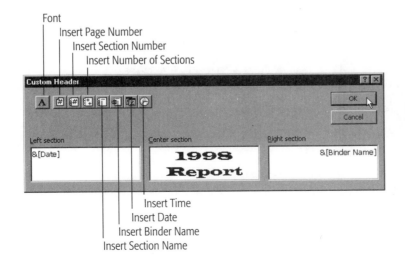

FIGURE 19.13:
Create a custom header in the Custom Header dialog box, and then click OK.

4. Next, either choose a ready-made footer from the Footer drop-down list, or click the Custom button to display the Custom Footer dialog box, which works just like the Custom Header dialog box. Click the OK button when you're finished.

5. Click the OK button to close the Binder Page Setup dialog box and apply the header and footer to the binder.

Printing a Binder

To print a binder, open it and choose File ➤ Print Binder to display the Print Binder dialog box (see Figure 19.14). Choose options for printing the binder just as you would for printing a Word document (look back to Chapter 3 for details), then click the OK button to print the binder.

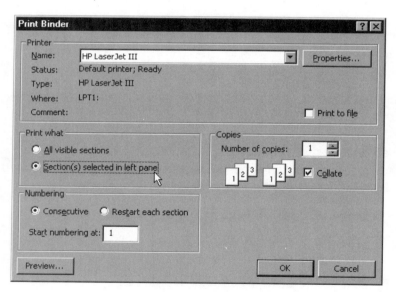

FIGURE 19.14: Choose options for printing the binder in the Print Binder dialog box, then click the OK button.

Chapter 20

WORD AND THE WEB

- **Creating Web pages using the Web Page Wizard**
- **Creating Web pages from Word**
- **Using Word as your e-mail editor**
- **Browsing the Web with Word**
- **Opening Web pages**

Over the last few years, the surge in popularity of the World Wide Web, and of internal corporate webs or *intranets*, has left many people wishing for an easy way to create Web pages from inside their word processor. Word 97 not only provides those capabilities, but also allows you to view both local and Internet Web pages. You can browse the Web (or your company's intranet) with Word, moving easily from page to page. You can open Web pages or intranet pages in Word, alter them, and (if you have the necessary rights), save the changes to the page on the Web site.

You can also use Word as an e-mail editor inside the Exchange client or the Outlook client. We'll look at this towards the end of the chapter.

At the risk of stating the obvious, to use the features described in this chapter, you need to have either an Internet connection, a network connection, or both.

Using Word to Browse the Web

We'll start off by looking at how you can use Word to browse the Web. If you've used a Web browser before, you'll find this straightforward; if you've used Microsoft's Internet Explorer, you'll find that Word's Web-browsing features look very familiar indeed.

The main tool for browsing the Web with Word is the Web toolbar (see Figure 20.1). You can display the Web toolbar by clicking the Web Toolbar button on the Standard toolbar, or by right-clicking the menu bar or any displayed toolbar and choosing Web from the context menu of toolbars. The Web toolbar will also pop up unsummoned when you start accessing a Web page (for example, from a hyperlink—a jump—in a Word document).

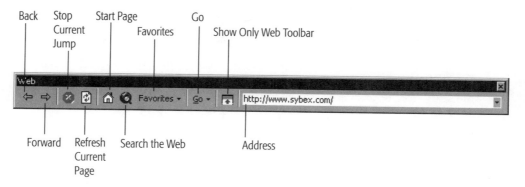

FIGURE 20.1: Use the Web toolbar for browsing the Web (and the Internet) with Word.

Here's what the buttons on the Web toolbar do:

- **Back** moves to the previous page you were on.
- **Forward** moves forward again to a page you were on before you clicked the Back button.
- **Stop Current Jump** stops Word from pursuing a jump that's in progress. (For example, you might want to click this button if a jump has stalled or if a page is dreadfully slow in loading.)
- **Refresh Current Page** makes Word reload the current page. You may want

to do this if part of the page fails to transfer properly, or if you've had the page open for a while and you suspect it may have been updated in the interim.

- **Start Page** jumps to your *start page* (the Web location your Web browser heads to when you start it; also known as your *home page*).
- **Search the Web** displays your chosen Web search tool.
- **Favorites** displays the Favorites menu. *Favorites* are pages whose address you tell Windows to store so you can return to them quickly; other browsers call them *bookmarks*. To add the current page to your list of favorites, choose Add to Favorites, enter the name you want for the favorite in the File Name text box in the Add to Favorites dialog box, and click the Add button. To open a favorite Web page, either choose it from the list of favorites on the Favorites menu or choose Open Favorites, select the favorite in the Favorites dialog box, and click the Open button to jump to it.
- **Go** displays a menu of actions and jumps you can make from the current page:

    Open displays the Open Internet Address dialog box, where you can enter a Web address to go to or click the Browse button to open a file or an address by using the Browse dialog box. Select the Open in New Window check box in the Open Internet Address dialog box if you want to open the page in a new window rather than using the same window and leaving the current page.

    Back and **Forward** move you back and forward through the series of pages you've visited.

    Start Page takes you to your start page.

    Search the Web displays your Web search tool.

    Set Start Page offers to set your start page to the page currently displayed. Click the Yes button to accept the offer.

    Set Search Page offers to set your search page to the page currently displayed. Again, click the Yes button to accept.

    The bottom of the Go menu provides a list of jumps you can take from the current page.

- **Show Only Web Toolbar** toggles on and off the display of all displayed toolbars other than the Web toolbar. This is good for quickly freeing up screen real estate so that you can better view Web pages—and for restoring the toolbars you were using before when you need them again.
- **Address** enters an address to go to, or chooses an address from the drop-down list of addresses you've previously visited.

Opening a Document on a Web or Intranet

To open a document at an HTTP site on the Web or on an intranet, you can use the Address box on the Web toolbar as described in the previous section. To open the index of an HTTP site, omit the name of the document. To reopen a page you've visited before, choose it from the Address drop-down list.

Figure 20.2 shows a Web page opened in Word. You'll see that Word has opened the page as a read-only document because I do not have rights to change it. Hyperlinks to Internet locations appear as underlined red text, while hyperlinks to local files appear as underlined blue text.

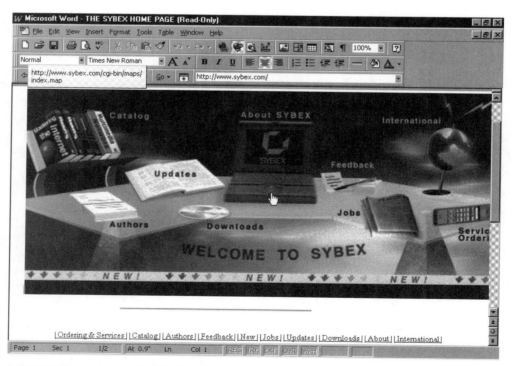

FIGURE 20.2: Browsing the World Wide Web in Word

> **NOTE** You can also open Gopher documents: Simply enter the address in the format `gopher://gopher.location.page` in the Address box.

Adding FTP Sites

Before you can open a file at an FTP site, you have to add that site's address to Word's list of FTP sites:

1. Choose File ➤ Open to display the Open dialog box (see Figure 20.3).

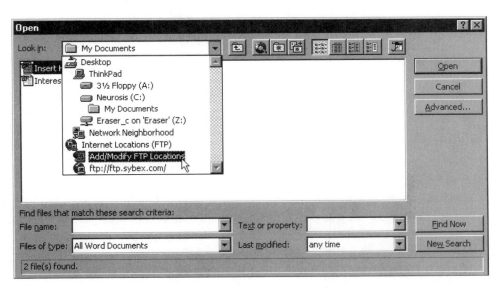

FIGURE 20.3: Use the Open dialog box to navigate to an FTP site.

2. Select the Add/Modify FTP Locations item in the Look In drop-down list to display the Add/Modify FTP Locations dialog box (see Figure 20.4).

3. In the Name of FTP Site text box, enter the full address of the FTP site (e.g., `ftp.sybex.com`).

4. In the Log On As group box, choose how to log on to the site. If you do not have an account at the site, leave the Anonymous option button selected. If you do have an account at the site, select the User option button and enter your user name in the text box.

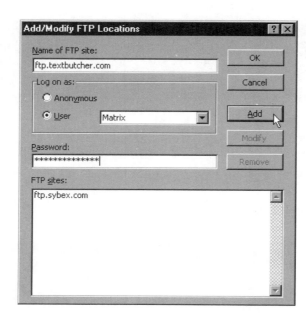

FIGURE 20.4:
Set up your FTP locations in the Add/Modify FTP Locations dialog box.

5. Enter your password in the Password text box. For sites that you log onto as Anonymous, you'll typically use your e-mail address as your password; for sites where you're known by user name, you'll need to specify your personal password.

6. Click the Add button to add the site to your list of FTP sites. (Once you've created a site, you can modify it by selecting it in the FTP Sites list box, changing the information in the appropriate boxes, and clicking the Modify button; or you can remove the site from your list by clicking the Remove button.)

7. Click the OK button to close the Add/Modify FTP Locations dialog box.

Opening a File from an FTP Site

To open a file from an FTP site, use the Internet Locations (FTP) feature from the Open dialog box:

1. Choose File ➤ Open to display the Open dialog box (see Figure 20.5).

2. In the Look In drop-down list, choose the FTP site from the Internet Locations (FTP) category. If you see no FTP sites listed, add sites as described in the previous section.

3. Navigate to the folder that contains the document you want to open, and then click the Open button to open it.

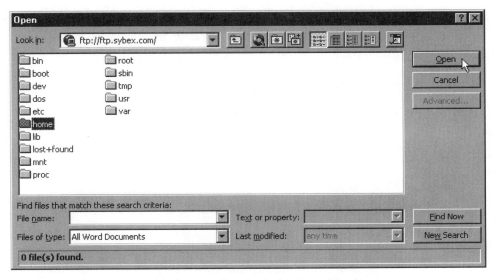

FIGURE 20.5: Opening a folder in an FTP location in the Open dialog box

Creating Web Pages with Word

You can create Web pages with Word in three ways: First, you can use the Web Page Wizard to walk you through the steps of creating a Web page. Second, you can use one of Word's Web templates to create a particular type of page. Third, you can convert a regular Word document to a Web page.

Web pages are formatted using the HyperText Markup Language, or HTML, which consists of large numbers of ugly codes within angle brackets. The good news is that not only does Word handle all the creation of, or conversion to, HTML codes for you, but Word can also display these codes for you if you're curious about how they look.

Creating Web Pages with the Web Page Wizard

To create a Web page with the Web Page Wizard:

1. Choose File ➤ New to display the New dialog box.
2. Click the Web Pages tab to display it at the front of the dialog box. (If you don't see a Web pages tab in the New dialog box, whoever installed Word on your computer probably didn't install the Web templates. See the Appendix for instructions for installing Word components.)

3. Click the Web Page Wizard icon, then click the OK button. Word will start the Web Page Wizard and display the first Web Page Wizard dialog box (see Figure 20.6).

FIGURE 20.6:
In the first Web Page Wizard dialog box, choose the type of Web page you want to create.

4. Choose the type of Web page you want to create, and then click the Next button. (For this example, I'll choose Personal Home Page, which is a good place to start.) Word will display the next Web Page Wizard dialog box (see Figure 20.7).

FIGURE 20.7:
In the second Web Page Wizard dialog box, choose a style for your Web page.

5. Choose the style for your Web page, and then click the Finish button to create the page. Word will display the skeleton for the type of Web page you chose in the style you selected (see Figure 20.8).

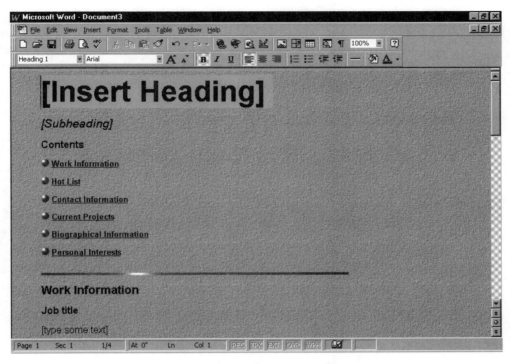

FIGURE 20.8: Word will create the skeleton for the type of Web page you chose.

6. Save the page so that you can add hyperlinks to it. (We'll get to this in a moment.)
7. Add text to the placeholders in the page by clicking each placeholder and then typing in your text. For example, to add a heading to the Personal Home Page, click in the Insert Heading placeholder and enter the text you want. Rinse and repeat for other heading placeholders in the page, such as any Subheading placeholders.
8. Replace any sample text with suitable text of your own.
9. Edit the page to suit your needs: Add, cut, and edit the text as necessary. Use the blue hyperlinks to move quickly to a linked part of the page.
10. Save the page when you're finished.

Using Web Templates

Instead of using the Web Page Wizard, you can start a Web file by choosing one of the templates on the Web Pages tab of the New dialog box (File ➤ New).

> **NOTE** You can download additional Web templates from the Microsoft Web site, http://www.microsoft.com.

Saving a Word Document as an HTML File

You can also save a regular Word document as an HTML file by choosing File ➤ Save As HTML and specifying a location and a file name in the Save As HTML dialog box.

> **WARNING** When saving a regular Word document as an HTML file, you need to be aware that some Word elements do not translate properly to HTML. These include complex tables, bulleted and numbered lists, and graphics. If you need to include these items in your HTML documents, you may do better to create the HTML documents and then place these items in them.

Saving an HTML File as a Word Document

You can also save an HTML file as a Word document. To do so, choose File ➤ Save As Word Document. Specify a name for the document in the Save As dialog box, and then click the Save button.

Creating Hyperlinks

A hyperlink, as we mentioned earlier, is a jump to another location. This location can be either part of an Office file (for example, part of a spreadsheet, or of another Word document, or even of the same Word document), an entire Office file (for example, a PowerPoint presentation), or a Web page either on the local computer, on a local intranet, or on the World Wide Web. You can mix and match these different types of hyperlinks to suit you.

You can create a hyperlink in any of three ways, as we'll see in the following sections.

Inserting a Hyperlink Manually

To insert a hyperlink:

1. Enter the text or graphical object that you want to have displayed for the hyperlink.

2. Select that text or graphical object.

3. Click the Insert Hyperlink button on the Standard toolbar, or choose Insert ➤ Hyperlink, to display the Insert Hyperlink dialog box (see Figure 20.9).

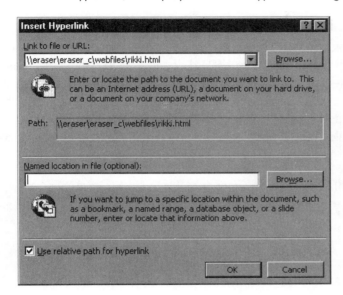

FIGURE 20.9:
In the Insert Hyperlink dialog box, specify the details for the hyperlink.

4. In the Link to File or URL text box, enter the path and name of the file for the hyperlink. Either type in the path and name, or click the Browse button, use the Link to File dialog box to select the file, and click the OK button to enter the filename and path in the Link to File or URL text box.

TIP

If you're using Internet Explorer 3.0 or a later version, or Netscape Navigator 2.0 or a later version, you can quickly enter a URL by leaving the Link to File or URL text box empty and the Insert Hyperlink dialog box onscreen. Then use Internet Explorer or Navigator to go to the site, and then switch back to Word.

5. In the Named Location in File text box, you can enter the part of the file you want the hyperlink to jump to. You can jump to a bookmark in a Word document, a range in an Excel spreadsheet, an object in an Access database, or a particular slide in a PowerPoint presentation. Click the Browse button to display a dialog box containing a list of the objects in that file that a hyperlink can jump to.

6. Click the OK button to insert the hyperlink in your document.

Once you've inserted a hyperlink in a document, you can click the hyperlink to jump to the document or Web page to which it is connected.

Creating Automatic Hyperlinks from File Names

Word's AutoFormat feature (discussed in Chapter 2) can automatically create a hyperlink when you type the name of a file into a Word document. To enable this feature, choose Tools ➤ AutoCorrect to display the AutoCorrect dialog box. Click the AutoFormat As You Type tab and select the Internet and Network Paths with Hyperlinks check box; click the AutoFormat tab, and select the check box there too. Then click the OK button to close the AutoCorrect dialog box. Thereafter, when you type an URL or a network path and filename into a document, Word will automatically format it as a hyperlink.

> **NOTE** To turn URLs and file paths in an existing document into hyperlinks, use the Format ➤ AutoFormat command. Make sure that the Internet and Network Paths with Hyperlinks check box on the AutoFormat tab of the AutoCorrect dialog box is selected as described in the previous paragraph.

Creating a Hyperlink by Dragging

You can also create a hyperlink to an Office document by dragging the object to be linked from the application to the Word document that should receive the hyperlink. For example, you can create a hyperlink from a range of cells in Excel, a slide in PowerPoint, an Access database object, or even part of another Word document.

To create a hyperlink, display Word and the other application (or two windows in Word) onscreen at the same time. Then right-click and right-drag the object to where you want it to appear in the Word publication. Word will display a context menu; choose Create Hyperlink Here to create the hyperlink.

Creating a Hyperlink by Copying

To create a hyperlink by copying, select the material in its source application (or in another Word document) and copy it by right-clicking and choosing Copy, clicking the Copy button, or choosing Edit ➤ Copy. Then switch to Word (or to the Word document that will receive the hyperlink), position the insertion point where the hyperlink should go, and choose Edit ➤ Paste as Hyperlink.

Viewing HTML Source Code

To view the source code of an HTML file in all its glory, choose View ➤ HTML Source. If you're experienced in HTML, you can then troubleshoot formatting problems in your HTML file by editing the codes directly. Choose View ➤ Exit HTML Source or click the Exit HTML Source button that Word displays on the Standard toolbar to return to the graphical view of the file.

> **TIP**
>
> I've made viewing HTML source code sound particularly un-appealing—and indeed, you'll probably want to take advantage of Word's ability to create and read HTML to keep your involvement with HTML codes to a minimum. But you can use the View ➤ HTML Source feature as a way of seeing how people create particular effects in HTML. For example, if you run into a Web page that has impressive effects, you could use this feature to sneak a look at the code they're using—and perhaps even try some of the same techniques in your own files.

Saving a Document to an FTP Site

To save a Word document or an HTML file to an FTP site, choose File ➤ Save As and choose the FTP site from the Internet Locations (FTP) section of the Save In drop-down list. (If you don't see any FTP sites listed there, you need to add them as described in *Adding FTP Sites*, earlier in the chapter.)

Using Word as Your E-Mail Editor

If you're using Microsoft Outlook or Microsoft Exchange as your messaging client, either for a dial-up Internet connection or through a network running Exchange, you can use Word as your e-mail editor instead of the Outlook e-mail editor or the Exchange e-mail editor. The advantages of using Word are that you have more formatting options at your fingertips and that you can easily move between messages you're creating and Word documents you're working with. And because WordMail tracks changes made to e-mail messages, you can quickly see who has added which part to an e-mail message that has passed through a number of hands before reaching you.

Before you can use Word as your e-mail editor, you need to tell Exchange or Outlook (whichever you're using) that you intend to do so. (You also need to have installed the WordMail component during Setup.)

Setting Word Up as Your E-Mail Editor

In Outlook, choose Tools ➤ Options to display the Options dialog box. Click the E-mail tab to bring it to the front of the dialog box, and then select the Use Microsoft Word As the E-Mail Editor check box. (To stop using Word as your e-mail editor, clear this check box again.) Word provides a template named *Email.dot* as the default for e-mail using Word, but you can change this by clicking the Template button, choosing the template in the resulting WordMail Template dialog box, and clicking the Select button.

In Exchange, choose Compose ➤ WordMail Options to display the WordMail Options dialog box. Select the Enable Word as E-Mail Editor check box to turn WordMail on; clear this check box to turn WordMail off again.

Starting WordMail

WordMail integrates with the Exchange client or the Outlook client (whichever you're using) and springs to life when necessary—you don't have to start it manually. To start WordMail, open Exchange or Outlook and proceed as usual. When you start a new message, or when you open a message you've received, WordMail will open as a window for handling the message (see Figure 20.10). (For other items you send and receive, such as message requests and task requests, you still use the Outlook client or Exchange client.)

Using WordMail

WordMail works in a similar way to the Exchange and Outlook clients, which you're probably already familiar with. In this section, we won't go over the basics of Exchange and Outlook; instead, we'll look at the special features that WordMail brings to e-mail.

WARNING When using WordMail's features, be aware that recipients of your messages will need to be using WordMail as well to see them in all their glory. For example, if you include borders, tables, or floating graphics in your messages to people who are using a text-only e-mail program, they will see only the text of your messages, and any effort or creativity you put into the messages will be wasted.

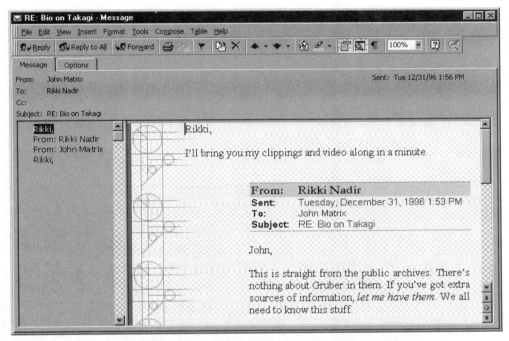

FIGURE 20.10: WordMail integrates with Exchange or Outlook and springs to life when you need to use it for reading or writing a message.

Templates

Apart from setting your default WordMail template for e-mail, as we saw at the beginning of this section, you can also use the other templates that WordMail provides. To start a WordMail message based on a template other than your default template:

- In Outlook, choose Compose ➤ Choose Template, select the template you want to use in the Choose Template dialog box, and click the OK button.
- In Exchange, choose Compose ➤ WordMail Options to display the WordMail Options dialog box, select the template in the Template box, and click the Compose button.

You can also create further WordMail templates of your own design. For example, you can create canned responses for queries you often receive so that you can shoot out an answer with little more than the click of a button.

- In Outlook, start a new WordMail message based on a suitable template, and enter the text you need in the message. Then choose File ➤ Save As to display the Save As dialog box, enter a name for the template in the File Name text box, choose Outlook Template in the Save As Type drop-down list, and click the Save button.

- In Exchange, create the template in Word as usual. Then choose Compose ➤ WordMail Options to display the WordMail Options dialog box, and click the Add button to add the template to the Template list.

Formatting

WordMail lets you use a much wider selection of formatting than Outlook or Exchange alone can provide. By using styles from the Formatting toolbar, you may be able to avoid having to attach files to e-mail messages, instead including the information in the message and formatting it there.

> **WARNING** **Formatting can be a double-edged sword. As we saw earlier, the recipient of your messages has to be using WordMail, or your effort is wasted. And even if the recipient *is* using WordMail, many times it will be better to attach a document to a message than to spend time formatting the message itself. Also, just because you can add formatting to e-mail messages doesn't mean that you should: Many messages are just as effective—if not more so—as plain text.**

Views

Formatting may be a dubious advantage for WordMail, but its capability to provide Word's views for messages is a definite plus. As in Word itself, you can choose views either from the View menu or by using the buttons at the left end of the horizontal scroll bar:

- **Page Layout view** provides a view of the message as it is currently formatted. This is most useful when you're working with styles and need to see the effect they will produce.
- **Online Layout view** adjusts the fonts to a suitable size for onscreen viewing.
- **Outline view** lets you collapse a long e-mail message so that just its salient parts are displayed.
- **Normal view** removes from view any decorative elements and can make your messages easier to read.
- **Document Map** in Outlook gives you the dual benefit of the outline of the message in the left pane and the full text of the message in the right pane.

Appendix

INSTALLING WORD 97

In this Appendix, we'll look at installing Word on your PC. Because it's most likely you'll be installing Word as part of Office 97, we'll concentrate on that. Installing the stand-alone version of Word works in a similar way, but the installation is simpler.

System Requirements

You can install and run Word 97 on any computer capable of running Windows 95 or Windows NT Workstation 3.51 or higher. That means, in practice, a 486 or higher Intel processor (Pentium, Pentium Pro) or equivalent (AMD 486 or K5, Cyrix 5x86 or 6x86, and so forth) with 8MB or more of RAM for Windows 95 or 12MB or more of RAM for Windows NT Workstation.

> **NOTE** Technically, you can run Word 97 on a 386DX with 6MB of RAM. In practice, this will be horribly slow.

As we'll see in a moment, Word includes a number of optional components that you can install if you want. If you have plenty of hard disk space, my advice is to install Word with all the trimmings—in fact, if you really have plenty of space, install Office 97 with all the options. This way you'll be equipped to use all the features of Word (and Office). If you find that you don't need certain features and you want to reclaim the disk space they're hogging, you can remove selected components of Word (or Office); we'll look at this later in this appendix.

Installing Word

Installing Word is a straightforward process, but one that involves more dialog boxes than we can comfortably show in a book this size. This section will set you on the right path to installing Word, but will not guide you along every step of the way.

To install Word or Office:

1. Place the CD-ROM in your CD drive. If AutoPlay is enabled on your computer, a CD-browsing window will open automatically; click the Install Microsoft Word or Install Microsoft Office button to start the installation routine, and go to step 7. Otherwise, choose Start ➤ Settings ➤ Control Panel to display the Control Panel window.

    *   If you're installing on NT Workstation 3.51, choose File ➤ Run to display the Run dialog box. In the Command Line text box, enter ***cd*:\setup.exe**, where ***cd*** is the drive letter assigned to your CD-ROM drive, and click the OK button. Go directly to step 7 (do not pass Go, do not collect $200…).

2. Double-click the Add/Remove Programs icon to display the Add/Remove Programs Properties dialog box (see Figure A.1).

3. Click the Install button to display the Install Program from Floppy Disk or CD-ROM dialog box.

4. Click the Next button. Windows will display the Run Installation Program dialog box and will suggest the installation program to run (SETUP.EXE on the drive containing the CD-ROM).

5. If this is the correct installation program, click the Finish button. (If by some mischance Windows has selected an installation program on an inappropriate disk—for example, if you have multiple diskette drives or CD-ROM drives containing installation programs—correct the choice and then click Finish.) Setup will display the Microsoft Word 97 Setup or Microsoft Office 97 Setup dialog box warning you to close any open applications and reminding you that you can install each copy of Word or Office on only a single computer.

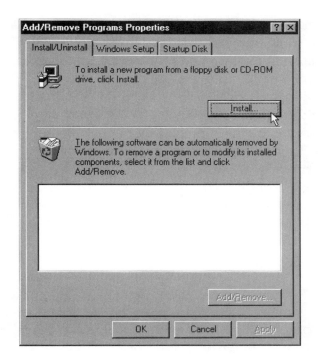

FIGURE A.1:
Click the Install button in the Add/Remove Programs Properties dialog box.

6. Click the Continue button to continue with Setup. You'll see the Name and Organization Information dialog box.

7. Enter your name and organization information and click the OK button. Confirm these in the Confirm Name and Organization Information dialog box.

8. Enter your Product ID number or CD Key number in the next dialog box. You should find this number either on the Certificate of Authenticity in the CD-ROM's sleeve or on a sticker on the CD-ROM's jewel case. Type the ID number into the boxes and click the OK button.

9. Record the Product ID number that Setup gives you in the next dialog box. You'll need this if you call for technical support;. you can get this number any time from the Help About dialog box. Click OK to continue.

10. If you're upgrading to Word or Office, the Setup program will check for a qualifying product for the upgrade.
   • Qualifying products for Word range from Ami Pro to XyWrite and include one-time favorites such as MultiMate and DisplayWrite. You'll find a full list of qualifying products on the Word box.

- Qualifying products for Office also include almost every spreadsheet and database known to humankind. Again, you'll find a full list on the Office box.
- If you've uninstalled the qualifying product, Word will ask you to insert the product's setup disk, which it will then quiz and approve.

11. Next, Setup will suggest a destination folder for the installation of Word or Office (e.g., **C:\Program Files\Microsoft Office**). Accept this by clicking OK, or first click the Change Folder button and pick a more appropriate folder in the Change Folder dialog box. (If the folder doesn't exist, Setup will invite you to create it. Choose Yes.)

12. In the next Setup dialog box, choose the setup option that suits you: Typical, Compact, or Custom. For Office, Setup offers you a fourth option—to run from the CD-ROM drive. This places approximately 50MB of files on your hard disk and leaves the others on the CD-ROM. You'll save disk space, but the applications will run more slowly (and you won't be able to play BTO as you work).

13. If you choose Typical or Compact (or Run from CD-ROM for Office), Setup will go ahead and install those Word options for you. If you choose Custom, Setup will display the Microsoft Word 97 - Custom dialog box or the Microsoft Office 97 - Custom dialog box (see Figure A.2), in which you get to choose which options to install. Options whose check boxes are selected will be installed wholesale; options whose check boxes are selected but grayed out will be installed with the selected subset of their available suboptions; and options whose check boxes are cleared will not be installed.
    - To select all the options (for a full installation), click the Select All button.
    - To reach the Word options from Office Setup, click Microsoft Word in the Options box and then click the Change Option button.
    - To change one of the options, select it. To select options for an option (yes, this gets deep), click the Change Option button to view a list of the options after first selecting the "main" option. Again, select the check boxes for the options you want to install, and then click the OK button. (You may need to drill down to a further layer of options for some options.)
    - When you've selected all the options you want, click the Continue button to install them.

14. Setup will install the options you chose. If setup detects a previous version of Word or Office on your computer, the Upgrade Wizard will offer to remove it for you. Choose Yes or No.

15. Once installation is complete, Setup will offer to walk you through Online Registration, which is handled via the Microsoft Network. If you have a modem up and running, registering electronically can save you the cost of a stamp.

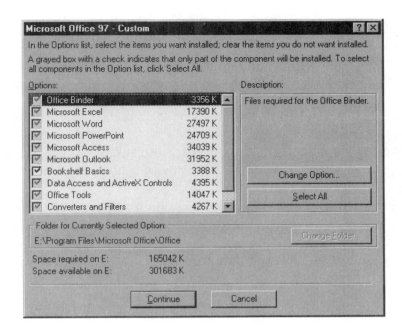

FIGURE A.2:
Choose the parts of Office you want to install.

Installing and Uninstalling Items

Depending on how you (or whoever) originally installed Word or Office on your computer, you may need to install extra items:

- If you need to work with text or graphics files created in another application, you may need to install extra text or graphics converter files. Word and the other Office applications use these files when opening text or graphics files created in another application (or another format) and when saving Office documents as other file formats for use with other applications.
- You may need to install extra templates or Wizards.

> **TIP**
>
> If you have enough disk space, go ahead and install all the converter files. Besides exercising squatters' rights on part of your hard disk, they won't do you any damage, and you'll be equipped to handle almost any type of file your colleagues choose to throw at you.

- You may need to install specific Help files (e.g., the Visual Basic Help files).
- You may want to uninstall items you never use to save disk space.

To install or uninstall Word or Office items:

1. Choose Start ➤ Settings ➤ Control Panel to display the Control Panel window.

2. Double-click the Add/Remove Programs icon to display the Add/Remove Programs Properties dialog box.

3. In the list box, select Microsoft Word 97 or Microsoft Office 97 (or Microsoft Office 97 Professional) and click the Add/Remove button. Setup will prompt you to insert your Word CD or Office CD.

4. Insert the CD and click OK. Setup will check your computer to see which Word items or Office items are already installed and then display the Setup dialog box.

5. Click the Add/Remove button to display the Maintenance dialog box, which shows which Word or Office components you currently have installed.

6. Choose which components to install and which to uninstall:
   - To install components, select their check boxes as described in step 13 of the list in the previous section.
   - To uninstall components, clear their check boxes.

WARNING This dialog box is somewhat counterintuitive: Think of it not as a list of what you want to install, but what you want to *have on your computer* at the end of the installation. For example, if you already have most of Word's features installed and want to install the remainder, select the check boxes for the missing items and *leave the other check boxes selected*. If you clear the check boxes for the items that are already installed, Setup will uninstall them.

7. Click the Continue button to continue with the installation. (If you chose to uninstall components, Setup will display the Confirm Component Removal dialog box. Click the OK button to proceed.) When Setup is complete, you'll see a message box informing you of this. Click the OK button to return to the Add/Remove Programs Properties dialog box and click the OK button to close it.

Glossary

access key   The underlined character in a menu or on a button or other interface element that allows you to access it by pressing that character (in some cases, in combination with the Alt key). For example, *F* is the access key for the File menu.

alignment   Specifying how text is aligned with the margins of the page. Word supports left alignment (the default), center alignment, right alignment, and justified alignment (in which each line of the paragraph is aligned with both the left margin and the right margin).

anchor   An icon indicating that an object (for example, a text box) is attached to a particular paragraph or an exact position on the page.

AutoCorrect   A feature for automatically correcting typos and expanding predefined abbreviations into their replacement text.

AutoFormat   A set of automatic formatting features that Word offers—for example, automatically creating a heading when you enter text in an appropriate configuration.

AutoText   A feature for storing boilerplate text so that you can easily and swiftly insert that text into your documents. AutoText is similar to *glossary* features found in other word processing applications.

bookmark   A feature for electronically marking a section of text (or a graphic or other object) so you can return to it easily or automatically. Bookmarks are hidden by default, but you can display them by selecting the Bookmarks check box on the View tab of the Options dialog box (Tools ➤ Options).

border   A line around a paragraph, an object, or a table.

cell   A table unit formed by the intersection of a row and a column.

center alignment   An alignment option that spaces text at an equal distance from the left margin and the right margin.

center tab   A tab stop around which Word centers text.

change case   A feature for quickly changing the case (capitalization) of selected text. The choices are sentence case (in which the first letter of the first word of each sentence is capitalized), lowercase, uppercase, title case (in which the first letter of each word is capitalized), and toggle case (which reverses the current capitalization).

character style   A collection of character formatting information that can be applied quickly to selected text. Character styles are used within paragraphs formatted with paragraph styles.

check box   A box in a dialog box or other interface element that can be *selected* (checked with an *x*) or *cleared* (without an *x*).

click   To press and release the primary (usually the left) button on the mouse.

Clipboard   An area of reserved memory in Windows for storing one piece of information at a time. The Copy command copies an item to the Clipboard, while the Cut command moves an item to it; then the Paste command places a copy of the item from the Clipboard in a document or file.

column   A tool for creating newspaper-style columns of text.

command bar   A new term in Word 97 that encompasses both the menu bar and toolbars.

comment   A feature for attaching a note (text or an audio message) to part of a document. Comments are useful for collaborating with your colleagues on documents.

concordance file   A file used for indexing a document quickly. It consists of a table containing the terms to be indexed and their corresponding index entries.

context menu   A menu of commands appropriate to the current item or current selection. To display a context menu, right-click an item.

copy   To place a duplicate of the current selection on the Windows Clipboard ready for pasting elsewhere.

cut   To remove the current selection from the document and place it on the Clipboard ready for pasting elsewhere.

data file   A file (for example, a Word document, or an Excel spreadsheet, or an Access database) used to provide the information for merging in a mail merge operation.

decimal tab   A type of tab at which text or numbers are aligned at the period or decimal point.

dialog box   A box that Word displays onscreen with choices for the current operation. For example, the Print dialog box displays a selection of printing options.

docked   Used in reference to a toolbar or menu bar that is attached to one side of the screen rather than undocked (free-floating).

document   A Word file.

Document Map   A feature that displays a panel of variable width at the left side of the Word window containing the outline of the current document.

double-click   To quickly press and release the primary (usually the left) mouse button twice.

double-numbering   Page numbering that uses the chapter or section number and the page number within the chapter or section (e.g., **Page 2-24**).

Draft Font view   A view option for Normal or Outline view, it uses standard fonts (with underline to indicate formatting) to speed up the display of text.

drag   To move the mouse with the primary mouse button held down. For example, to select an area of text, click (depress the mouse button) and drag with the mouse button held down until you have selected all you want to select.

drag and drop   To move or copy a selected object with the mouse by clicking in the object and dragging it to where you want it to appear. Hold down the Ctrl key as you drag and drop if you want to copy the object rather than move it.

embedding   A way of including information (an object) from another Word document or another application in a Word document. Embedding places in the Word document all the information needed to display the object.

field   An item of information in a record. For example, one field in a database might contain a person's first name; another field might contain the person's last name.

field code   An instruction that tells Word to insert variable information in a document.

field result   The information produced by a field code.

Find   A feature for searching the current document for a specified string of text or for a specified item.

font   A set of characters that share a particular design (also known as a *typeface*).

formatting   Choosing the appearance of a document or part of a document.

full justification   *See* justified.

Grammar checker   A feature for checking the grammatical soundness of your text, either on-the-fly as you type or at times of your choosing.

gutter   The area on the inside of each page that will be hidden or unusable when the page is bound into a book.

handles   Small black rectangles that Word displays around a graphic object or text box when you select it. You can drag a handle to resize the object or text box.

header row   A row of field-name headings identifying the columns in a data source.

hidden text   Characters formatted with the Hidden effect in the Font dialog box. Hidden text is normally not displayed onscreen or printed out, but you can choose to display it or print it as necessary.

hot key   Another name for an access key.

hot link   *See* hyperlink.

HTML   *See* HyperText Markup Language.

hyperlink   A link to either a different location in the same document or to a different document. Hypertext links can lead to documents on a local drive, on an intranet, or on the World Wide Web.

HyperText Markup Language   A system of formatting codes used to create web pages for either the World Wide Web or a corporate intranet.

indentation   The space between a paragraph and the left margin or the right margin.

input box   A simple dialog box that you use for entering information in a macro.

Insert Mode   The default mode for entering text in Word. Characters you type are inserted at the position on the insertion point, and characters to the right of the insertion point are pushed along. Compare with Overtype Mode.

insertion point   A blinking vertical bar that marks the current position in the document. Characters you type are inserted to the right of the insertion point.

kerning   The space used between letters so that no letter appears too far from its neighbor; adjusting this space changes the proximity the letters to one another.

justified   Aligned so that both the left and right ends of a full line are aligned with their respective margin. Also known as *full justification* and *justified alignment*.

label   In Visual Basic for Applications, a word (followed by a colon) used to identify or go to a part of the code.

landscape   The orientation of a sheet of paper in which it is wider than it is tall.

language formatting   A way of defining text as being in a different language (no matter which language it is actually in).

left-aligned   Aligned so that the left end of each line in a paragraph is flush with the left margin.

linking   A way of including information (an object) from another Word document or another application in a Word document. Linking places a connection between the Word document and the other file that allows the information to be updated as necessary.

lock   To protect a document against unauthorized changes; to prevent a field from being updated.

macro   A series of actions that you can repeat with one keystroke, click, or menu choice. You can record macros by using the Macro Recorder, and you can edit recorded macros—or write macros from scratch—in the Visual Basic Editor.

mail merge   To combine information from a data file with a main document to produce form letters, catalogs, envelopes, or lables.

main document   The document in a mail merge that contains the skeleton into which you fit the variable information from the data file.

master document   A document made up of a number of subdocuments.

maximize   To enlarge a document window to its largest possible size; to enlarge an application window to fill the entire screen.

menu bar   The bar that contains the menu names. Like the other command bars, this can be attached to any side of the Word window, or it can appear as a free-floating panel.

merge   To combine information from a data file with a main document to produce form letters, catalogs, envelopes, or labels.

merge cells   To combine the contents of two or more cells into one cell.

merge field   A code used to tell Word where in a merge document to put information from the data file.

message box   A simple dialog box that presents information and lets you make choices by clicking one of several buttons.

minimize   To reduce a document to a small section of its title bar; to reduce an application to an icon on the Taskbar.

mirror margins   Margins for facing pages, so that the outside margin of each page (the left margin of the left page and the right margin of the right page) is equal and the inside margin of each page (the right margin of the left page and the left margin of the right page) is equal. Mirror margins are often used for bound books (though not for this one).

mnemonic   Another name for an access key.

module   A Visual Basic for Applications container in which the code for macros is stored.

move   To remove text or an object from one part of a document, or from one document, and place it in another part of the same document or in another document. You can move text or an object by using drag and drop or the Cut and Paste commands.

no proofing   A language-formatting choice (Tools ➤ Language ➤ Set Language) that tells Word not to spell-check the text.

nonbreaking hyphen   A hyphen you use to tell Word not to break a hyphenated phrase. Press Ctrl+Shift+— (Ctrl+Shift+hyphen) to enter a nonbreaking hyphen.

nonbreaking space   A space you use to tell Word not to break a line between two words. To enter a nonbreaking space, press Ctrl+Shift+spacebar.

object   A chunk of information (data) that knows which application it was created in—for example, a group of spreadsheet cells that knows it was created in Excel.

Office Assistant   The animated-character help system for Microsoft Office 97. You can summon the Office Assistant by pressing the F1 key or by clicking any convenient Help button.

Online Layout view   A new view in Word 97 used for viewing online documents. Online Layout view displays the Document Map at the left side of the Word window and increases the size of text in any font that is below a specified size to ensure that documents are easy to read.

option button   A dialog box element used for presenting two or more mutually exclusive options. You can select only one option button in any set at once. Selecting one option button deselects the previously selected option button.

optional hyphen   A hyphen that appears only when it's needed to break a word at the end of a line. Word uses optional hyphens for automatic hyphenation; you can press Ctrl+— (Ctrl+hyphen) to enter an optional hyphen manually.

Options dialog box   The dialog box that contains settings for many preferences.

orphan   The typesetting term for when the first line of a paragraph appears by itself at the foot of a page.

outdent   A hanging indent, one that makes the first line of the paragraph hang out to the left of the rest of the paragraph.

Outline view   A view that lets you collapse your documents to a specified number of heading level; very useful for structuring long documents.

Overtype Mode　An optional mode for entering text in Word. Each character you type replaces the character to the right of the insertion point. Compare with Insert Mode.

page break　A division Word uses to mark the end of one page and the beginning of the next. Word automatically breaks text from page to page, but you can enter hard page breaks manually by pressing Ctrl+Enter.

page numbering　A feature for automatically inserting the correct page number on each page.

paragraph style　A collection of paragraph formatting information comprising character formatting, paragraph formatting (including alignment), tabs, language formatting, and even borders and shading. Every paragraph has a style applied to it and can have only one style applied to it at a time.

password to modify　A protection option for a document. Once password to modify is set, the user can only save changes to a file if they supply the correct password when opening the file.

paste　To insert a copy of the contents of the Clipboard at the insertion point.

portrait　The orientation of a sheet of paper in which it is taller than it is wide.

Print Preview　A view that shows you the result you'll get when you print your document on the currently selected printer.

read-only recommended　An option for saving a document. Whenever someone opens the file, Word displays a message box recommending that they open it as a read-only file; if they do so, they cannot save changes to the original.

records　A division of information that Word uses for sorting data. A record will typically make up one of the items you want to sort and will consist of a number of fields, each of which contains one piece of the information that makes up the record.

redo　To restore one or more actions you've undone using the Undo feature.

repeat   To perform the operation you've just performed. (The operation can be any-thing from entering the last chunk of text to applying formatting to a paragraph.) To repeat an operation, press F4 or choose Edit ➤ Repeat.

Replace   A feature for locating specified text or a certain element in a document and inserting other specified text or another element instead. You can also replace for-matting with other formatting, or formatting with text, or text with formatting.

restore   To return a window to the size it was before you maximized or minimized it.

revision marking   The old name for the Track Changes feature.

right tab   A type of tab at which text is right-aligned (i.e., the text is to the left of the tab stop).

right-aligned   Aligned so that the right end of each line in a paragraph is flush with the right margin.

right-click   To press and release the non-primary (usually the right) mouse button. Right-clicking in Windows applications displays the context menu.

rulers   Word provides a horizontal ruler for all views and a vertical ruler for layout views (such as Page Layout view and Print Preview). To display the ruler onscreen, choose View ➤ Ruler. To pop the ruler up momentarily, move the mouse pointer to the thin bar at the top of the Word window (for the horizontal ruler) or the left of the Word window (for the vertical ruler).

section   A defined portion of a document, usually used for applying different page layouts or different sizes of paper to a document.

section break   The division between two sections.

select   To choose text or an object with the keyboard or the mouse so that you can work with it. Selected text appears highlighted, while a selected object has handles around it.

Shrink to Fit   A Print Preview feature for reducing a document so that it will fit on one page less than it does currently.

Spelling checker   A feature for checking the spelling in the current document. Word can check spelling either on-the-fly as you type or at times of your choosing.

split   To divide one table cell into two or more cells.

SQL   *See* Structured Query Language.

status bar   The bar across the bottom of the Word window that contains information on the position of the insertion point, the number of pages, whether you're using Insert Mode or Overtype Mode, and more.

string   In Visual Basic for Applications, a variable used for storing text information.

Structured Query Language (SQL)   The computer language used for putting together queries for databases.

style   A collection of formatting information that you can apply quickly to selected text. Word supports both character styles and paragraph styles.

style area   A vertical bar at the left side of the Word window that displays the style name for each paragraph.

subdocument   A component document of a master document.

tab stop   A tab position set on the ruler. When you press the Tab key, Word moves the insertion point to the next tab stop.

table   A tool for laying out text in columns made up of rows of cells.

template   A special type of document used for producing cookie-cutter documents. Templates can contain styles, AutoText entries, toolbars, and macros. By attaching a document to a different template, you can change its styles and its look instantly.

text box   A container that Word uses to position items (pictures, text, and so on) in an exact place on the page. Text boxes can be held in place by *anchors*.

Thesaurus   A feature for finding synonyms (words with similar meanings) and antonyms (words with opposite meanings) for any given word.

toolbar   A set of buttons for performing commands in Word. Toolbars, like the menu bar, are command bars. Word automatically displays toolbars appropriate to elements you're working with: For example, if you insert or select a picture, Word will display the Picture toolbar. You can also display the toolbars you want to use, and you can create new toolbars and customize toolbars to contain the buttons and menus you need.

Track Changes   A feature for tracking the edits (additions and deletions) made to a document by a team of users and which user made which edits. Track Changes was known as *revision marking* in previous versions of Word.

undo   A feature for canceling one or more previous actions, starting with the most recent action. Once you've undone one or more actions, you can use the Redo feature to redo them if necessary.

undocked   Used in reference to a toolbar or menu bar that is displayed as free floating rather than docked (attached to one side of the screen).

unlink   To unhook a field result from its field code so that it cannot be updated.

VBA   *See* Visual Basic for Applications.

Visual Basic Editor   A program shared among the Office applications for creating and editing macros.

Visual Basic for Applications (VBA)   Any of several dialects of the Visual Basic programming language, used for recording and writing macros in the Office applications. Word, Excel, Access, and PowerPoint use different dialects of Visual Basic for Applications.

Web page   A document formatted with HTML, the Hypertext Markup Language.

Web Page Wizard   A feature for creating Web pages formatted with HTML codes.

widow   The typesetting term for when the last line of a paragraph appears on its own at the top of a page.

wildcard   A character used to stand for a number of other characters (e.g., a range of characters, or a string of characters at the beginning of a word) in a Find or Replace operation. You can also use wildcards when working with file names.

word wrap   A standard word processing feature whereby the program starts a new line when you type a word that will not fit on the current line.

World Wide Web   A graphical section of the Internet. The Web (as it is commonly called) runs on the HyperText Transport Protocol (HTTP) and uses the HyperText Markup Language (HTML) for formatting its pages (documents). You can view Web pages either directly in Word or by using a Web browser such as Microsoft Internet Explorer or Netscape Navigator.

Wrap to Window   A view option for Normal view and Online Layout view that wraps lines to optimize the amount of text displayed. Wrap to Window wraps long lines so that they fit in the document window as it's sized and wraps short lines to display as much text as possible.

zoom   To enlarge or reduce the onscreen display of a document so that you can see more or less of it. Zooming affects only the display of the document—it does not alter the font sizes.

Index

Note to the Reader: First level entries are in **bold**. Page numbers in **bold** indicate the principal discussion of a topic or the definition of a term. Page numbers in *italic* indicate illustrations.

D

W